Resettlement and famine in Ethiopia

Resettlement and famine in Ethiopia

The villagers' experience

ALULA PANKHURST

Manchester University Press
Manchester and New York

distributed exclusively in the USA and Canada by St Martin's Press

363.8
P19 r

Published by Manchester University Press
Oxford Road, Manchester M13 9PL, England
and Room 400, 175 Fifth Avenue, New York, NY 10010, USA

Distributed exclusively in the USA and Canada
by St. Martin's Press, Inc., 175 Fifth Avenue, New York, NY 10010, USA

A catalogue record for this book is available from the British Library

Library of Congress cataloging in publication data
Pankhurst, Alula, 1962–
    Resettlement and famine in Ethiopia: the villagers' experience /
Alula Pankhurst.
        p.   cm.
    Includes bibliographical references (p.   ) and index.
    ISBN 0–7190–3537–6 (hardback)
    1. Famines–Ethiopia.   2. Land settlement–Ethiopia.   1. Title.
HC845.Z9F357   1992
363.8'0963–dc20   91–18748

ISBN 0 7190 3537 6 *hardback*

JP

Phototypeset by Intype, London
Printed in Great Britain
by Biddles Ltd, Guildford and King's Lynn

Contents

Tables

Illustrations

Maps

Acknowledgements

More people than can be mentioned helped to make this book possible. A grant from the Economic and Social Research Council of Great Britain enabled me to undertake the study. In Ethiopia I received constant support from Addis Ababa University, notably the Institute of Ethiopian Studies, the Institute of Development Research and the Social Science Faculty. Thanks are due to Dr Taddese Beyene, Dr Taddesse Tamrat and Dr Dessalegn Rahmato, whose inspiration will be apparent to the reader. The staff of the Sociology Department have offered me a stimulating teaching environment during the editing work. In Addis Ababa my kind hosts were Ato Lemma Firehiwot and Ato Debebe Habte Yohannes.

Travel to resettlement areas was facilitated by the Relief and Rehabilitation Commission (RRC). I am grateful to Ato Teferi Wosen and Ato Tamrat Kebede for their help. Hezekiel Gabissa accompanied on a study tour of settlements; he and his family became good friends. In the settlement areas I received full cooperation from WPE administrators, and extension agents of the RRC, and the Ministries of Agriculture and Health. I wish to thank Isayas Dagne, and am indebted to Taddese Wolde and Haile Mikaél Nigusé for their insights into the early days of resettlement.

I am grateful to several international organisations, including Canadian International Development Agency, Concern, Save the Children (US, UK and Norway), Secours Populaire Français, UNICEF, UN Office for Emergency Operations in Ethiopia and the World Bank. In particular, I am indebted to Jack Finucane, Alice Bavent, Gery Salole, Angela Raven-Roberts, Michael Priestley, Dag Hareide and Peter Hawkins. Heartfelt thanks go to successive teams of volunteers from the two agencies working in Qéto: Concern and SPF, especially to Aidan Leonard and Dr Claude Tillard and Dr Pascale Mardon.

In Village Three settlers and Government workers shared their experiences with me, and put up with my questioning. This book is the outcome of their experiences and the insights I gained from living with them. Special thanks got to Wendwesen, an outsider, and Qegnu, an insider.

At Manchester University the Department of Social Anthropology encouraged my work. I am especially grateful to Professor Marilyn Strathern, and Drs Paul Baxter, Jeanette Edwards and Tim Allen. In writing the thesis, I benefited from comments from Drs Adrian Wood, Norman

Singer, Eva Poluha and Ken Wilson, and Deborah Hicks; Liz Stone has
made invaluable suggestions for the book. Responsibility for mistakes
and inadequacies remains my own.

My greatest debt is to Dr David Turton, without whose judicious
guidance over five years the study could not have been completed. Finally,
I wish to express my deepest gratitude to my parents Rita and Richard,
my sister Helen, Rockie Arnold and Hirut Tafara for their constant
faithful support.

Transliteration and dating

To minimise on diacritical marks the following simplified system has been adopted for transcription, except for proper names where usage is well established. The seven vowel orders are represented as follows: e, u, i, a, é, i, o. Glottalised explosives have been omitted except for k, represented as q. For names used by settlers I have retained their pronunciation rather than more established forms e.g. Mehammad instead of Muhammad, and Seyd instead of Sa'id.

Most dates have been translated from the Ethiopian calendar into the Gregorian, except for those of newspapers and certain important cases, e.g. the use of '1977', i.e. 1977 in the Ethiopian calendar, which was associated by settlers with the 1984–5 famine.

Acronyms

AMC	Agricultural Marketing Corporation
CSO	Central Statistical Office
FAO	Food and Agriculture Organisation
EDDC	Ethiopian Domestic Distribution Corporation
EHRS	Ethiopian Highlands Reclamation Study
IBRD	International Bank for Reconstruction and Development (World Bank)
IDR	Institute of Development Research, Addis Ababa
ILO	International Labour Organisation
ITDG	Intermediate Technology Development Group
MOA(S)	Ministry of Agriculture (and Settlement)
MOE	Ministry of Education
MOH	Ministry of Health
MLRA	Ministry of Land Reform and Administration
MNCD	Ministry of National Community Development
NRCP	National Revolutionary Production Campaign
CPSC	Central Planning Supreme Council
ONCCP	Office of the National Committee for Central Planning
PCO	Planning Commission Office
PDRE	People's Democratic Republic of Ethiopia
PMAC	Provisional Military Administrative Council
RRC	Relief and Rehabilitation Commission
SPF	Secours Populaire Français
TBA	Traditional Birth Attendant
UNDP	United Nations Development Programme
UNESCO	United Nations Educational, Scientific and Cultural Organisation
UNHCR	United Nations High Commission for Refugees
UNICEF	United Nations International Children's Emergency Fund
WFP	World Food Programme
WHO	World Health Organisation
WPE	Workers' Party of Ethiopia

Glossary
of Amharic and Oromo terms

Abba Werra	household head, literally 'father of people'
Arrash	Woman who looks after another during childbirth
Awrajja	Until recently the second level of the country's three-tier administrative structure
Berberé	Chilli; the chief condiment in Ethiopian cuisine
Béteseb	Household, literally 'house of people'
Birr	Currency of Ethiopia. One United States dollar equals 2.07 *birr*
Budin	Work and residential team
Chat	Mild narcotic
Huddu Gela	Temporary shelter
Imbidadé	Community boycott of an offender
Injera	Pancake-like bread; basic component of the diet
Medebegna	Conventional Resettlement Site
Mehaber	Christian religious association
Merdo	Mourning for absent deceased
Netib	Work points
Sigsega	Integrated Resettlement Site
Téf	Eragrostis téf; a cereal traditionally grown only in Ethiopia
Tim	Orphan
Tiré	Literally 'raw', grain
Tigab	Literally 'satiety'; denotes impetuous, arrogant behaviour
Qallichcha	Muslim religious leader
Qiré	Bural association
Qub	Rotating credit association, known as Iqqub in most of Ethiopia
Wabi	Literally 'giver', the guarantor of the gift
Wedaja	Muslim ceremony, often associated with healing
Wereda	Third and lowest tier of administration
Wet	Spicy sauce; a staple component of the diet

To my parents

Introduction

My research in Ethiopia lasted one year and nine months, from September 1986 until June 1988. I first visited Ethiopian resettlement sites in January 1986, travelling with a team comprising members of the Ethiopian Government Relief and Rehabilitation Commission (RRC) and the United Nations Office for Emergency Operations in Ethiopia. The team spent a week in the north of the country visiting famine shelters in Wello and Tigray Administrative Regions, and a reception shelter near the town of Desé. We then spent a week in western Ethiopia, visiting resettlement areas in different regions.[1] This brief tour gave me a sense of the diversity of resettlement projects and of the magnitude of this controversial operation.

The choice of an area in which to conduct intensive field research was complicated by the variety of schemes carried out in a vast area of western Ethiopia, within five Administrative Regions. In addition to settlements established by the RRC in the late 1970s, two major types of new schemes were established in 1984. 'Conventional' Settlements are large-scale, mechanised complexes of linked villages sited mainly in the lowlands; 'Integrated' Settlements are much smaller sites, more widely distributed among local Peasants' Associations (PAs) in the highlands, and received far less Government support. The resettlement mix also varied according to the settlers' backgrounds and the local populations among whom they were relocated. Settlers came from four Administrative Regions, speaking several languages, and adhering to different religions and local traditions. They were settled among a variety of peoples with diverse backgrounds and social and economic means of livelihood.

Before narrowing the focus to one area I decided to visit different kinds of settlement sites within one region. Wellegga was the obvious choice, since it was the only region in which all resettlement types could be found; moreover, it hosted the largest settler population (43%). In October and November 1986 I spent a month visiting settlements in Wellegga. This tour alerted me to the problems the old settlements were facing in attaining self-sufficiency while relying on mechanised agriculture to produce low-value cereals. I also became aware that Integrated Sites varied considerably in performance according to size, amount and type of land, and the ratio of plough oxen to households. Conventional Settlements received considerable inputs in extension personnel and materials, but were also subject to stringent Government directives; as Producers' Cooperatives (PCs), with the exception of small private plots, land was under communal production.

At first I planned to carry out a detailed study in one area, comparing the adaptation of settlers in Conventional and Integrated Settlements, and examining the relationship of settlers with the local population. I selected the Qéto resettlement area situated in Qéllem *Awrajja* in south-western Wellegga, since it was the only area where a Conventional Settlement complex could be found side by side with Integrated Sites. Settlers in Qéto were receiving support from two aid agencies, Concern and Secours Populaire Français, and I was interested in the effect of aid on settler adaptation.

I narrowed down the study to one of the twenty Qéto villages in order to be able to observe settler life through participation, in accordance with the canons of social anthropology. I selected Village Three, later renamed 'Fruit of Struggle', for three main reasons. First, it was the only Conventional Site with fields adjacent to an Integrated Site, which I hoped to study by way of comparison. Secondly, I felt that the diversity of language, religion and area of origin would make for an interesting study of integration. In particular, my decision was influenced by the fact that Village Three comprised a majority of speakers of Amharic, the language in which 'I untied my mouth' (the Amharic idiom for 'maternal language'), but also speakers of Oromo, a language I had begun to learn as a teenager. Last, but not least, Village Three appealed to me because it was built on a slope leading down to the river Chebel with a lovely view of Welel, a sacred Oromo mountain, in the background.

The settlement had an irregular shape owing to ravines, and had a small central meeting area at the top of the hill. The village was surrounded in part by tropical riverine forests of dense vegetation as well as savannah plains interspersed with acacia trees, the habitat of a variety of wildlife, including lions, buffaloes, antelopes, wild boars, pythons, babboons and monkeys. The village hosted twelve outsiders, the 'Government workers',[2] who lived in a compound of huts at the top of the hill.

After spending the first few nights in a tent, I shared a hut with a series of Government workers: two agricultural extension agents, followed by two literacy teachers, an RRC food distributor and a health worker. I usually spent the day with settlers but often had morning tea and either lunch or supper with my housemates. Living at close quarters with men and women who were outsiders in the village gave me an insight into the relationship between the settlers and these representatives of the State.

I lived in Village Three for fourteen months between January 1987 and June 1988, returning to Addis Ababa every two or three months. On these occasions settlers would ask me to purchase scarce items for them, notably watches, shoes, rat traps and cloth for dresses. I also became acquainted with settlers' relatives in the capital. I became aware of the extent to which settlers were linked to relatives throughout the country.

In September 1987 I paid a second brief visit to Wello, the settlers' homeland. I was given over a hundred letters for relatives, and visited a PA near the town of Kombolcha in Desé *Awrajja*. The visit gave me a visual impression of the homeland the settlers had left behind. I gained a clearer understanding of why settlers moved, and became more aware of the strength of their links with their homeland.

At first my presence in Village Three was viewed with some suspicion by the Government workers and with incredulity by settlers, especially since I spoke Amharic. The former could not understand why I wished to remain in the village and what I wished to know beyond what I had been told about the statistics on production, population, etc. If I had questions why did I not ask them? Settlers initially tended to identify me with the Government workers; however I did not fit the established categories. On one occasion a little orphan girl was asked by her elder sister to say which jobs the various Government workers performed. When it came to my turn, she said: 'Alula counts people.' Later I was able to help settlers by buying them things they wanted from the capital. Some saw me as the postman who delivered letters to their relatives in Addis Ababa. For many I was the repairer of digital watches, which had become a sign of prestige and power in a society where work was strictly related to time. Children came to me to borrow books.

Although I got on well with most settlers and Government workers, I kept my distance from the leadership. The deputy chairman of the PA would sometimes joke with me that he would have me removed from the village. There were a few individuals whose demands I disliked; on one occasion I was taken to the village Law Court by a settler who thought I was going to leave without returning a watch he had given to me for repair. One source of tension was photographs; settlers were very keen to have their picture taken, and once I had given a few people prints demands became so persistent that I stopped taking photographs altogether.

Initially I was at a loss to decide what aspect of settlement life should form the main focus of my study. From an anthropological standpoint I sought spontaneous forms of social organisation. However, the settlers' new lives were highly regimented in ways determined from 'above'. They went out to work when a bell was rung at six in the morning, and received daily work points. Agriculture was largely planned and directed by cadres, or Party activists, and extension agents. Most economic activities were carried out within the framework set up by the PA. Spontaneous activities were largely restricted to the social field; settlers gathered for religious events, marriages and funerals, and to form credit associations.

To start with I was careful not to ask too many questions, especially given the sensitive nature of the role of Government in organising resettle-ment, and the suspicion with which my work was seen. I therefore did not ask direct questions, but sought out situations and forums where settlers expressed their views to each other. Given my interest in language I was also predisposed to look into areas of debate. However, I found PA meetings rather stilted and the deliberations of the Law Court uninspiring.

My interest was aroused by a committee of elders appointed to look into marriage and divorce. Much of what went on during the proceedings remained obscure until I began to understand the relations between people and the issues with which they were concerned. This forum gave me an insight into the meaning of resettlement for settlers, for in the course of litigation spouses and elders spoke about their relationships, problems, fears and aspirations with directness and spontaneity.

During the second half of my fieldwork I carried out an almost com-plete village survey, which complemented the population data I obtained from the PA. I interviewed each household head and his or her spouse if they did not come together. The interviews were informal and concen-trated on how people came to resettle and the relationships they formed after arrival. Sometimes settlers told tragic stories of loss. For me there was a disturbingly poignant contrast between my interest as an avid listener and the bleak life stories many shared with me in a matter-of-fact way. Most were more than happy to relate their life story. Some, however, did not feel like talking about a past on which they had turned their backs, while a few recalled their former lives with nostalgia, once or twice shedding a tear or lapsing into silent memories. The time I spent in the village was a most exciting and enjoyable period of my life. However, I found the contrast between my feelings of happiness and the bleak, ardu-ous and restricted settler life disturbing.

Attending the sessions of the Marriage and Divorce Committee gave me a view of resettlement life from the inside and brought me back to the pervasive influence of the State in settlers' lives. Choices and chances during my fieldwork led me to change my research designs. The popu-lation of a little over 1,800 people was too large for me to become closely acquainted with all the settlers. Towards the end of my stay I began to know all the villagers by face, but could not name most of them on sight. Living with the Government workers, and trying to understand the whole village, I did not get to know one family intimately, although I developed close friendships with quite a few. This meant that I did not gather detailed daily data on a sample of households, although the Marriage and Divorce Committee sessions afforded a window on domestic life.

I became so involved in studying Village Three that after six months' fieldwork I abandoned my original plan to undertake a comparative study in the adjacent Integrated Site of Iggu Kofalé. I also gave up the idea of spending a portion of my time in an Oromo PA in order to understand the effects of resettlement on the local population. I made both these decisions because I felt I was a long way from understanding what resettlement meant to the settlers in Village Three. The focus of the study altered to issues of adaptation and integration within one settler community.

In reworking my thesis, and reducing it by a third, I have omitted a chapter on 'Labour, Capital and Land', which reviewed anthropological literature on Amhara society, as well as Amharic quotations, data of primarily linguistic interest, and anecdotal material, including numerous settler 'stories'. However, the book has benefited from insights gained during two subsequent visits to the village in April 1989 and January 1991, at a time when dramatic changes were in the making.

Apart from my own observations, the primary source for this work is hundreds of settlers' accounts. Such reminiscences provide an understanding of the backgrounds which pushed settlers into leaving their homelands and lured them to settle for a new world. In selecting material to create a text I have highlighted moving and unusual cases while silencing more drab and ordinary accounts.

The outcome of the resettlement programme was greatly influenced by the administrative framework set up by exogenous agents of the State: WPE cadres, agricultural, health and literacy extension agents. I have tried to give them a voice too, by using the files of three generations of cadres, interviewing as well as corresponding with the leader of the first round of cadres. He was one of the first organisers of the Qéto complex, who lent me his detailed diaries. Having lived with the Government workers, I also became familiar with their views and attitudes on a daily basis.

I have likewise consulted Ethiopian Government documents and reports, notably those produced by the MOA, the RRC, the Office of the National Committee for Central Planning, the Council of Ministers and the Central Statistical Office. The leading Ethiopian daily newspapers, *Addis Zemen* and *Ethiopian Herald*, gave me an understanding of how resettlement was presented in national terms, and provided an insight into the Government's rationale for embarking on such a massive programme.

In the first chapter I discuss the notions of resettlement and its history in the Ethiopian context. The rest of the book is in two parts. The first, entitled 'The logic of resettlement', seeks to explain the economic, political and social forces which gave rise to resettlement. The second, 'settling for a new world', presents the life of the settlers from the time of their departure from northern Ethiopia until August 1991, the time of my last visit to Village Three. This section focuses on the period during which I was most closely acquainted with the village, during 1987 and the first half of 1988.

Settlers' views of the famine and the aid environment form the basis of

Chapter II. I discuss peasant survival strategies, and suggest that the aid environment pressurised peasants to resettle.

In Chapter III I seek to explain the then Government's motives for launching a massive resettlement programme. The rationale, I argue, was to be found in Ethiopia's independent past, the crisis of the famine, and the Mengistu Government's vision of a self-reliant future based on socialist transformation. I describe the implementation of the programme and discuss key problems, such as coercion and family separation.

The diversity and complexity of interrelated settler motives are the subject of Chapter IV. Age, wealth and gender were found to be the most important individual factors, but these operated within the social context of family, peer and community pressures.

Chapter V begins with preparations for the settlers' arrival and their journey west. The crisis in the transit camps and the Qéto shelter are depicted in the words of settlers and an administrator. Finally, I describe the settlement of the sites, notably Village Three, and the struggle to start a new life with insufficient means.

The social organisation of production and exchange is the subject of Chapter VI. The paramount relationship between settlers and the State is discussed and the mediation of the agents of the Government is considered. I describe the collectivisation of production and explain the crucial role of the market in settler adaptation. I conclude with a discussion of changes in production and exchange during the village's five years' history.

Chapter VII focuses on settler social life within the constraints imposed by the new order and considers life cycle events, the role of religion and credit associations, and relations between settlers and the outside world.

In Chapter VIII I examine the negotiations between forces of tradition and change in the context of marriage and divorce. I discuss the role of the bridal dress as a symbolic and economic measure of commitment to marriage, and consider the involvement of the State in domestic affairs through the establishment of a Marriage and Divorce Committee, whose rise and demise and power struggle with neighbourhood elders are described. Issues relating to the 1987 Constitution form the focus of an analysis of State-settler relations.

The concluding chapter sums up the resettlement experience and looks to the future. The relationships of settlers and the State is reviewed, and the wider significance of the study is outlined. Finally, in the epilogue I seek to place this study in the context of changes observed during my last three visits to the village, in 1989 and 1991. I discuss the consequences of changes due to liberalisation in the final year of the Mengistu regime, describe the emergence of a sense of community and a new identity, and outline the implications of the dramatic changes in government which swept across Ethiopia from April 1991 onwards.

Notes

1 Metekkel in Gojjam, Asosa in Wellegga, Gambélla in Ilubabor, and Kishé in Kefa.
2 The twelve included three *cadres* from the Workers' Party of Ethiopia, five agricultural extension agents, two health assistants, an RRC food distributor, and an Ethiopian Nutrition Institute agent.

I

Resettlement in Ethiopia

It would be pleasant to believe that one of the virtues of anthropology is its humane interest in social process – in growing up, marrying and dying, solving disputes and making a living. A concern for the human 'passions', which once animated social philosophy, has become lost in contemporary social science . . . *we must surely regret that the social fabric of a modern land settlement scheme has never been contemplated with the thoroughness which Fourier applied to his projects.*

Robertson (1984, p. 302; emphasis added)

The involvement of the State tends to be peripheral to most anthropological studies of indigenous peoples. In this study the relationship between village and State is central. The settlement owed its very existence to Government policy. The account is primarily concerned with life in a settlement village in western Ethiopia. The village was part of a massive resettlement scheme set up by the Government; over half a million people were moved from the famine areas of northern Ethiopia to the west of the country, between November 1984 and February 1986.

In Ethiopia prior to the Revolution anthropologists tended to study either the central highlands, notably the Amhara, or societies far from the centre of the State, mainly in the south-west. The relationship between the centre and the periphery has since become a prominent theme of a collaborative work of anthropologists and historians edited by Donham and James (1986). The present study is, in a sense, a continuation of this trend, firstly, since the concern is with people from the centre now living on the periphery, and, secondly, because the relationship between the people and the State is paramount. The study also fits in with a post-revolutionary trend towards 'problem-oriented' anthropology. Other case studies have also considered issues raised by State policies, such as cooperativisation[1] and villagisation,[2] thus complementing the growing literature in related disciplines, notably economic and development studies.

In the book I seek to explain the motivations of settlers and the Government, and analyse the political, social and economic forces involved. I argue that stereotypes of resettlement as either purely enduced by famine or enforced by the Government are equally misleading simplifications. Settler perceptions of their new environment are described. Living in a mechanised collective represented a dramatic change of life-style. Settlers were being transformed from independent small-scale producers into wage-labourers. Land was held 'communally' except for small garden plots, which were initially restricted to a mere tenth of a hectare. Capital, in the form of tractors, was controlled by the State. Labour was channelled into communal production, and remuneration depended on a system of work points.

The most surprising aspect of resettlement life was the way settlers seemed to adapt to such radical changes in their way of life. Some expressed a sense of passive resignation. Others spoke of resettlement as a deal with the Government. A few expressed sincere thanks to the latter for having saved them at a time when 'people were falling like leaves'. One elder put it this way: '[The famine] was like a burning house. The Government came to our rescue and dispersed us in different directions, like someone throwing out belongings about to burn.'

However, in exchange for offering them the chance of a new life, the Government imposed its vision of change. The result was not what settlers, left to their own devices, would have chosen. However some saw it as a kind of contract which they were ready to accept. Many decided that settlement life was not for them and returned home or became wage-labourers elsewhere.[3] Most, however, decided to remain, and make the best of settling for a new world.

Settler responses were not simply or predominantly passive. There was much subtle resistance in the ways in which traditions were adhered to, rituals revived, and religious concerns kept alive despite the constraints imposed by the administration. Settlers took the dramatic changes to their lives in their stride and thrived, despite the restrictions imposed from outside. Settlers relentlessly pursued private concerns and revealed considerable determination, notably in the way in which grain was invested in livestock. During my stay in Village Three I was constantly struck by the settlers' vitality, endurance and ability to adapt.

The resettlement milieu was one in which the State was for the first time directly altering the means and relations of production through imposed collectivisation. The State's influence depended on the mediatory role of cadres and extension agents, whose relationships with settlers portray some resemblances to the traditional system of clientage. Labour relations also explained stratification, much in the same way as 'big men' emerged through patronage in former times. All settlers were at first practically destitute and were allocated equally small plots; yet a marked hierarchy rapidly emerged. Settlers rose to prominence partly through the ability to wield a pen or a gun, much in the traditional way in which ecclesiastical and military elites were formed, and partly through manipulating relationships with the representatives of the State and other settlers.

Although it would be hard to conceive of a more radical and dramatic transformation of peasant life, the inescapable conclusion one is left with is that continuity rather than change was the underlying text revealed beneath the turmoil of reform. *Plus ça change, plus c'est la même chose*, which may explain the puzzle of the settlers' remarkable ability to adapt.

Resettlement: concepts, theories and practices

The term 'resettlement' covers such a wide range of issues, approaches and experiences that it can best be understood as a catch-all term, of descriptive rather than analytical value. Historically, the term 'resettlement' has been used mainly to convey the idea of people returning to an area they had, or were supposed to have lived in previously.[4] From the eighteenth century the term was used to describe the exodus of Jews from Egypt to Judaea. After World War I it was applied to demobilised servicemen returning. Since World War II it has frequently been applied to the forced transfer of urban black South Africans to their putative rural 'homelands'.

As Chambers suggests, resettlement is characterised by two main features: 'A movement of population; and an element of planning and control' (1969, p. 11). The notion of movement may serve to differentiate resettlement from two other policies: 'villagisation', where the basic notion is regroupment, which may or may not involve moving significant distances; and 'sedentarisaton', which aims to settle pastoralists, a process which need not involve moving away from the area in which the people were living (Apthorpe, 1966, p. 11). However, migration needs to be qualified by the second, arguably more central notion, that of *the movement of people organised by the State*. In this sense resettlement may be distinguished from 'spontaneous migration', initiated and undertaken by people on their own. Resettlement may also be distinguished from the exodus of refugees fleeing from one State to another. However, once refugees have crossed a border and sought asylum in a different State, the latter may decide to 'resettle' them. A State may also promote the migration of people from one country to another for a variety of reasons.

Resettlement has increasingly been undertaken to further a wide range of political, economic and social objectives. In some cases it has been used primarily for repressive purposes, such as the early deportation of convicts to Australia or dissidents to Siberia, the removal of South African blacks from towns; or resettlement may have repressive consequences, for instance in slum clearances and evictions of urban unemployed. Resettlement has also been used to state claims to land, to strengthen border defences, or to change the existing population balance, e.g. the eviction of native Kenyans from land restricted to white settlers, and the Israeli policy of settling the West Bank with Jews.

In recent times resettlement has been used to address problems created by sudden natural or man-made disasters, such as famine, floods, hurricanes, chemical or nuclear accidents and, last but not least, warfare. Resettlement has also become a by-product of large-scale development projects, including dams, factories and national parks. Finally, resettlement has been used to promote long-term development strategies to alter the ratio between population and land. This may be justified as a means of relieving population pressure and addressing the problem of land shortage, as in the Indonesian 'transmigration' programme, or it may be a way of opening up new lands, as in the Latin American 'colonisation' schemes.

Resettlement schemes have mushroomed all over the world, along with the increase in State intervention in 'development'. For planners resettlement has been seen as an opportunity to introduce social change rapidly (Chambers, 1969, p. 258); for social scientists it has offered the chance of well-defined test cases to monitor the effects of change. Resettlement of people to make way for dams is a case in point. In Africa the social effects of three large dams, Volta, Kariba and Aswan, have been the subject of several studies.

However, attempts at formulating a 'relocation theory' are disappointing, no doubt because resettlement circumstances are so varied. Scudder and Colson suggested that 'rural communities undergoing resettlement respond in the same general fashion irrespective of their socio-cultural background and of the policy of the resettlement authorities' (1979, p. 246). However, a consideration of the growing body of literature on relocation, notably Colson and Scudder's own pioneering long-term study, suggests that the reverse is true: both cultural factors and the administration's policies are crucial to understanding resettlement, and the interaction between the two systems is intrinsic to the nature of relocation.

Relocation theory relies on vague notions of 'stress', 'crisis' and 'adaptation'. Scudder suggests that communities behave as if they were closed systems. This is what he terms 'cultural involution' (1973, pp. 51–5). Three facets may be distinguished: conservatism, retrenchment and simplification. The first is a 'security orientation': people cling to familiar behavioural goals and institutions. Secondly, settlers initially fall back on close relatives, living together until they feel able to branch out again. Thirdly, resettled communities exhibit 'a reduction in the cultural inventory'; some aspects of behaviour become irrelevant or inappropriate. Rituals may be abandoned or simplified. In fact accounts of relocated 'communities' show that the situation is more complex; some rituals are kept alive despite the cost involved, others are dropped temporarily and later revived, yet others are altered or substituted. In some cases the practices of local populations are adopted, in others new 'traditions' emerge.

Relocation theory is based on an organic analogy which assumes that communities are discrete, integrated and undifferentiated isolates. Such a schema does little justice to the variety of responses within communities, and underestimates the adaptability and inventiveness which accounts of resettlement portray. In many cases it was the resettlement process itself which created the very 'community' under discussion. People learn new skills, develop new relationships, and show a range of social responses, which vary according to factors such as sex, age, religion, occupation and ethnicity.

Finally, relocation theory has not concentrated sufficiently on the crucial issue of interactions between cultures and States. The extent of State organisation of resettlement varies, as does the degree of consultation, coercion, compensation, commitment to development and interference in settlers' lives. In his study of the Zande scheme, Reining suggested that officials as well as the people in the scheme should be part of the research, and that 'the totality of the development project should be studied rather than just the people being developed' (1966, p. 261). Chambers has suggested that resettlement can be meaningfully understood only as an inter-active system between indigenous and exogenous sub-systems. One of the most interesting conclusions of Colson and Scudder's long-term study of the Gwembe Tonga is that resettlement pro-moted and hastened the settlers' integration process within the Zambian economy.[5]

History of resettlement in Ethiopia

In Ethiopia resettlement, in the restricted sense of State-organised migration, is of recent origin. However, migrations explain much of the history of population distributions. During the early part of this millennium small groups of Semitic peoples moved across the Red Sea and expanded their influence southward, dominating the Hamitic inhabitants of the highlands.[6] From the sixteenth cen-tury Oromo pastoralists expanded north and settled in the high-lands, where they became sedentary cultivators.

However, it was in the second half of the nineteenth century that the modern Ethiopian empire was formed through conquests by the rulers of the central State of the peripheries mainly to the south. From then onwards the direction of settlement was largely southwards. As Emperor Menelik expanded the empire he rewarded soldiers with grants in the conquered territories. Mene-lik's policy was continued and extended by Emperor Haile Sellasie in lieu of providing pensions.[7]

During the twentieth century the development of a bureaucracy and the growth of administration and communications provided a stimulus for migration. The extent of spontaneous migration can only be guessed. Wood suggests that the area under cultivation may have expanded by 25% in the period 1950–74, and that more than one million people resettled (1982, p. 157). Projections from data on ethnicity in the 1981 Demographic Survey reveal that over a million people living in southern regions claim Amhara ethnicity.[8]

Considerable spontaneous migration occurred in response to 'push factors' in the north and 'pull factors' in the south. The former included land degradation and population pressure, a system of land tenure which led to fragmentation of holdings, evictions resulting from the establishment of large mechanised estates,[9] and periodic and increasing incidence of famine. 'Pull factors' included availability of land and opportunities for wage-labour and trade.

Over the past thirty years State-sponsored resettlement has become an increasingly prominent aspect of central planning and Government policy. A parallel exists between modern State-sponsored settlements set up from the 1960s and the imposition of soldier-settlers at the end of the nineteenth century. Some of the early schemes were planned for ex-soldiers. Both Imperial and Revolutionary Governments appropriated local land and labour for settlements. The former disregard for traditional land rights was continued with the assumption that lands not under continuous cultivation were not used.

With the latest phase of massive resettlement the analogy between colonisation at the end of the last century and the current programme has been developed by writers who suggest that the former 'garrisons towns' were the model for the modern settlements.[10] The claim has also been made by liberation movements, which have attacked settlements on several occasions. However, superficial similarities mask significant differences. Although political objectives of control and integration were an aspect of resettlement policy, the primary objectives were not military conquest and pacification, but to provide new opportunities for famine victims and increase agricultural production. In the past, grants to soldier-settlers in lieu of pensions gave them almost unlimited rights to exploit the labour of their 'tenants' and exact tribute. In the recent resettlement, though local people were initially mobilised to build huts for settlers and plough land for them, settlers thereafter had no further rights over them. The relationships of settlers with local people were mediated through the market, except for those settlers who left their villages and become dependants or 'tenants' of local people.

Prior to the Revolution in 1974, resettlement was not a major Government concern. Schemes were set up on an *ad hoc* basis on the initiative of administrators, notably the Governor of Sidamo, aid agencies, such as Association Solidarité et Développement; and religious organisations, in particular the Ethiopian Evangelical

Church Mekane Yesus. This led to the creation of what Robertson termed 'aid fiefdoms' (1984, p. 203). Government concern with resettlement was mainly a consequence of projects aimed at agricultural or community development. Without coordination and with little central planning, resettlement was used to promote an assortment of economic, social and political objectives. Settlers comprised landless peasants, evicted tenants, pastoralists and shifting cultivators, urban unemployed and ex-servicemen.

Resettlement became an issue of Government concern with the establishment in 1966 of the Ministry of Land Reform and Administration. In the Third Five Year Development Plan, published in 1968, settlement schemes were seen as necessary to relieve population pressure in the northern highlands, and to raise production by exploiting underdeveloped lands in the south. In 1972 a committee was set up to carry out feasibility studies. Delegations were sent to tour settlement schemes in Kenya and Tanzania. The Ministry commissioned several studies.[11] A first proposal was considered too costly for a small number of settlers. Other suggestions were too far-reaching to be implemented by a Government which relied on the backing of the landed elite, and had neither the power nor the will to introduce land reforms. The Planning Commission Office also recommended resettlement as a means of creating employment and solving the problem of the growing excess labour force.

By the time of the Revolution resettlement had made little impact on the economy. Simpson concluded: 'Settlement programmes made a negligible contribution to Ethiopia's rural development' (1976, p. 150). Some forty settlement sites with about 10,000 households had been established at a cost of US$8 million. This represented less than 0.2% of rural households, compared with over 5% of households which settled spontaneously (Wood, 1985, p. 92). The results were poor and the viability of many schemes remained open to question. Although small-scale and low-cost schemes fared best, the Government was involved mainly in large-scale high-input schemes (ILO, 1970, p. 29; Dessalegn, 1989, pp. 23–4). Schemes involving settlers without agricultural or settled backgrounds, including pastoralists,[12] shifting cultivators and ex-soldiers, showed little sign of success and even schemes for land-short peasants were fraught with difficulties.[13]

After the Revolution the pace of resettlement increased dramatically. Within ten years some 46,000 households, comprising about 187,000 people, were resettled on eighty-eight sites in eleven

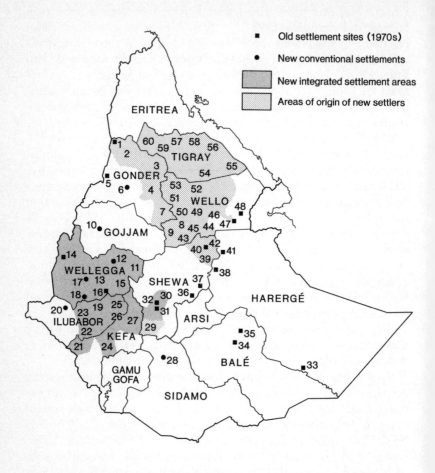

The location of settlement sites. *1* Humera, *2* Wegera, *3* Semén, *4*
Libo, *5* Metemma, *6* Chilga, *7* Gayint, *8* Were Himeno, *9* Borena,
10 Metekkel, *11* Horro Gudru, *12* Anger Guttin, *13* Gimbi, *14* Asosa,
15 Neqemté, *16* Dimtu, *17* Jarso, *18* Qéto, *19* Sor and Geba, *20*
Gambélla, *21* Gimira, *22* Mocha, *23* Goré, *24* Kefa, *25* Buno Bedellé,
26 Limu, *27* Jimma, *28* Dila, *29* Kembata and Hadiya, *30* Chebo and
Guragé, *31* Tadelé, *32* Harolé, *33* Godé, *34* Melka Oda, *35* Harawa,
36 Wenji, *37* Metehara, *38* Amibara, *39* Yifat and Timuga, *40* Menz
and Gishé, *41* Gewané, *42* Jewana, *43* Werre Ilu, *44* Qallu, *45* Desé
Zurya, *46* Ambasel, *47* Dubti, *48* Asaita, *49* Yejju, *50* Wadla Delanta,
51 Lasta, *52* Raya and Qobo, *53* Wag, *54* Raya and Azebo, *55* Inderta,
56 Hulet Awlelo, *57* Adwa, *58* Agamé, *59* Axum, *60* Shiré.

regions. Three factors explain this increase. (1) The land reform of 1975 nationalised rural land, thereby removing the greatest obstacle to implementing earlier proposals. (2) Two successive nation-wide famines within the span of a decade highlighted the need for long-term solutions. (3) The Government set up agencies with responsibilities for resettlement. In 1973 the Relief and Rehabilitation Commission (RRC) was created and became the implementing agency of the Inter-ministerial Group on Land Settlement; in 1976 a Settlement Authority was set up as an autonomous unit within the Ministry of Agriculture (MOA), which was renamed Ministry of Agriculture and Settlement; finally, in 1979, a merger of the old RRC, the Settlement Authority and the Awash Valley Authority led to the establishment of a new RRC.

Major changes in settlement patterns took place during the first post-Revolution decade. Famine victims gradually became the dominant component (Wood, 1985, p. 106). Nonetheless, resettlement continued to be seen as a remedy for all ills and a way of furthering a hotchpotch of economic, social and political objectives for dealing with famine, providing land to the landless, increasing agricultural production, introducing new technologies, establishing cooperatives, removing urban unemployed and 'undesirables', stopping charcoal burning, settling pastoralists and shifting agriculturists, forming defences on the Somali border and rehabilitating repatriated refugees. Resettlement was increasingly used to promote cooperativisation. The Settlement Authority envisaged a resettlement model involving the *melba*, or first of three stages of collectivisation. The RRC launched a plan in July 1981 to transform large-scale settlements into the *welba*, or second degree of collectivisation, with minimal private holdings of 0.1 ha.[14]

Despite the increase in numbers since the Revolution the results during the 1970s were mediocre and did little to relieve highland population pressure. By 1982 a mere 0.6% of total rural households had been resettled.[15] The Settlement Authority planned to settle 20,000 households annually. By the time of its abolition in 1979, the Authority was responsible for 20,000 households (some 75,000 people), some of whom belonged to schemes set up before the Revolution. Reports pointed to high social and economic costs,[16] and reliance on State inputs. Although settlements were assumed to become self-sufficient within five years, a decade after their establishment the Government was still supporting many schemes. On the eve of the 1984 famine many settlements had not become self-sufficient and required food aid. Evidence of low productivity and declining yields, particularly in high-input schemes, raised doubts about their economic viability and sustainability. Ten years after they were set up only about a quarter of the original tractors were operational. Socially, the results were disastrous. The schemes paid no regard to the local population. The attempt to settle urban unemployed and pastoralists, often against their will, led to massive desertions, and the policy of settling men without their families proved so unpopular that it was abandoned (Colaris, 1985, p. 53). Collectivisation was resented and high-profile cooperatives showed the greatest desertion rates. By 1983 the RRC had come to the conclusion that these ventures were unworkable. A new approach was proposed in September 1984, in which emphasis was placed on small-scale projects, with oxen as the means of draught power. Existing mechanised cooperatives were to be scaled down and gradually phased out.

To conclude, the history of resettlement schemes in Ethiopia has little to commend itself. On the eve of the great famine of 1984–5, resettlement contributed a mere 0.2% to agricultural production (ONCCP, 1984c, p. 162), and the country's resettlement programme was in crisis. Dessalegn concluded (1989, p. 45):

> Resettlement failed to live up to its expectations. It had absolutely no impact on the unemployment problem in the urban areas, and did little to ease the agricultural or environmental crises facing the country. Indeed, there is reason to believe that the damage caused by resettlement far outweighs its benefits, and the vast resources wasted on the various programmes would have been more profitably employed elsewhere.

The final chapter in the history of Ethiopian resettlement opened with the devastating famine of 1984–5; this was followed by a massive relocation programme, the consequences of which form the basis of this book.

Notes

1 Poluha (1989).
2 H. Pankhurst (1990).
3 A. Pankhurst (1991a).
4 *Oxford English Dictionary* (1989), p. 705.

5 The authors conclude: 'Big dams, for all their negative impacts, are a very effective mechanism for incorporating local populations into a wider regional and often national framework' (1979, p. 228).

6 It is interesting to note that perhaps the first reference to resettlement is in an inscription of the fourth century, in which King Ezana claimed to have settled some 4,000 people whom he supplied with new land and 25,140 cattle (Budge, 1928, I, pp. 245–6).

7 This was recommended to promote assimilation by Tedla Haile Modja in his thesis submitted to the Belgian Colonial University of Anvers (1930, p. 42). From 1942 Emperor Haile Sellasie instituted 'Land Grant Orders'. Some 8.5 million hectares were defined as 'Government land', about 2 million of which were distributed between 1942 and 1974 (Ministry of Land Reform and Administration, 1972a, p. 30; 1972b, p. 16).

8 Central Statistical Office (1985a, pp. 94–108); A. Pankhurst (1988b, p. 5). Ethnicity is, of course, constantly being created.

9 The Awash Valley Authority deprived Afar pastoralists of dry-season grazing lands and attempted to transform them into settled wage-labourers (Flood, 1976, p. 66).

10 E.g. Clay and Holcomb (1985, p. 164), Mekuria Bulcha (1988, pp, 118–23).

11 Burke and Thornley (1969), ILO (1970), MacArthur (1971, 1972), Wetterhall (1972), MLRA (1972a, 1974).

12 The policy of sedentarisation was a result of prevailing prejudice against pastoralists, often described as 'following the tails of their cattle'.

13 See Simpson (1975, 1976), Van Santen (1980), Wood (1985), Eshetu Chole and Teshome Mulat (1988), Dessalegn Rahmato (1989).

14 It is revealing that in the structure of the RRC resettlement was placed in a section named 'Settlers Administration and Cooperative Department'.

15 The Ethiopian Highlands Reclamation Study estimated that 4.3 million people will have become landless by the year 2010. The study's Resettlement Strategy Proposals suggested the need for 645,000 families to be resettled over twenty-five years, i.e. an annual rate of 25,800 families or 129,000 people (Colaris, 1985, pp. 65–6).

16 Annual expenditure rose from less than US$1 million before the Revolution to US$5 million under the Settlement Authority, US$24 million under the new RRC by 1979, and US$30 million in the early 1980s. In the five years prior to the 1984 famine, operating costs incurred by Government were probably more than US$150 million (Colaris, 1985, pp. 38–44; Eshetu Chole and Teshome Mulat, 1988; Wood, 1985, pp. 92, 108; Dessalegn, 1989, p. 46).

PART ONE

The logic of resettlement

II

'The cruel days':
survival and surrender

The dramatic drop in the price of cattle and the mass
migration of peasants out of rural areas that one observes
at a particular point in a famine is merely the closing scene
of a drama whose most important and most decisive acts
have already been played out behind closed curtains.

Dessalegn Rahmato (1987, p. 24)

In this chapter I seek to place resettlement in the context of the
1984–5 famine. The media image of passive resignation is contrasted with settlers' accounts of determined struggle. After a brief
overview of the famine the perspective shifts to peasant conceptions
of the drought, and the links they saw between the famine and
their resettlement.

In the second part I describe the main options pursued by
peasants during the famine: remaining on their land, looking for
work as wage-labourers and seeking assistance from relatives. Settler accounts relate their attempts to survive without becoming
dependent on others or on food hand-outs in the disease-ridden
shelters. The stories reveal how the restrictive nature of the aid
environment placed pressure on peasants to resettle.

Finally, the narrative depicts failure, defeat and capitulation, as
peasants surrender their way of life and place themselves at the
mercy of the State.

The 1984–5 Ethiopian famine

The Ethiopian famine, as remembered by the world, is largely a
fabrication of the visual media projected on a hitherto unheard-of
scale.[1] The famine became a modern myth of apocalyptic magnitude. The vision of living skeletons shown on television screens
propagated a message of passive resignation and silent despair.[2]

The image was a powerful and effective scoop, in more senses than one. First, it was a simple image, self-contained in time and space: helpless victims with no former lives, no present identity, no future, moving relentlessly from famine camps to the grave. Secondly, the spectacle was glaringly explicit: human suffering exposed with almost pornographic vividness. Thirdly, the message was clear and contained an emotive plea for help. It was calculated to elicit repugnance at the sight of contorted naked figures stripped of their humanity, shame at being spectators of the tragedy, and pity for the victims. The pictures triggered an unprecedented response, symbolised internationally by effervescence of phenomena such as Band Aid, Live Aid and Sports Aid. In Ethiopia all sections of the population were mobilised to combat famine, and the Government embarked upon the resettlement of over half a million people.

The muted *images* moulded by the media contrast with the accounts of those who lived through the famine; the latter reveal determination to find ways of surviving. However, visions of a holocaust were not merely a media fabrication. The stories related by those who lived through the famine are also filled with tales of bitter hardships and tragic death. But these were only part of complex stories. Consider, for instance the case of Fantayé:

> What can you do? The crops withered, all twelve fields were empty, as if they had not been sown. They said, 'Flour and clothes are being distributed in Lalibela.' I got up with my husband. I was pregnant and carrying a child on my back. There was nothing to eat, let alone clothes. My husband caught a disease in town and became severely ill when we got home. I stayed ten days by the fireplace until he died. On the eleventh day we ate together, and he died at night. It was raining; I cried and called his relatives who lived in the neighbourhood, but they would not come, fearing the illness.

She struggled to prepare the corpse for burial while an enemy of her husband gloated at his death.

> I pulled down the door, placed stones underneath at the corners and managed to lift the corpse on to the door; I washed it with leaves. I spent the night alone with the corpse and the next day an enemy of my husband came to the door and looked in. He said, 'Did he die on you?' I could not answer, my throat was blocked.

He ran back to his wife and put on his smart clothes. I dragged my husband out, and began crying; people were frightened. As they approached I said, 'Let me bury my husband. Those of you who have betrayed me do not come to my doorway. Don't let that man come close, let me bury my corpse in peace.' They stopped him; may God reward them.

After her husband's death Fantayé no longer had any reason to stay behind among people by whom she felt betrayed.

After the burial I went round the mountain and left, without telling anyone, without so much as a glance backwards. I did not say to the spirit of my country, 'Follow me.' I said, 'Take me to a place where there is bread, so that I can work to make dough to eat and live. Do not return me to my country, send me away!' I turned round and left with my child.

Aid workers in the shelters recall that for every living corpse the cameramen homed in on there were a hundred dignified under-nourished people awaiting their fate. Likewise, for every person who decided to walk to the shelters, there were hundreds who sought different ways to eke out a living: gathering wild plants, rationing reserves and selling assets, migrating in search of wage-labour, seeking assistance from wealthier relatives in less affected areas, taking part in food-for-work projects . . . anything to avoid coming to the shelters, usually a last resort and an admission of defeat.

The Ethiopian famine of 1984–5 has been the subject of much writing from the point of view of aid administration. The involve-ment of international aid agencies and governments, and the slow response to the crisis have been well documented.[3] What is still lacking is an understanding of how peasants and pastoralists respond to famine, and the ways in which aid affects their response.[4] This is beyond the scope of this study, based on the accounts of those who left their homeland. The following narrative cannot convey the complexity of survival strategies nor the ways in which communities coped.[5] However, the perspective of those who failed to maintain their way of life may shed some light on the other side of the survival coin.

Famine is nothing new in the history of Ethiopia. Since the first written reference, in the ninth century, many major famines have been recorded, sometimes several a century.[6] Most notable was the

Great Famine of 1888–92, exceptional both in its duration and in its rapid spread across Ethiopia and beyond. In the last quarter of this century two famines have associated Ethiopia in the minds of most outsiders with images of starvation of biblical proportion. During the first, in 1973, the Imperial Government's neglect was seen as an important catalyst for the 1974 Revolution. The second, in 1984–5, like that of 1888–92, was unusual in the extent of the country it affected and the time span it covered.

Throughout history, famine in Ethiopia has resulted in extensive migration. In 1888–92, people migrated from the central highlands in almost all directions: to the coast and to Harer in the east, to Gojjam in the west, and to Kefa in the south-west (R. Pankhurst, 1986, pp. 93–8). During both the 1973 and the 1984 famines, people on the move were signs that alerted the authorities to the gravity of the situation. Wello region bore the brunt of six major famines this century (Dessalegn, 1987, pp. 114–17), and the propensity of its inhabitants to migrate in the face of dire crisis gave rise to the remark: 'The people of Wello flee taking even their dogs with them.'

A brief sketch of the 1984–5 famine is required to contextualise settler views and accounts. In 1984 the crucial short rains, known as *belg*, usually expected between March and April, failed completely in many areas. The RRC appealed to donors in March. The failure of the short rains was compounded by insufficient *meher*, long rains, normally expected between June and September. In 1984 the main rains started late and ceased prematurely; in some areas they were almost non-existent. By August the RRC estimated that 8 million people were affected (RRC, 1985, p. 172). International assistance was slow to gather momentum, until the television break-through in October.[7] Soon after that, the port of Aseb became flooded with grain which could not be off-loaded fast enough. In November international donors resorted to costly grain airlifts, described in the following way by a settler from Werre Ilu in southern Wello:

> The air[craft] did not land; when it reached the height of trees it opened the window and dropped sacks on the plain. The first time we rushed forward to open the sacks; we were surprised to find that they were not full of grain, but held three or four smaller sacks and sometimes empty ones, perhaps to stop the sacks from exploding as they hit the ground.

The man described how the collection organised by a PA broke down as peasants rushed forward:

> The PA organised the collection. Donkeys were tied and people lined up waiting. The plane came five times in one day; we could get about three *qunna* [about 30 kg]. Sometimes it would spray the grain without sacks as if it wanted to sow it. The grain would fill holes. People would rush forth with their sticks and blankets. You had to put your blanket over a full hole and scratch the ground close by, like a chicken looking for grains. Should anyone challenge you, you warned him off with your stick.

Peasant views of famine and resettlement

The drought and ensuing famine were not perceived by all settlers in the same way. Opinion among settlers was divided as to whether the famine was a one-year event or a gradual worsening of conditions. The dominant conviction was that the 1984–5 famine was unprecedented, and the worst within living memory. Total rain failure was considered exceptional, as expressed in the following saying: 'Hamlé and death never fail,' i.e. the rains of the month of July always come.

Many settlers were quick to point out that it was their inability to find ways of tiding them over for a few months which accounted for their resettlement, as a settler named Yimam explained: 'It was a short-term problem: how to "cross over" from March to April. We could not last out till the main rains crop. If we could have survived through that period, we wouldn't have resettled.'

Settlers sometimes suggested that the drought weakened people's capacity to withstand drought over a period of years. Some could remember the main rains diminishing in intensity and length for three consecutive years. A man from Meqét claimed that the main rains had started later than in the past and were interrupted earlier: 'We listened three years for the rains, but each year they were less and were cut short; in '77 [i.e. 1984–5] they were silent.'

A few peasants were even able to remember exact dates. One man from Desé recalled the rainfall pattern in detail: 'In '74 [i.e. 1982] the rains started on 18 Hamlé and stopped on 15 Nehasé; in '75 [1983] they began on 22 Hamlé and ended on 18 Nehasé, and as for '76 [1984], the clouds remained an empty promise'.

That some perceived the famine as a one-off event, while others saw it as a 'creeping drought', may be partly explained by regional variations and partly by differences in recall. Settler accounts suggest that the famine in northern Wello, particularly in Lasta, was prolonged, resulting in gradual cumulative famine. In central Wello, notably the Desé Zurya area, however, the famine was mainly seen as the result of a one-year drought.[8] Even within regions differences existed. For instance, within Lasta, the Lalibela area was for several years much more severely affected than the Meqét region, which seems to have suffered from only two years of rain shortfalls. In the following case a husband from Meqét began to describe the famine where he came from:

> The famine came over two years. Before, I used to harvest fifteen to twenty sacks of beans, ten to twelve of barley and six to nine of *téf*, depending on the year, and plenty of oats. The first drought year I threshed only enough to fill three sacks of beans, three of oats and one of *téf*. The plants that had been protected from the sun by stones in the field survived. The year we left for resettlement, I threshed a mere *bédo* [20 kg] of barley, another of oats and a little *téf*.

Innannu, the man's wife, who came from Lalibela and married him on the journey, listened to her husband's account and then gave her own version of events. She argued that the famine was far more acute and disruptive where she came from:

> *Theirs* was not a real famine! It was easy; *they* simply became unnerved. The troubles afflicted *us* for three years. We sold our belongings over several years; we hardly had any crops for three years; there was no rain; no point in sowing. Where *we* came from, people were left unburied; hyenas took livestock and even dragged corpses out of houses. People uprooted themselves when the livestock were finished. We sold, ate and went to Lalibela. There was no one left, the land became a desert, a wilderness; people became bandits. While we still had a cow left, people made us give them milk.

In considering peasant responses, it is important to bear in mind that famine conditions were not uniform. In 1984 some areas received no rain at all during the main rainy season, others received a little. To the west and south other areas obtained enough rainfall for normal harvests.

Settlers also noted marked differences between highland and lowland areas. The drought was perceived as having originated in the lowlands and spread upwards.[9] Moreover, in a number of lowland areas it was compounded by insect pests: army worms called *dayri* and a termite-like pest called *degeza*. A woman from Lasta recalled: 'The *dayri* drought finished us off: they munched the crops down to the earth, leaving it bare like a bread pan.'

Although some settlers saw the famine as an event which developed over three years, few related it directly to environmental degradation or earlier disasters. Even among the elderly there was little mention of earlier famines. The Great Famine of 1888–92 was a distant memory. However, an old woman from Lasta and two old men from Desé recalled their fathers speaking about it. They referred to it as the 'four-year "ceasing" of rain', a time when 'people ate skins which they soaked and cut up in order to survive'.[10]

Although younger settlers usually did not know of the Great Famine at the end of the last century, linguistic usage draws a parallel between these two calamities. The most common expression describing the 1984–5 famine was 'the Cruel Days', the same term employed for the earliest remembered famine. The period is also sometimes called 'the Evil Days'. Direct reference to the famine is often avoided by using the elliptical expression 'the days', as in the phrase: 'We had hoped the days would pass.'

In popular consciousness earlier famines tended to be linked to political events, battles or events associated with local or national leaders. Settlers from Wello spoke of famine at the time of the Segelé battle of 1916, when Ras Mikaél was defeated. Some recalled the failure of the small rains during the Italian fascist invasion in 1936. More recently the 1974 famine was perceived as directly linked to the overthrow of the former order. It was referred to as the famine 'which uprooted Jan Hoy [Haile Sellasie]'.

When asked to relate how they left their homeland, settlers often spoke of a direct causal link between the famine and their resettlement. The drought was often seen as the crucial factor which influenced their destiny. Common expressions used included 'It was the sun which untied us' and 'Drought expelled us from our homeland.' The verbs contain an imagery of violence: 'uprooting', 'untying', 'sending into exile'. The agency is often attributed to the sun, the sky, or the land: 'The sun made the land silent,' 'It was the quarrel of the sky that made us go out [leave]', 'The land betrayed us.'

Most settlers did not speak of drought or famine so much as of hunger. The most common expression settlers used in referring to their motives was 'It was a matter of "grain [and] water" that sent us into exile.' Settlers would often say: 'I came saying [i.e. because of] my stomach.' One man added: 'The stomach is cruel; unless you give it to eat, it won't let you sleep.' An elderly woman exclaimed: 'Hunger is powerful. It makes the feeble leave with staffs, the blind with leaders, all must go.'

Some of the elderly and devout interpreted the famine and consequent resettlement as a sign of God's wrath:[11] it came 'from the Lord above'. Kedija, an elderly woman, put it succinctly: 'When Allah is angry he does not [need to] cut a staff.' Divine retribution seemed meted out to the people of Wello for insolent behaviour. An old man explained:

> People had grown reckless in years of plenty. They used to compete at shooting bullets through their stacks of harvested grain, boasting that their stack was so thick that the bullet would not go through. It was such arrogance which brought God's wrath down upon us.

A feeling of resignation in the face of the will of the Almighty was often expressed by Muslim religious leaders, one of whom commented: 'If God would not help, how could it be [resolved] by people's help [alone]?' A young man once quizzed a religious leader why the famine was not 'written in the book', and why religious leaders had not predicted it. He retorted: 'Nobody asked us.' An ironic couplet explains the lack of assistance from God on the grounds that He too, was resettled.

> As I looked up to the sky it appeared to me too light
> It seems they have taken Allah too for resettlement.

Among the Christians the concept of Divine retribution was also common. However, Christ was also portrayed as forgiving, as in the following story:

> Jesus said to his disciples that it would not rain, so they sat without sowing. But the ignorant peasants did not know this and planted all the same: Jesus then sent plenty of rain. The disciples said to

him: 'Why did you do this to us?' He replied, 'I could not let my people starve.' Then he gave his disciples the chick-pea which can be sown late in Pagumé,[12] so that they would not go hungry.

Among the young, no doubt influenced by the media, secular conceptions were more prevalent.[13] One of the commonest expressions was: 'It was Nature that sent us into exile.' The word for 'Nature', *tefetro*, is usually associated with the expression 'natural (or environmental) problems', a formula which gained currency in official discourse on the famine. The term became so closely associated with drought that settlers would sometimes simply say, 'Nature came,' to explain their resettlement. Other common expressions refer to changes in climate, e.g. 'the air altering', 'the air changing' or 'the sky being perturbed'.

Settlers often felt the need to justify their departure. One man from Desé suggested that migration was natural: 'Men and pack animals die on the road, chickens die in their houses, crowing. Pack animals seek out areas where there has been some rain; so must men.' An old woman from Meqét persuaded several friends to join her in resettling by suggesting that those who left prospered, while those who remained behind stagnated. She quoted the following saying: '[Only] the simple-minded and grass do not leave the threshing floor.'[14]

An interesting example of how resettlement was perceived as an act of Divine retribution for the evil practices of the settlers' forefathers during the days of slave trading was mentioned by a man from Lasta:

> In our fathers' days our people came from Wello to this country in caravans, and took many Shanqilla[15] as slaves. They were gagged with cloth balls [to prevent them from screaming], and were taken back to Wello; there they were used to perform household tasks. Now we have come from the country they were sold in; we have been taken to the country they were captured in.

In this way misfortune was explained and the settlers could feel exonerated from direct responsibility for their fate. The process of rationalising resettlement even resulted in prophetic sanction as in the following account, in which the river at the bottom of Village Three was said to have been blessed for the Wello people:

> Ahmed Yimer Tijani was a Welloyé who had been to Mecca. At

the time of the Italian invasion he travelled with a caravan to Dembi
Dollo; on the way back they heard lions and fled. They lost their
way and found themselves near here. Then a storm raged and a bolt
of lightning came growling towards the sheltering party. Ahmed
Tijani caught the bolt before it reached the ground; it turned to
iron. The Italians hearing the story came to see this wonder; they
decided they would take the piece of metal to their country, but no
one could lift it. They summoned Tijani, who lifted the object with
one hand and placed it in the car. Then the car would not start [so
heavy was the weight of the metal]. When Tijani got in, the car
started easily. They travelled near the Qéto river, where Tijani
decided to have a drink. He said, 'This water is sweet, I bless it for
the Wello people, they will come and settle here.'[16]

Survival strategies

Settlers who moved because of the 1984–5 famine usually tried
other options before seeking aid or resettling. Three main strategies
were considered: (1) remaining on the land; (2) looking for work as
wage-labourers, and (3) seeking assistance from relatives elsewhere.
Although, for purposes of discussion, these are considered separately, peasants pursued these strategies simultaneously as well as
consecutively. As we shall see, survival options were also conditioned by externally created contexts of availability of aid and
the possibility of resettlement.

The strategy of remaining on the land comprised three elements:
working the land in the hope that the rains would come; disposing
of assets, and rationing consumption while gathering wild plants.
Peasants did not easily abandon hope of rain. Normally they
expected at least one of the two rainy seasons to be successful.
When the rains failed those with oxen ploughed over the same
land and sowed again, sometimes as many as three times. When
their own seed reserves were exhausted they bought seed from the
market to try again. During the long rains a little rainfall gave rise
to false hopes. The rains were interrupted and the crops 'were
burnt by the sun'. The following account by Hasen is typical:

The long rains pretended they would come, the cloudy skies tricked
us into planting. On my mother's land, in the highlands above
where we lived, I had planted barley and wheat, lentils and peas.
On my father's land in the lowlands, I had planted *téf*, beans,

sorghum and maize. The beans flowered, the maize was pregnant. When the seedlings began to dry, we let the cattle loose on to them, ploughed the land over and started again. Once more the seedlings sprouted; but the rains were silent; we started one last time. The beans flowered and drooped, the peas grew high enough to hide a cat and withered, the maize was bearing fruit, but did not give birth. The main crop had been silenced by September, and there was no sign of the short rains.

The famine was often described as a 'cattle hunger'. The lack of rain meant no fodder. Peasants repeatedly emphasised that the sale

The Wellegga region

of their cattle was a crucial factor in their decision to resettle. The sale of livestock jeopardised the likelihood of recovery as self-reliant peasants. They could plough only by borrowing and becoming dependent on others. Peasants even began to sell food crops to buy fodder but, as supplies dwindled and prices rose, there was no option left but to sell livestock. Mehammed Husén explained the logic of a famine in which, as he put it, 'the cattle ate the cattle'.

> What I mean is that, as the drought worsened, there was nothing for the cattle to eat. We would pull the thatch from our huts to feed them, but that could not last. The only way out was to sell some livestock to save the rest. One animal would be sold to buy fodder for the others. But even this sacrifice was not enough. People ate the livestock. Once we had sold and eaten our cattle what 'way-of-standing' did we have? A human hunger is better; it was the loss of our animals which 'killed us'. Then we took to the road.

After the cattle famine came the human hunger. As the famine worsened, peasants began to consume their seed reserves. Grain prices rose sharply and 'reached the sky'. A plate of grain cost between three and five *birr*, depending on the type of grain and severity of famine. Peasants became dependent on, and at the mercy of, market forces which, paradoxically, ensured as well as threatened their survival. As grain prices rose, so livestock prices fell, for peasants were obliged to sell animals to survive. Those who sold livestock earlier in the famine received far higher prices than those who tried to hold on to their cattle in the hope of managing to eke out a subsistence, while retaining their oxen for ploughing. An ox worth 300 *birr* in good times would be sold for 100 *birr* early in the famine, and for as little as thirty *birr* at the height of the calamity. In the end, no one would buy or exchange livestock for grain. The market collapsed. The only option was to slaughter and eat the livestock.[17] Settlers commented on the incongruity of eating meat at the height of the famine.

Ironically, during the famine, the meat industry expanded. Restaurants and consumers in the large towns and the meat tinning factory at Kombolcha obtained livestock at extremely low prices. Cattle were exported from Wello to other regions, across borders and through the port of Aseb, as reflected in the following couplet:

Woe, '77, the [terrible] things that you did [to us].
[You sent] our cattle to Aseb and us to resettlement.

The option of staying on the land and selling assets to meet
food needs became increasingly difficult as the famine worsened.
However, many settlers stressed the fact that if only they could
have found a way of 'crossing' a few months, they would not have
resettled. Peasants ate less variety of foods and reduced the number
of meals. Many resorted to eating wild berries, leaves and roots.
Yimer commented that people less well off than his family survived
in this way:

> Some 'below us' managed to survive by gathering fruits and roots;
> they cut the leaves, washed them, left them to dry, and mixed them
> with whatever grain they had left in order to make it last longer.
> Today they are prosperous, yoke oxen and milk cows. We lacked
> a way of lasting out those few months from May to July.

People could not live indefinitely on wild produce and the livestock could not survive without fodder. Women sold clothing and
jewellery, men tools and weapons; households even sold the wood
from their houses. The final blow was the consumption of animals,
which was an inevitable form of self-destruction, leaving people
with little alternative to departure. Welela, one of the oldest women
in Village Three, declared succinctly:

> There is no judge for those whom [the year] '77 [i.e. 1984–5]
> 'buried'.[18] The water dried up: no grass. Neither did the cattle have
> fodder, nor could people survive on wild leaves. Both 'roads' were
> closed; people and livestock were finished . . . The cattle raised their
> eyes mournfully towards the sky. Who would buy them in the
> market? We just slaughtered them. We ate them and left.

The option of seeking wage-labour was usually pursued by men,
and was the main strategy chosen by those without livestock. Three
patterns of migration may be discerned: (1) going to towns; (2)
working on State farms or Government projects, and (3) working
for private smallholders in less affected areas. Those who went to
towns sought day labour, generally as porters. The aid industry,
which required sacks to be transported, provided a boost to the
flagging labour market. However, opportunities for work became
limited, since, despite attempts to restrict movement, towns were

flooded with migrants and prices were higher in urban areas. Some peasants were nevertheless able to use connections with relatives in trade or employment to obtain jobs. A few went as far as Addis Ababa to contact relatives and ask for help in obtaining work.

Most peasants looked for work in rural areas. Some went to State agricultural projects, for instance cotton plantations in the Awash valley, or sesame farms around Humera. Seasonal wage-labour before the famine had been an important strategy for those without oxen. Peasants who went to large projects had often worked in them before and had established connections. The work was arduous in these arid lowland regions and opportunities were limited. The third and most commonly practised option was to travel to areas where there had been some rain, and to look for work among smallholders at peak agricultural times.

Two major patterns of rural migration may be distinguished: from lowlands to highlands, and from poor to better areas of rainfall. Those who migrated from the lowlands, where drought and army worm had destroyed crops, to the nearby highland areas looked for work during the harvest. They often stayed with relatives, sometimes leaving children with them when they left.

As famine conditions spread, people travelled further, often into other regions.[19] Some peasants would stay away for two to three months. One man claimed to have earned 500 *birr* during six months in Begemdir. People worked on the harvest, at a rate of one *birr* per day plus food, or two to three *birr* without food. Sometimes payment was made in food alone, usually two to three tins (of about 450 g) of whatever grain was being harvested.

Although labour migration was largely a male domain, women also travelled in search of work. They were involved in both urban and rural migration, and, in both short-distance lowland–highland migration, and long-distance interregional migration. While men tended to opt for rural migration, women were more likely to go to the towns. They could not easily compete with men in agricultural work. Many relied on begging, as Bayush recalled: 'We became [like] baboons looking for grain. At first you could get a handful of grain by sweeping the threshing floors but later the beggars became too numerous and no work was left.'

In towns women found work more easily as servants and in beer houses. The poorest carried water and firewood for sale; the most desperate resorted to begging. Collecting wood was an arduous job involving at least half a day's walking. In addition there was the threat from forestry guards; Fantayé recalled:

> In Lalibela, we would go to collect wood, rising well before dawn and returning around one in the afternoon. It was difficult to find good wood and there were guards in the forests. We also brought back some *gilmina*, a white tree, which we would pound and eat. We could sell a good load of wood for three and a half *birr*, and a poorer one for one *birr*, enough for one day's food, a single meal. At that time a tin of grain cost two *birr*.

Wage-labour was an honourable way of trying to get through the famine. Unless they were fairly well off, or had reserves of grain or livestock, peasants usually sought paid employment. However, the demand for wage-labour fell. In towns migration from the countryside increased and the cost of living spiralled. Moreover, people from rural areas lived illegally in towns and were in danger of being evicted or taken to resettlement. In rural areas opportunities for work decreased as the drought intensified. This largely ruled out the possibility of migration to highland regions, and there were attempts by highland PAs to control in-migration. Some recall being told not to welcome migrants who could carry 'lowland diseases'. Even long-distance migration to other regions was limited, because of State restrictions on travel, and large numbers of rural unemployed at the end of the harvest season. Those able to return with money earned as migrants were adversely affected by the increasingly unfavourable terms of trade. The price of grain rocketed so that they could no longer sustain themselves until the next year.

Many returned to find their families had departed for the shelters. The famine had also spawned disease; men often returned only to find that loved ones had died. Such was the case of Abbay, who returned to find his sister in a shelter:

> I left with Birhanu to look for work in Bugna [in Lasta]. After two months working for two *birr* a day we decided to return to visit our families, before returning to work. Hungry people had gathered in Lalibela; when we arrived the town was full. We found our families; they had closed the door to our houses and become refugees. I said to my sister, 'What happened?' She answered, 'We uprooted our household and came.' She said, 'Don't go back to

your house.' I asked, 'Is my daughter all right?' She lied, saying, 'Yes, she and the family are all fine.'

The following day Abbay found out that his daughter and cousin had died; he was so distraught that he resolved to leave for resettlement.

I spent the night in the shelter and was about to set off [home] the next day, when my sister said, 'Why do you want to go? Your child has died; so has Allellign, Misa and her children.' I was silenced out of shock, I became [like] a stone. I cried, and said, 'Why should I stay in this vindictive land?' If they had not died I would not have turned my face this way.

Abbay found his wife at her parents' house. Although he did not tell them, his wife guessed that he was about to leave for good.

My wife's father said, 'Listen to me, don't go into the town, look for work on the edges.' I pretended to agree, and told me wife I was about to leave. She said, 'What for?' I answered, 'I will work and return.' She had a small child by another; he wrapped himself round my legs; I gave her a *birr* to buy sweets for the child, and gave her twenty *birr* for herself. As I departed she said to me, 'Abbay, what have you got left to come back to me for. If only my [other] child had died, not the one [which I bore] from you.

During the famine peasants received help from better-off relatives or those living in less affected areas. Many famine victims went to stay with relatives. Evidence suggests that people became weary of assisting relatives. One woman put it thus: 'It became like the saying, "People come, problems come". Relatives are no use; there are no relatives in times of difficulty.'

The highlands were the traditional refuge for those from the drought-prone lowlands, but the highlanders began to tire of the refugees, as one man from Desé observed: 'The highland people disliked us and began to look to their money.' However, this was by no means a simple case of 'aid fatigue'. Many often insisted that they did not want to ask for assistance, and actually turned down offers of help from relatives who invited them to stay, for two reasons. First, they did not want to be a burden; second, they did not wish to be dependent, and preferred to brave the uncertainties of a new life. Having sold their livestock, those who might otherwise have accepted help or sought loans were reluctant to face the likelihood of long-term dependence. Husén recalls his cousin saying: 'Let us stay together; if things get worse we will all leave together.' I answered: 'The sky has been "disrupted". Rather than harming you, I will leave, lest the day refuses to be reconciled with us.'

This attitude was in part an indication of altruism. Settlers often used the verb 'to weigh down on someone' to describe this situation. The case of Tazzeze, a young man from Lasta, illustrates this point. He had been to Gonder to work; when he came back he found that his mother had left. He went to see his father, who lived in a different area; the old man said: 'Don't go, I will support you,' but he answered, 'I won't denude my father. What I eat could be for my sister.'

This attitude reveals a strong sense of pride and independence, deeply embedded values of the Wello peasant. Tazzeze had not been living with his father after his mother divorced him. To return to him, and accept his protection, would have meant becoming subservient.

Peasants did not want to become clients of other independent householders even though the latter were keen to offer assistance. To avoid disapproval, people often did not tell their relatives that they were planning to leave, or claimed they were going to look for work locally. Relatives who found out expressed anger. Husén, the brother of a woman who resettled with her husband, worked as a petrol pump attendant in Addis Ababa. He sent her money but was resentful of her husband, whom he blamed for not having appealed to him before leaving: 'If only he had sent me a message! I would have sent them 300 *birr* to tide them over until the rains. With that they could easily have bought a sack of grain.'

Abba Seyd had a son who owned a bar and had tried in vain to dissuade his father from resettling. Abba Seyd wrote to his son several times, but never received a reply. Finally, he sent a letter by hand. He recalled: 'When the messenger told my son that he had a letter from his resettled relatives his only response was: "I have no settler relatives".'

The discussion so far has treated three strategies – staying on the land; looking for work, and seeking help from relatives – as though they could be considered separately. The reader, however, will have noticed that there is a good deal of overlap. Patterns of survival were in fact closely interwoven. Moreover, members of one family often pursued different strategies, as the following example shows:

> Mehammed lived near Harbu in Qallu region. At the beginning of the famine he sent his wife with his two youngest children to stay with his brother, who lived in a nearby highland region. Meanwhile he and a teenage son attempted to plough their fields again. His eldest son first went to town to look for employment with his uncle, and later worked on a food-for-work project, planting seed-lings. When the famine worsened Mehammed and his son aban-doned their fields and drove the remaining ox, their cow and three goats to the highlands. He then left his son to take care of the livestock, while he went looking for work in Borena, where he received a handful of grain for each load he threshed. He returned home to find that his eldest son had registered for resettlement, since he could no longer find work. His son suggested that they should leave together, but Mehammed would not depart without the rest of his family. By the time he had fetched them, the batch in which his son was had already left. The famine was still intense and Mehammed thought he might find his son, so he and his family also registered.

When the various strategies failed the only remaining options were to seek assistance and/or resettle. For most it was by no means an easy decision, as revealed in the dominant imagery in the expression 'We uprooted ourselves to come.'

Aid and surrender to the State

In an era of world food surpluses alongside mass starvation, inter-national intervention saved the lives of millions. Without the mass-ive relief effort, the famine of the mid 1980s might have assumed the proportions of the calamity of 1888–92. Some thirty shelters run by a dozen aid agencies were established in Wello between 1983 and 1984 (Dessalegn, 1987, p. 121). However, the relief operations engendered their own problems and inequities. The shelters, which the cameras needed to trigger the release of vitally needed assist-ance, were part of the problem. The high-profile tragedies of the camps told only part of the story. Beyond lay the invisible world of those struggling to survive in a multitude of ways. Settlers' accounts make it clear that wholesale migration to the shelters was very much a strategy of last resort. People tried to avoid the shelters, which they knew to be breeding grounds for disease. The Government and foreign agencies also gradually became aware that shelters generated self-perpetuating problems. As a result a policy was adopted which discouraged people from going to shelters and provided food for people to take back to their villages. By the time I visited Wello in January 1986 the camps had all but disbanded.

During the famine peasants found the aid environment uneven and unpredictable. In some areas food-for-work programmes were set up, while in others food distribution was free. This discrepancy gave rise to some resentment among peasants relying on food-for-work programmes. A settler from Desé recalled: 'We had to work for grain; we built the very road the buses used to take us away from our homeland. While we worked for food, others received aid free.'

Given limited assistance, Government and aid agencies sought ways of targeting aid, and treating the problem as if it could be contained within the shelters. One approach was to restrict assistance to the population already in the shelters and exclude others from entering. This had the result of turning shelters into privileged islands. Another practice was to limit assistance to a particular group of people. In one area in northern Wello, when supplies ran short, an aid agency used a ticket system in order to provide assistance to a limited number of people from one district. This led to a situation where the 'ticket owners' profiteered by selling aid grain at high prices. They bought livestock and other items at rock-bottom prices from destitute peasants who were then left with little option but to resettle. A third solution was to target the vulnerable, particularly mothers with small children, the elderly and sick. This selectivity was seen by many as arbitrary, and the priority given to babies who were likely to die seemed pointless. This increased family separation as women with babies went to the shelters while men sought work. However, peasants were quick to find ways of getting round the system. Young mothers, for example, could obtain food through their babies. Iténat, a young woman from Lalibela whose parents and brother had died, described how she and her sister managed to survive by 'sharing' her sister's child. 'We took turns at carrying the child to the feeding centre. That is how we survived the drought from July to October. Then one of the workers recognised us and I was told: "You are single, go to resettlement".'

Since food aid was tailored to perceived needs and could be tapped only by certain categories of the destitute, families deployed their members accordingly. One young boy from Lasta explained:

> My father and older brother went looking for work; my mother and I went to the town. While she went to collect firewood for sale, she sent me to the shelter to sit. If I sat in a queue long enough, looked unwell and was lucky, I might get some food. You could only get food by sitting and waiting.

The towns and shelters were feared for the diseases they spawned, but often people had no choice. Abeba recalled:

> My elder sister died, leaving behind her daughter of three months. Everyone insisted that I must look after the infant; I weaned my baby and took care of hers. They said, 'There is aid in Lalibela,' so I slung the baby on my back, and went there to try to save her. The foreigners told me that I could receive aid 'through the child' if I registered and stayed in the shelter. I said, 'What! Looking after someone else's child while mine die at home!' I took what they would give me and returned to my country. When I arrived my children, who had been longing for me, kissed my hands and feet. Then I fell ill with a disease that I had picked up in the shelter and lay unconscious for three days.

Abeba went on to recount the story of the death of her aunt and her daughter:

> While I was delirious my mother's elder sister came to visit. She spent the night at my house and died the next day. We had no people around; our relatives had gone to Lalibela. My son, Demillé, put a cloth over her, and they removed me from the house she died in. Unbeknown to me, my dead sister's child also died by my side when she had nothing to suck. An aunt of mine came with her brothers to take the corpse. I said, 'The child has died too, bury her.' They said, 'We cannot carry two corpses.' My brother came the next day and took the infant to the graveyard on his own.

Abeba's continued with the story of her children's death:

> I became ill again. Demillé was also affected; he went out in the middle of the night by moonlight. The Lord watched over him for me; the hyena did not eat him, nor did he fall down one of the

precipices which our country abounds in. I was delirious in the
house and he outside. After a few days we both regained consciousness. I returned to my own house, as the one they had taken me to
was oppressive. I had a daughter; I used to call her Innatiyyé. She
was a beautiful girl, very pretty; she was fair. One morning she
played outside until ten o'clock, came in and sat by the stove. I
said; 'Come, the fire will burn you.' She said, 'I want to get warm.'
She came towards me to the couch, pulled herself up, and sat down;
she fell over head first. I picked her up, saying, 'What is wrong?'
She had died. I became [numb like] a stone. To say I cannot take
what He gives is false, I suffered patiently; I laid her out and closed
her mouth, prepared her for burial. I stayed with her that day and
night, and the next day her father's brother came, as well as my
relatives. I was too weak to go to the graveyard; three of them
buried her.

Abeba's trials were not over. Shortly after the death of her
daughter, she lost her youngest son.

Now I had a good son aged nine whom I call Takkele, her elder
brother. Three days after Innatiyyé died, Takkele went out in the
morning. He came and lay down beside me. He said to me, 'Tatey,
get up'; when I got up he said, 'Tatey, give me water.' He tried to
swallow it; it came spurting out of his nose. I said, 'My Takkele,
what is the matter?' He fell down trembling. I embraced him just
as he died. Once again I did not say, 'I cannot take what He gives
me.' I laid him out, tied him down and prepared the corpse. I spent
the night 'being ground and roasted'. The next day, I sent for my
relatives. The previous time when my daughter died, I could not
even get up; I sat on the couch. This time I hobbled to the door –
you can see the road all the way down to the church. My eyes
watched until they reached there.

After all these tribulations Abeba could not see any reason to
remain in her homeland. When her brother left to resettle, followed
by her eldest son, she could stand the loss no longer and decided
to leave with the rest of her family.

I tried to regain my strength; when I went out, I could see the earth
my daughter had piled for her make-believe mill, and the sticks the
boy had sharpened and the stones he had piled, saying he would
build a house, and my husband's seat. [It was as if] I had entered
a desert. What is a house to me? What is a country to me? I took

nothing with me except one container and a food basket. I closed the door and got up to go to Lalibela. This is how I suffered in [the year of] '77. Death and disease, not famine, made me leave my homeland. Then my brother Abbay returned from looking for work to find all this death; his daughter had also died and he decided to resettle. Demillé followed him, and I could not stand losing yet another child, so I took the little ones and joined them.

Peasants who went to receive food often walked for several days and tried to keep out of the shelters. The price of food, water, and even the barest room in town, became prohibitive. This put pressure on those with young children who could not walk from their villages to remain in shelters. Their closing and the restriction of aid to certain categories of the destitute pushed people to resettle. One young woman from Lalibela recalls:

We had been receiving aid for up to five months; then they said, 'We have no aid for you. If you are able to work and eat, go to resettlement.' I panicked and simply slung my child [on my back] and registered to leave.

The way in which dependence on food aid placed pressure on people was recalled in the following bitter poem:

What sort of grain was it which deceived us?
What kind of wheat was it which deceived us?
It returned to its country, and sent us to the forest.

The story of Innannu presents a poignant testimony of the stress that the famine and the harsh aid environment placed on peasant families. Innannu first went to the town with her husband in the hope of being able to return with aid:

My husband sold one of our two calves for thirty *birr*. He had a brother in the highlands. We closed the door, drove out the cow and the remaining calf, and loaded our mats and skins on our two donkeys. We left the cattle and children with his brother and proceeded with the donkeys to Lalibela, thinking we might be able to get food aid, and bring it back. When we arrived they said, 'There is no aid: only peasants who are willing to be registered for resettlement will be given food.' People were in tents, ill, dying. We were not ill and did not want to go in. We rented a room for five *birr* a month without water or anything. We became thirsty

and the cold was killing us; there was no wood. Water too had to
be bought; we sold the little we had to buy food. There was no
grass or fodder; my husband took the donkeys to his brother,
saying, 'They shall not die with me; let him do with them what he
will; let the hyena eat them, or perhaps times will improve.'

Thirst, cold and hunger drove Innannu to suggest to her husband
that they should look for work or resettle. He refused to leave
while they still had livestock, and rejected resettlement out of hand,
with a strength of feeling indicative of how many people viewed
it.

I said to my husband, 'The children are suffering; thirst is killing
us. Let us find some water, and wood for heat. What can we do?
Why don't we look for work?' He refused, saying, 'I won't go while
my livestock are not exhausted.' I said, 'Why don't we resettle?' He
started trembling and exclaimed, 'What! By the Holy Saviour of
the world, let me be seen [alive] in the morning and die in the
evening [rather than go to resettlement].'

Exasperated, Innannu told the children she was leaving, and
asked them to follow her if they so wished:

At that time I was mistaken; I said to my children, 'Let us go, this
man is not helping us. Now if you will follow me do so, I will go;
at least we will die having drunk water.' They agreed. We got up,
taking with us one food basket, a pan and a skin; I left him the
rest. I did not ask him for five cents. I sold the skin and the basket
in town; with that I bought three tins of beans and we set off. We
drank our fill at the river and continued our journey.

Innannu intended to seek work to see her through the difficult
times, but by the time they reached the town of Filaqit two of the
three children were ill and they decided to enter the resettlement
shelter. Their mother could not dissuade them. She remained outside all day before joining them.

I was planning to go to Gonder or Gojjam, and return when things
improved. But then this boy became ill and this girl also; so much
affliction. When we reached Filaqit the children said, 'Let us go in.'
I refused; we quarrelled. They said, 'We will enter'. I said, 'I won't.'
They went into the compound; I stayed behind, and sat outside the
fence. People started saying, 'What kind of woman is she? What is

wrong with this woman? Does she want to watch these children die? While one can eat bread inside, does she want to murder them?' I spent the day outside, and gave in towards the evening.

Registering for resettlement was an acceptance of defeat. After describing how famine reduced him to destitution one man recalled how he volunteered to resettle at a meeting: 'It was hands up and off to resettlement.'

'Reception shelters' were places where peasants gave up their independence and entrusted their fate to the State. These shelters were dotted about Wello near the main towns. While some settlers left within a few days of arriving, others spent more than a month before departure. Just as famine conditions varied, so the situation in the shelters was not uniform. In some shelters settlers were free to move between their homes and the shelter until the departure date. This allowed them time to dispose of assets, and bid farewell to friends and relatives. They could also take the grain they received to be ground at the mill in town. In many other shelters, however, settlers were not allowed to leave once they had entered. Camps were guarded in an attempt to prevent transit shelters from turning into famine camps.

Settlers sometimes changed their minds after registering, and wished to stay behind, but were not allowed to do so. This partly accounts for some of the incidents of coercion reported in the foreign press. One man from Desé commented: 'If we could have slipped out after eating our fill we would have done so.' Another likened the transit camp to a rat trap with food available to ensnare people. Nonetheless the guards could not prevent people from escaping. In one shelter so many people were deserting that guards accompanied people going to the latrines at night. The shelters held hundreds and sometimes thousands of people. Some twenty-five families would live in one tent. A team leader was designated to receive grain rations on behalf of all the members of a tent. Team leaders tended to exaggerate the number of people in their tent in order to receive more rations. Relatives who tried to join family members in the shelters had difficulty gaining admission and finding those they were looking for among the crowds, as Yesuf recalled. He had been sent to fetch his sister, who was living in another area. By the time he had returned home, he found their house closed.

At Kombolcha the guard would not let me in. I went round to
another entrance and said to another guard: 'Please, my family are
inside. I have just arrived.' He let me in. There was a multitude of
tents with different names; I looked in those which said Desé and
eventually discovered my family . . . We stayed fifteen days in the
[transit] shelter; in one day alone 500 people arrived in lorries.

Yimam recalled his amazement at the size of the reception
shelter, and described life sitting and waiting idly in conditions of
poor sanitation.

The tents were like pebbles; one who sees the multitude wonders
how many there must be in the world. You could find your tent
only by the name of the tent leader. We were given bread to eat;
we had nothing to do; we just sat there talking all day waiting to
leave. The problem was the latrines. You could see one person
standing holding his bum until somebody came out.

The atmosphere of the shelters was by no means sombre, quite
the contrary. At times it was somewhat reminiscent of the preparations for a war campaign in bygone days. Yimam described the
festive mood, which he likens to a wedding, as the loudspeakers
blared catchy tones:

The megaphone was strung up like telephone wires. If you lost a
wife or a child you went and stood under it, and it would proclaim
your name, saying, 'So-and-so' from such and such a PA. Sometimes
the loudspeaker chanted; when I heard the music it awakened my
feelings. The blowing of the *shembeqqo* [a reed flute] and the string-
ing of the *masinqo* [a violin-like instrument] made me forget my
former poverty and pushed me as if I were the one wearing the
lion's mane.[20] He [the Government] made me a best man.

Yesuf recalled the story of a man who was so good at playing
the flute that the officials tried in vain to persuade him not to
resettle:

A man was blowing a flute. The sound came out of the three
loudspeakers; it was something quite extraordinary. There was no
one who was not affected when he performed – if only you had
seen! The officials put him in a car and gave him cigarettes, saying,
'Don't go, you are going to a forest, stay with us.' He refused; he
thought it would be novel and fun [to see the world], and came

with us till Bakko. When they gave him this boiled grain, he said, 'Am I supposed to eat this!'[21] He went back to Addis Ababa; they say he is now working in a bar.

In the shelters the settlers were provided with food, blankets, clothing and oil in yellow plastic containers called 'rubber', which have become standard water carriers and beer containers throughout resettlement land. Teferi, an old man who came on his own without his family, described the distribution of aid at Kombolcha shelter.[22]

When we arrived those who accompanied us said, 'Take care of these people for they have come from Geregera and are exhausted. Feed them well.' Then they registered us, asking, 'Do you have dependants?' I did not mention that I had children. They said, 'Have you not given birth at all!' I said 'No'; had I counted my children I would have received more blankets!

Conclusion

This chapter introduced the famine which formed the background to resettlement. The image of hopeless resignation and apathetic despair fabricated by the international media was contrasted with the accounts of those who struggled to survive the crisis. Settlers' descriptions reveal a variety of experiences and regional differences. Drought was perceived as a powerfully disruptive force. Resettlement was rationalised as an inevitable outcome of the crisis. While the young adhered to the official idiom of 'natural disasters', some of the elderly and more devout conceptualised famine as a form of Divine retribution.

Strategies pursued by peasants during the famine were described. Staying on the land soon became impossible and the terms of trade between grain and livestock forced peasants to sell off their assets, notably the oxen upon which they relied for an independent livelihood. Wage-labour was the most commonly followed strategy, involving different kinds of migration: urban as well as rural, short-distance to highland areas, and long-distance to regions unaffected by the famine. Some worked on Government projects, but most depended on working for smallholders. Reliance on relatives was commonly rejected by destitute peasants, who had no wish to enter a cycle of dependence. Most settlers had followed several strategies consecutively or simultaneously before resorting to the aid option.

Aid shelters were shunned as centres of disease and death. Like the famine, the pattern of aid was not uniform. Restriction of aid to specific groups, by area or category, created islands of privilege to which those seeking assistance often vainly tried to gain admission. In a climate where aid was scarce, many who had pursued other alternatives had no option but to resettle. Having abandoned their homes, they resigned themselves to the fate the Government held in store for them.

Notes

1 The film which broke the news to the world was shown on no fewer than 425 of the world's television networks (Goyder and Goyder, 1988, p. 93).
2 It is no accident that in films with telling titles, such as *Human Calvary*, the victims are silent, their voices blotted out by Messianic music.
3 Cutler and Stephenson (1984); Hancock (1985); RRC (1985); Gill (1986); Goyder and Goyder (1986); Jansson *et al.* (1987); Curtis *et al.* (1988); Webb and Braun (1989).
4 Goyder and Goyder wrote, 'work on this subject has indicated a number of serious gaps in our understanding about how Ethiopian famines affect individual households and how they cope with famine, (1986, p. 75).
5 See A. Pankhurst (1985); Dessalegn Rahmato (1987).
6 For a history of early famines in Ethiopia see R. Pankhurst (1986). Twentieth-century famines are discussed by Mesfin Wolde-Mariam (1984) and in Lasta by McCann (1987).
7 Goyder and Goyder (1986, pp. 82–3); Gill (1986).
8 See Dessalegn (1987, pp. 119–21) for regional variations.
9 This is confirmed in Dessalegn's study (1987, p. 119).
10 This was noted in other accounts (R. Pankhurst, 1986, pp. 82–3).
11 See Dessalegn (1987, pp. 118–9) and de Waal (1989, p. 79) for similar findings.
12 The thirteenth month of the Ethiopian calendar.
13 Dessalegn (1987, p. 119).
14 The threshing floor is symbolic of the homeland.
15 A derogatory term for black people from the border areas.
16 I once heard this legend told with an ending in which Tijani is supposed to have predicted that the Wello people would make the land productive, but that after four years things would begin to go wrong; the settlers would become discontented and return to their homeland! The abandonment of the settlement was thus justified.
17 The slaughter of animals was also carried out by Muslims and Christians for sacrificial purposes as part of propitiatory rituals (Dessalegn, 1987, p. 163).
18 Unlike a murderer, the 'year' which resulted in so many deaths could not be tried by a judge.
19 From Lasta to Raya, but when famine struck there, to Gonder Region; from

Desé to Gonder and even Gojjam, and from Qallu and Werre Ilu to Borena and Menz in northern Shewa.

20 Warriors wore a lion's mane head-dress for chants.

21 Boiled grain is looked down upon as an inadequate meal; it is considered a side dish or one which goes with coffee rather than a full meal in its own right.

22 Tamrat Kebede, former head of the RRC Settlement Division, wrote: 'Distribution of blankets and clothing gave the onlooker an impression of a massive flea-market' (RRC, 1987, p. 9).

III

The riddle of resettlement

Resettlement is the most condemned of all the policies of
Ethiopia's embattled administration, although, or perhaps
because, most of its critics know nothing whatever about
it.   Germaine Greer (1986, p. 277)

The resettlement of over half a million people between October
1984 and January 1986 was the most complex and ambitious operation in the history of the Ethiopian State. Chairman Mengistu
Haile Mariam described it as a means 'which will enable us to

A high-level team headed by Comrade Leggese Asfaw, Secretary of
the WPE Central Committee Drought Relief Committee, being
shown round Village Three by the first-round cadres

resolve the following riddle: while we have we lack, and when we could be lending we are beggars'. To foreign observers the timing of such a massive programme at the height of the worst famine in living memory presented a paradox: when resources were most stretched and the country was in dire straits, why embark on such a draconian measure? In the first part of this chapter I seek to explain how resettlement came to be seen as a national imperative. I argue that the logic is rooted in Ethiopia's independent past, the impact of the famine, and the then Government's misguided vision of a brighter future.

In the second part I discuss the resettlement plan and how the policies were implemented. Recruitment criteria were not always adhered to, and were sometimes mutually incompatible. I use examples from Village Three to illustrate controversial issues and distinguish different types of coercion and family separation. The hasty manner in which the programme was carried out left little time for planning, resulting in harmful mistakes and much hardship. Most of the costs remained hidden, resulting in dependence on State inputs, which left settlers orphans of the Government.

A national imperative

The struggle to make [the settlers] productive is clear proof of victory which gives pride to the nation, a symbol of the brilliant avenue upon which we have set forth.
Chairman Mengistu Haile Mariam[1]

During the last quarter of 1984 resettlement was transformed within a matter of months from a minor component of agricultural policy into a national priority of the highest order. The areas designated for resettlement were visited by the then Head of State and prominent officials. The WPE mobilised all sections of society, from local PAs to university staff and students. The resettlement policy attained such importance that it was enshrined in the Constitution.[2]

How is this rise of resettlement to national prominence to be explained? Why did the Government venture along the costly road of moving so many people at the very moment when the country was economically bankrupt, and while famine was taking its devastating toll of people and resources? Although the logic was not evident, or seemed perverse to foreign eyes, the appeal of launching a resettlement programme lay, I believe, in its value as a symbol of hope and proof of action.

Famine was symbolically linked with the overthrow of the old order and the birth of the Revolution. The neglect of the famine in the early 1970s had been a focal point for criticism of the Imperial Government, whose alleged indifference to the issue was turned into a symbol of oppression and a rallying cry for change. The haunting appearance of famine a decade later, as the Revolution was about to celebrate its tenth anniversary, was an omen of failure. The Revolutionary Government could not afford to neglect the issue. At the end of March 1984 a high-level committee, the National Committee for Drought Rehabilitation, was made directly responsible to the Council of Ministers. As the famine worsened the Government became anxious to do something positive. In October, after the tenth anniversary celebrations,[3] the Political Bureau of the Central Committee of the WPE formulated an Action Plan. This was a wide-ranging document envisaging short-term emergency relief and a range of longer-term projects. The resettlement component proposed relocating a million and a half people from the north to the west within two years.

There was a further side to the famine which dealt a galling blow to the national psyche. Famine had turned Ethiopia, a country proud of its age-old history, into a beggar at the mercy of donors. What seemed to add insult to injury was that most of the latter were Western countries which were perceived to have turned their backs on Ethiopia when it began its journey along a socialist path.[4] It was in this context of humiliation and frustration at dependence on foreign aid that resettlement was seen as a positive and purposive measure initiated by the Government under the leadership of the vanguard party. Resettlement was thus identified with the aims and success of the Revolution. Visiting resettlement sites, Chairman Mengistu commented:

> To see the first new life in new villages . . . is clear proof of the popular foundations of our Party and leadership. It is the achievement of deeds, the guarantee of our victory, a sign of our unity, with which the strength of our cooperation is measured, and is a further chapter testifying to another victory in the history of our Revolution.[5]

In the face of mounting criticism, resettlement was portrayed as a way for Ethiopia to reassert its age-old independence. The unwillingness of Western Governments and aid agencies to help[6] did not act as a deterrent, but rather spurred the Government to proceed regardless, in the way the country had done for millennia. Resettlement was thus presented as a nationalist venture, under-taken by an independent State capable of deciding on its own priorities; it was almost an act of defiance, requiring self-sacrifice.[7] The success of resettlement was also seen as discrediting the enemies of the country.[8]

Resettlement appeared as part of a strategy for reducing reliance on external aid, which concentrated on emergency assistance and woefully failed to address development issues.[9] Further justifi-cations for the programme were sought. Resettlement was por-trayed in the national press as part of the solution to the country's manifold problems. The programme was depicted as providing a means of livelihood for the famine victims, a way of facing the root causes of famine, and part of a strategy of combating excessive land degradation and deforestation. By moving people population pressure on over-exploited land could be relieved.

The value of resettlement as a means of reducing population pressure in the north of Ethiopia may be questioned. Resettlement involved 1.6% of the rural population. Even the region from which most resettlement occurred, Wello, saw only 11% of its rural population siphoned off. Given an annual growth of 2.9%, the resettlement can have had only a marginal impact on population in the northern highlands.

Resettlement was also portrayed as a way of exploiting hitherto underdeveloped fertile-looking areas of the country.[10] The belief in the existence of vast expanses of 'virgin' land was based on the assumption that lush-looking uncultivated lands were unused. This ignored the fact that dozens of small ethnic groups had survived in such lands for millennia by practising careful resource exploitation, involving shifting hoe agriculture, pastoralism, gathering and hunt-ing.[11] The existence of dense vegetation was also taken as evidence that continuous cultivation was possible, an assumption which, as we shall see, experience showed was not always valid.

Last but not least, resettlement was perceived as an opportunity to introduce social and economic change and, in particular, to pursue policies of socialist transformation. Three basic ideas were involved. (1) Mechanisation would liberate the peasantry from what was considered its archaic economic servitude resulting from dependence on the plough. (2) New settlements offered the possibility of introducing villagisation. Resettlement villages with an organised grid layout were a precursor of the massive villagisation campaign, which sought to transform the appearance of the Ethiopian countryside between 1986 and 1987, when settlements were rearranged according to the new design.[12] (3) Resettlement, by starting from scratch, allowed dramatic changes in the mode of production. The new villages were designed as PCs with minimal private holdings. Resettlement became an experiment in cutting out intermediary stages towards collectivisation devised by the theoreticians of rural socialist transformation. This was pre-eminently the role of the WPE campaigners who were sent to organise the settlements.

Resettlement thus presented a challenge to the newly formed Workers' Party of Ethiopia (WPE), which organised the whole venture; it was a way of putting into practice the socialist ideology of the newly formed Party. Just as the 'National Development through Cooperation' campaign in the early stages of the Revolution had mobilised thousands of students to teach peasants the aims of the Revolution,[13] so resettlement was a testing ground for the WPE and its Marxist–Leninist convictions. No fewer than 2,259 cadres were sent out to work in resettlement areas during the first year.[14] This was both a test of their allegiance and commitment to the Party and an opportunity for 'spreading the word'.[15] As the leading national daily put it, the cadres were to be involved in 'the national struggle to lay strong foundations for a lasting socialist economy'.[16]

The Action Plan and its implementation

The Action Plan proposed moving 300,000 family heads (an estimated 1.5 million people) over two years in two phases:
  Phase 1: 50,000 families (half from Wello, half from Tigray)
  Phase 2: 250,000 families (125,000 from Wello, 75,000 from Tigray, and 50,000 from Gonder, plus an undetermined number from Shewa)
Resettlement was carried out with extreme haste. The Action Plan was drawn up in October 1984 and the programme was launched on 14 November. Ten days later 15,000 settlers had already been moved.[17] In the five months up to the beginning of

April 1985 almost 239,000 people had been transported from Wello, Shewa and Tigray.[18] In less than a year and a half, between October 1984 and January 1986, two-thirds of the target had been reached. Over 200,000 households, comprising nearly 600,000 people from five regions in the north, had been resettled in six regions in the west and south-west.

Table 1: Settlers by region of resettlement and origin

Region of resettlement			Region of origin					
Region	Settlers	%	Wello	%	Shewa	%	Tigray	%
Wellegga	253,282	42.7	220,636	87.1	11,279	4.4	21,367	8.4
Ilubabor	146,216	24.7	72,226	49.4	28,275	26.2	45,715	31.2
Gojjam*	101,122	17.1	29,839	29.5	54,858	54.2		
Kefa	79,838	13.4	50,690	63.5	6,514	8.1	22,634	28.3
Gonder**	6,397	1.1						
Shewa	6,149	1.0			6,149	100.0		
Total	593,004	100.0	373,392	63.0	107,075	18.1	89,716	15.2

* The total of 101,122 settlers in Gojjam includes 16,425 (16.2%) resettled from within the same region.
** All settlers in Gonder were resettled within the region.
Source: RRC (1986).

Most settlers (96%) originated from three regions: Wello (63%), Shewa (18%) and Tigray (15%). Most (96%) were relocated in four regions: Wellegga (42%), Ilubabor (24%), Gojjam (17%) and Kefa (13%). Two significant changes took place during implementation. First, the size of the programme was scaled down. Only two-thirds of the planned numbers were moved during the year and a half from October 1984 to January 1986, when the programme was halted for 'consolidation'. Over 200,000 households were relocated, but this represented only 600,000 people, as the actual average household size was only around three persons rather than the estimated five. The second change involved areas of origin. The early plans by the RRC and the Central Planning Committee envisaged settling only famine victims from Wello, Tigray and Gonder. Subsequently the decision was taken to settle peasants from Shewa, notably from its densely populated Kambata and Hadiyya area in the south.

The main pattern to emerge from the 'sending areas' was that accessibility rather than intensity of famine was the major factor in recruiting large numbers, notably in the late stages of the programme. Though famine was more intense in Tigray, military activity hindered recruitment. More people were moved from Shewa and three times as many were moved from Wello. Similarly, within Wello more people were moved from the more accessible areas in the centre and south than from the worst-hit *awrajjas* in the north.

In the 'receiving areas' there was a clear inverse correlation between population density and numbers of persons resettled. (See Table 2.) Areas with a lower density received far more settlers than those with a high density.[19] When they arrived settlers represented 6% of the population of resettlement *awrajjas*. However, this disguised considerable variations. Settlers constituted over a third of the population in Gambélla (42.5%), a quarter in Metekkel (25.5%; if we take the later RRC figures the proportion rises to 31 per cent), and more than 10% in four other *awrajjas*. On the other hand they represented less than 1% in three of the most densely populated *awrajjas*. In the resettlement areas as a whole the average density increased from thirty-five to thirty-seven persons per square kilometre. Although the overall impact on the demography of the settlement areas may be small, in some areas the concentration of settlers considerably increased population pressure on the environment and dramatically altered the ethnic composition.

The new resettlement sites were chosen with haste, sometimes during a helicopter tour.[20] As we shall see, a number of ill-advised choices of site had to be abandoned after much waste of resources, labour and time. Although some resettlement was carried out near existing settlements, such as Asosa, Anger Guttin and Didessa in Wellegga, and Metemma in Gonder, new large-scale complexes were established with little prior study in Gambélla *Awrajja* of Ilubabor, Pawé in Metekkel *Awrajja* of Gojjam, and Qéto and Jarso in Wellegga.

The rush with which resettlement was undertaken hardly left time for planning. A critical appraisal, submitted to the Council of Ministers in 1988, details the programme's shortcomings.[21] There was no attempt to assess at a local level how many people the Government should move, nor how many in designated areas were willing and ready to leave. No thought was given to sending settlers to regions climatically, linguistically or culturally similar

Table 2: Local and settler populations and changes in density

Region	Area (km²)	Population	Dens.	Settlers	%	New pop.	Set %	New dens.
Wellegga Sub-region	70,497	2,489,003	35.3	253,282	40.7	2,742,173	12.5	38.9
Asosa	15,270	239,536	15.6	48,973	10.4	288,509	16.9	18.9
Horro Gudru	16,578	481,394	29.0	24,671	5.2	506,065	4.8	30.5
Neqemté	7,009	345,765	49.3	17,146	3.6	362,911	4.7	51.7
Qéllem	10,739	470,409	43.8	59,217	12.6	529,626	11.1	49.3
Gimbi	16,828	746,192	44.3	30,098	6.4	776,289	3.8	46.1
Arjo	4,073	205,707	50.5	4,505	1.0	210,212	2.1	51.6
Ilubabor Sub-region	46,366	964,440	20.8	146,216	24.7	1,109,268	13.0	23.9
Gambélla	24,276	69,464	2.8	51,531	10.3	120,995	42.5	5.0
Sor + Geba	3,935	245,761	62.4	38,023	8.1	283,784	13.4	72.1
Buno	7,541	417,527	55.3	21,386	4.5	438,913	4.8	58.2
Goré	4,020	114,545	28.5	23,784	5.0	138,329	17.2	34.4
Mocha	6,594	117,143	17.7	10,209	2.2	127,352	8.0	19.3
Gojjam Sub-region	61,224	3,199,413	52.2	101,122	17.1	3,300,535	2.4	53.5
Metekkel	28,681	223,453	7.8	76,644	16.2	300,097	25.5	10.4
Kefa Sub-region	66,633	2,456,722	36.8	79,838	13.4	2,536,560	2.2	38.1
Limu	7,672	485,612	63.3	12,095	2.6	497,707	2.4	64.8
Jimma	8,897	950,454	106.8	11,643	2.5	962,097	1.2	108.1
Kulo Konta	6,704	287,025	42.8	654	0.1	287,679	0.2	42.9
Kefa	11,174	540,373	48.3	15,953	3.4	556,326	2.8	49.7
Gimira	7,383	132,488	18.2	14,004	3.0	146,492	9.5	19.8
Gonder Sub-region	79,579	2,869,269	36.0	6,397	1.1	2,875,666	0.1	36.1
Chilga	21,280	350,042	16.4	4,816	1.0	354,858	1.3	16.6
Shewa Sub-region	85,093	7,911,492	92.9	6,149	1.0	7,917,641	0.07	93.0
Chebo	9,144	1,247,236	136.4	6,149	1.3	1,253,385	0.5	137.0
Total all regions	409,392	19,890,227	48.6	593,004	100.0	20,483,231	2.9	50.0
Total all regions except Shewa and Gonder	217,798	7,670,026	35.2	471,500	100.0	8,141,526	5.8	37.4

Note: These figures represent numbers resettled and do not take account of demographic changes due to mortality and departures from settlements.
Sources: CSO (1984, 1985a, 1985b, 1986); RRC (1986 figures). This table was compiled using area figures in CSO (1986), excluding decimal points; rural population projections for 1986 in CSO (1985b), part 3. (*Awrajja* figures were calculated from these projected increases.) Regional figures for settlers were the latest provided by the RRC, but the breakdown by *awrajja* does not include the latter phase of the resettlement programme.

to those from which they originated, nor to ensuring that settlers from one area ended up in the same locality. As a national policy, resettlement was actively encouraged by officials of the WPE sent to address meetings in PAs in accessible areas. The cadres were the intermediaries sent to promote resettlement. However, those involved in explaining the aims and implementation of resettlement were often themselves poorly informed. Settlers had no say as to where they were sent and were either not, or incorrectly, informed. This sometimes resulted in disappointment and bitterness.

The inducements

What aspects of the meetings, in which the State representatives put the case for resettlement, did settlers recall, and how did they interpret the message? Many in Village Three recount being persuaded by rhetoric, some of which gave rise to unrealistic expectations and attracted young people who were not seriously envisaging a settler's life. Settlers often reported that they were asked to volunteer. They were warned that famine relief would be targeted, or restricted, to the weak and elderly. Some recall being told that the drought would not pass away quickly and might last several years.[22] Settlers also remember being urged to leave to save their children. One woman was told that resettlement would be temporary: 'They said, "Brave ones, you will 'cross over' [survive the famine] and return".' Some young men claim that they were told they would be able to become soldiers if they resettled. Although a few had such hopes fulfilled, many were disappointed.

The most commonly mentioned attractions of settlements were land, housing and clothing. The main promise was that land would be plentiful. Expressions reported included 'virgin land' and 'bread land'. The new land was conceived of, much as in the American Wild West, as a frontier to be pioneered. A similar view of the south and west of the country was traditionally held by Ethiopians from the central highlands. Some recalled that they were told that the land would be ploughed for them by tractors; but they resented not being told that they would still have to dig, and that they would be working in a cooperative. Settlers also reported being told that the houses would be built for them: 'They said "You will simply be given the keys, there will be separate rooms for latrines, and lights in the houses." We found little more than temporary shelters.'

Other promises were that they would be given clothes, and did not need to bring tools and utensils with them:

> They said, 'There is no need to take clothes, they will be provided.' Although we are grateful for the clothes we received, had we known that there would be such a shortage we would have brought blankets, mats and spare clothes with us. If only we had brought our hand tools and more cooking equipment, we would have suffered less at the beginning.

Settlers often stated that they were persuaded to leave without having previously considered resettlement properly, as the following account suggests:

> The team of officials who came 'from above' arrived, and we were called together; they said; 'Save your lives!' They made our hearts turn. I had not thought it over. I did not not have to go, but I volunteered. My wife had gone to visit relatives. I did not consult her but simply registered both of us.

The decision was thus often taken by male household heads without consulting their families, who sometimes expressed resentment. Yesuf, a young man who came with his father and the rest of their family, confided: 'We were surprised at our father, we don't know what came over him. He was going to visit my sister when a meeting was called by the PA; he attended, and when he came back he had registered us all.'

The atmosphere of the meetings was one in which group pressure affected individual decisions. Misgan recalls how his friends influenced him in the meeting:

> We were told, 'The weak will receive aid, but the strong will not; put your hands up voluntarily.' My friends put their hands up and said to me, 'Put your hand up too.' I did so and came [to resettle], slipping out, without telling my father or my wife. I left saying I was going to buy grain in the market.

Individuals made decisions in a climate in which apprehension about the future, and the actions of members of their community, rendered the concept of individual will almost meaningless. Mehammed explained that he still had reserves of grain, as well as eucalyptus trees and coffee:

People said to me, 'You can survive by selling your coffee and wood,' but when I heard it said that those who had sold their oxen should resettle, I said [to myself], 'This must apply to me.' When you say, 'Wush!' to a donkey all the [other donkeys'] ears stand up!

Types of settlements

The level of Government intervention in resettlement schemes has been subject to several classifications which hinge on the extent of government and/or aid agency inputs and extension services.[23] The main distinction is between 'Conventional' and 'Integrated' schemes. The former represented 53% of the total, and are located mainly in the lowlands of Gojjam, Wellegga and Ilubabor. The latter represented 44%, mainly situated in the highlands of Ilubabor, Wellegga and Kefa. A third type, namely those integrated in existing settlement sites, accounts for the remaining 3%, or some 16,000 people.[24]

Although the terms Conventional and Integrated have gained currency, and are used in this work, neither represents an accurate translation of the Amharic. Conventional Settlements are referred to as *medebegna*, which may be translated as 'allocated', suggesting that specific areas were set aside, and that they were conceived of as the main type of settlement. Another term for Conventional Settlements was *kuta gettem*, literally 'cloth fitting together', signifying that many fields of individual holdings were united in the collective settlement land.[25] The Amharic word *sigsega*, used to designate Integrated or Integration Sites, conveys the idea of filling in empty spaces; a better rendering might have been 'Insertion Settlements', for the settlers were to be inserted in existing settlements or placed within local PAs (Council of Ministers, 1988b, p. 74).

Conventional Settlements involved mechanised and collectivised agriculture; sites were linked in complexes located mainly in the sparsely populated western lowlands, which required land clearance and disease and pest control. Integrated settlements were smaller and more isolated, mainly in the western highlands. They were supplied with plough oxen and seed, and tended to be dominated by private agriculture.

Three main differences between these types may be distinguished: scale, concentration and inputs. In theory, Conventional

Settlements were made up of villages of 500 households, while Integrated Settlements comprised about fifty households. In practice, Conventional Settlements were often above the target, while Integrated Settlements varied from a few households to several hundred. Conventional Settlements were organised in complexes, which usually comprised between 10,000 and 20,000 households, normally within a radius of 100 km. The concentration was seen as justifying expenditure on mechanised agriculture, collective facilities, such as schools, clinics, mills and cooperative shops. Integrated Settlements, by contrast, were relatively inaccessible, and sometimes widely scattered, being distributed in over 1,500 PAs.

In the initial stages of resettlement, Conventional and Integrated Settlements both received the same food ration (500 g of grain/person/day), but the former also sometimes obtained salt, pepper and a greater variety of food more regularly. The key difference was in the provision of extension services. Both types were provided with extension staff, but Conventional Settlements had resident campaigners, including WPE cadres, health workers, agricultural extension staff, literacy campaigners and RRC food distributors. Integrated Settlements, on the other hand, did not have on-site extension staff, but received visits from agricultural extension agents, each of whom supervised several sites.

Both types were provided by the RRC with agricultural hand tools and household equipment, and received seed from the MOA, but Conventional Settlements were provided with tractor services, while Integrated Settlements were given oxen. Both types built grain stores and had rooms for literacy and health care but Conventional Settlements were provided with better health and educational facilities. Complexes comprising a number of villages were established; two or more were linked administratively and formed a Service Cooperative with a store and a grinding mill. Feeder roads were cleared; offices for the Associations for Peasants, Women and Youth, as well as craft workshops, model houses and cultural centres were built. Integrated Settlements were assisted by local PAs, which were responsible for preparing provisional housing before settlers arrived and ploughed land in the first year. In many cases the PAs did much more, providing food, cooking and household utensils and water carriers, donating seed and loaning oxen. Close links sometimes developed between the local PA leadership and the settler executive committee. Integrated Settlements were thus dependent on the existing administrative structure, while Conventional complexes were provided with a separate administration run by the WPE. As with Government inputs, international assistance concentrated on Conventional Sites.

Registration, coercion and separation

Registration of settlers took place both in shelters for famine victims and in PAs. The following five guidelines were laid down:[26]

1 Prospective settlers should be willing to be resettled.
2 They should be able to participate in agricultural work.
3 They should be physically fit.
4 Household heads should be aged between fifteen and forty-five.
5 Households should be resettled as single units.

The above guidelines stemmed from the RRC's experience with earlier resettlement, which had proved that forced relocation of urban unemployed and pastoralists showed few signs of success, and that settling single men without their families was unpopular. The guidelines, however, were not always respected, and were sometimes mutually incompatible, often involving difficult and painful choices. Before dealing with the two most controversial issues, namely coercion and family separation, let us briefly consider the second, third and fourth guidelines.

A household head's willingness to resettle did not necessarily mean that s/he was prepared to partake in agricultural work. Three categories of persons showed little inclination to do so: the urban unemployed, most of whom left; a small number of pastoralists from the lowlands who were drought victims; former soldiers who had joined resettlement expecting to become militiamen.

Nor did a household head's willingness to resettle always entail physical ability to participate in agricultural work. An early report noted the presence of numerous handicapped persons, including deaf, blind and disabled persons.[27] At first sight the principle of fitness seems an eminently sound guideline, as it was inadvisable to let sick people travel. It was sometimes overruled by the wish of family members to remain together. The authorities and settler families were placed in a dilemma: if a sick person was to remain behind, should the family remain behind as well? This seemed sensible, since the sick person needed support; but in the meantime relatives, friends and people of the same area were leaving for an unknown destination in the west; the chances of finding them later were slim. Allegiances were divided. Sick persons pretended that they were well for fear of being separated from their relatives. This accentuated the hardships during the journey.[28]

How many died is not known, nor can one estimate how many of those who died on the way would have survived had they remained behind. What can be said with certainty is that remaining in the shelters was no solution, and that those who left promptly and reached their destination rapidly were more fortunate than those who languished in shelters in the north, or who tarried on the journey.

The age limits set for household heads were based on the premise that settlers should be able to take part in agricultural labour, and that those who were either too young or too old should be discouraged. Sometimes attempts were made to circumvent age requirements. Some teenagers saw resettlement as an opportunity to leave home and start a new life; fearing they would not be accepted, many pretended to be older than they were. Youngsters who tried to register for resettlement in their own PAs were often recognised as under-age and not allowed to leave, but went to registration centres in towns where they were not known.

> The PA Chairman refused to register me, saying, 'You are too young, your family can support you.' A friend of mine suggested that we should go to the town and look for work. When I saw people registering I joined them.

Although it was mainly the young who tried to evade the age restrictions, there was also the case of an elderly man, named Teferi, who registered. His wife had left and he was sitting despondently in a bar talking to a group of people when the conversation turned to resettlement. A lorry driver made a bet with him, claiming that he would not be accepted on account of his age. Teferi decided to take up the challenge:

> I said, 'What if I were to go and register?' He said, 'They won't accept you.' I decided to try; when I arrived a man said, 'Who are you?' 'A settler.' He said, 'Come in, then. How old are you?' I answered, 'Fifty-seven.' He said, 'Register him as forty-six.'

The use of force

Just as famine is engraved in the minds of television viewers in the image of the skeletal child with a bloated stomach, so resettlement is associated with people being bundled into planes at gunpoint. While the image of the famine was impressed on Western viewers through the immediacy of the screen, the foreign press, in the absence of visual evidence,[29] played on the *memory* of atrocities with which their readers were familiar to create a vivid impression of repression.

The issue of resettlement exploded in the international media because of the denunciation by the French medical agency Médecins sans Frontières at the end of 1985. The Ethiopian Government responded by expelling the agency, which, with the support of a number of French intellectuals, led a concerted attack on resettlement. The campaign was later taken on board and expanded by Cultural Survival in the USA and Survival International in the UK. The image constructed depended largely on creating an association between resettlement in Ethiopia and three emotive symbols of oppression: Stalinist collectivisation and deportations to Siberia, Nazi extermination of Jews, and the Khmers Rouges' 'killing fields' in Cambodia.[30] The imagery is clear in the titles and texts of pamphlets, articles and reports on Ethiopian resettlement, which contain such phrases as 'Mass Deportations', 'Forced Labour Camps', 'African Killing Fields'.

Initially the debate often had less to do with what was actually happening in Ethiopia than with speculation about what might have happened. Many of those who wrote had not visited Ethiopia and none had actually seen the settlements. Later accounts relied almost exclusively on the evidence of refugees and representatives of liberation fronts opposing the Government. The former were used to promote the thesis that resettlement was designed first and foremost as a political tool of control carried out with deliberate and ruthless repression. The latter were used to suggest that resettlement was a continuation of the military or colonial expansion of the former Imperial State. Resettlement, it was argued, was a way of both depopulating areas in the north under the control of the Tigray People's Liberation Front[31] and repopulating areas in the west with soldiers to counter the Oromo Liberation Front. Refugee testimony was employed to build up an account of mass deportations and brutally enforced collectivisation in labour camps.

The regionalist thesis was used to create an impression of garrison camps akin to the army *ketema* of Imperial times.

The evidence from Village Three clearly suggests that the polarised views of resettlement as entirely voluntary and composed only of famine victims[32] or as systematically designed as a forced relocation programme[33] are equally misleading. The notion of coercion is by no means clear-cut. We have already noted the ruthless force of the famine which turned peasants into refugees and the harshness of the aid environment which pressurised many to resettle, as well as the political climate of persuasion and propaganda which drove many to leave.

As for the use of force, three levels may be distinguished. (1) At the regional level, forced resettlement was carried out for reasons distinct from settling famine victims. (2) At the local level, notably in the later stages of the programme, targets were turned into quotas by officials competing to show excessive diligence. (3) At the PA level, peasants were forcibly resettled owing to disputes with the leadership of their Associations, notably over land tenure, because of an inability to pay taxes,[34] or personal grudges.[35] Coercion seems to have become widespread in the later stages of the programme from mid–1985, when rain renewed peasants' hopes of being able to survive on the land.[36] This led to paternalistic decision-making for rather than by poor peasants, a policy aptly labelled *beggo tetsiino*, i.e. 'well-meaning repression'.[37]

Several categories of settlers were forced to move: (a) so-called 'urban unemployed'; (b) peasants living on slopes designated for afforestation; (c) peasants moved off areas designated for development; (d) people unable to pay taxes; (e) people living in densely populated areas, and (f) pastoralists.

The extent of coercion is difficult to ascertain. A Government survey based on a sample of 1,275 settlers revealed a figure of 38% coercion.[38] Although the incidence of force among settlers now in Village Three was small, it must be emphasised that this village is not representative of all periods and areas of resettlement. Most settlers in the village left their homeland before April 1985 while the programme was largely voluntary. Several settlers, who were emphatic that they came of their own free will, mentioned hearing of relatives who had subsequently been forcibly resettled in Metekkel. Moreover, the incidence of reported coercion would have been much higher if the research had been carried out earlier, since many of those who left the settlement in the first two years had not wanted to come in the first place. Those still living in Village Three who were forcibly resettled include presumed 'urban unemployed', people moved off mountain slopes allocated for forests and for a development project, and people unable to pay their taxes.

Urban round-ups

The rationale of using resettlement to dispose of unwanted urban unemployment was akin to that which led to the despatch of convicts from Britain to Australia,[39] although in the case under discussion deportees had not been convicted of crimes. The policy of settling the urban unemployed had proved a failure in earlier resettlement schemes and had resulted in a high rate of desertion.[40] This was no less true when the policy was repeated in the later phase of resettlement. Three people interviewed in the village described being caught in such round-ups. The first was Shéhu, a young man who has since left. He traded in clothes and contraband goods, such as radios and watches, between Aseb and Desé. He recalled:

> I came to Desé with three mules, one carrying beans, one *téf*, and one wheat. I had all that weighed. As I went to receive the money, one mule disappeared. I ran after her; some traders caught her. I brought her back. I got my money, left it with my brother and went to buy hay. I hired a cart and, as I came near the army camp, I was picked up by soldiers who said, 'Who are you?' I answered, 'I am from a PA.' They said, 'You are lying,' and beat me, saying, 'You must go to resettlement.' I pleaded, saying, 'My relatives have resettled, but I am not destitute.' I was taken with about 120 young men. The others were town louts. I was the only one from the countryside.

Shéhu went on to describe how he ended up in Village Three:

> They put forty-four of us in a lorry, and drove us to Debre Birhan. We spent the night there under guard, and the next day reached Addis Ababa. We were taken to the Administration. They said, 'These are single men from the town.' We were put on buses, and were assigned to go to Gambélla. Our bus broke down and remained in Qéto; since we were single men we were distributed in various villages. The town youths left for the local towns or returned to Wello; I found my father's cousin. His wife found me

a wife, but she soon left; then I met a woman from my country at the market. I married her, but now we are quarrelling.

Although Shéhu was not a townsperson, his account confirms the view that urban settlers will not remain in agricultural settlement schemes. He eventually left after his second resettlement wife had accused him of selling their common property and consorting with other women.

The second case is that of Yeshi, a woman who had left her husband during the famine and came to Desé to find work. While her husband came voluntarily, following a disagreement with his mother, Yeshi was forcibly resettled.

> When finding fodder for cattle became difficult, we pulled the thatch from our roof [to feed the animals]. But things did not improve, and I quarrelled with Abbebe [her husband]; I left him and came to Desé, where I worked in a beer house. I had been there three months when one day they picked us up in town; I was wearing my good clothes for market. We were taken to the shelter where my husband found me. When he heard that I was in the shelter, he had me brought to him by the guards.

The third case is that of a young Oromo man who was picked up in the town of Dembi Dollo. He was one of fourteen young men taken to Village Three in a round-up which involved several hundred people:

> My parents had died while I was young, and my mother's brother looked after me. I was working as a labourer for three *birr* per day laying electricity lines. One evening, I was with my brother when we were picked off the street without a chance to explain who we were. The next day we were taken with eight others to Village Three. The others all left within a matter of days, but I remained.

This case, once more, shows the futility of trying to settle urban unemployed. This young man was the only member of the 'urban unemployed' who remained. Like Shéhu, his marriage to a woman from Lalo Qilé explains his decision to stay.

Afforestation and development

A dozen families from a PA near the town of Kombolcha had been forced to leave their land on account of afforestation plans. One woman recalled:

> We were called to a meeting and told 'Your land is on the mountain slope which is to be for forestry; you have to go to resettlement!' We didn't even eat the maize we had sown on our irrigated land. We sold one ox and left the other with my father, who stayed behind.

Several other families from the same PA were obliged to leave because their land was where a textile factory expansion was planned. However, most of those who came from this PA claimed to be famine victims who left of their own accord. Why should some have been suffering from drought while others were not? The answer became clear to me during a visit to this PA in September 1987. Peasants who were living on the mountain slopes were able to survive the drought unscathed because of their irrigated fields. Those living in the plain were seriously affected by shortages of rainfall. One settler summed up the situation thus: 'From above there was the forest development, from below was the town, and in between Mr Drought.'

Taxation

Several settlers from Lalo Qilé in western Wellegga were forcibly removed because they were unable to pay taxes. The area was one of the few parts of Wellegga where famine struck and where food was distributed. Several hundred families were resettled and placed within existing settlements in Qéto. Forty families from three PAs ended up in Village Three. Motives, once again, cannot be reduced to a common factor, and settlers gave a number of loosely interconnected reasons for their resettlement, including poor, then excessive rainfall, oxen mortality, infertile soils and inability to pay taxes.

The area had experienced two years of poor rainfall; then in 1984–5 there was a shortfall followed by excess. Several settlers also complained that hail had destroyed part of their meagre crops. Drought was compounded by an epizootic of a cattle disease called *mariyé* (perhaps rinderpest). The loss of oxen reduced many to working as labourers. The consequent dearth of manure was a further serious drawback, since the rotating of the cattle kraals was vital for fertilising poor soils in an intensively used land-holding system. Finally, several PAs decided that those who were unable to pay their taxes should be registered for resettlement whether they wanted to leave or not. While some spoke of having been led off, 'children first', without any choice, others welcomed the opportunity to resettle as 'a way of saving the children'.

Separation

The most problematical guideline was that concerning the need for households to travel together. Separation occurred in a number of ways, both deliberate and involuntary. Even where a family acted with one mind there were many reasons why settlers often did not wish to leave with their entire household. Splitting the household made sense, since those who remained behind had a better chance of survival. Given famine conditions, fewer mouths to feed enabled some to retain livestock. By leaving members behind the family could often maintain a claim to their land, as in the case of Abba Yimer, who came with his daughter and two sons.

> My eldest son, Mehammed, remained behind with his wife. We sold one of the two oxen to buy fodder for the other, and some food for the family. Mehammed later sold most of our sheep and goats. He kept the land and looked after the eucalyptus and *chat* plantations. He has written and says he has rebuilt a small herd and bought a cow. He has had a second child.

A second reason for families splitting occurred when sons held positions in the PA, or found jobs in towns, as in the case of Abba Seyd, whose two eldest sons remained behind.

> My first son, Husén, had joined the army and was in Asmara at the time of the famine. His brother, Ahmed, found a job in the cloth factory at Kombolcha. Husén had sent 600 *birr* to us by post; he was angry to hear we had left.

Women were often separated from their kin because of the prevalence of virilocal marriage. A woman living in Wello would tend more often than not to live far away from her parents. Since the pattern of drought was not uniform, a daughter might be living in a less affected area (or vice versa). She and her husband might feel able to plan a way of surviving the drought from which her parents had fled. Many a resettled mother thus lamented the distance from a daughter who, when they lived within fairly close proximity, could easily be visited.

The concept of the household resettling together also assumed that all its members had the same objectives and motivations. However, attitudes to resettlement differed according to age, gender, social standing or personal preference. Many young men and women resettled without their parents or spouses. Given the guideline that households should not be separated, many, for fear of not being accepted, pretended that they did not have spouses or relatives. Iténat, a young woman who had lost both parents in the famine, and had divorced her husband because of the hard times, went to register in Weldia; she recalled a disagreement between two of the registrars as to whether she should be allowed to resettle. 'One of them said, "She musn't go, she has no husband"; the other said, "Let her go, she will find one." I said: "For each the stomach is the husband".'

Spouses also sometimes separated during the crisis because of disputes. Single people who came alone encountered considerable pressure to pair up with other single persons. Many therefore found 'road spouses'. Innannu, whose story about the famine we have already encountered, was at first refused the right to resettle without her husband. She stood firm and would not marry 'for the road', remaining contentedly in the shelter 'eating her bread' while others left.

> When I went to register in the shelter I at first lied, saying that I did not have a husband. The man said, 'Have you children?' 'Yes.' 'How many are they?' 'Four.' He said, 'They must go with their father.' I said, 'They have no father.' The man answered, 'You cannot enter with them without their father.' I said, 'How could I go back after having left him?' Then they said, 'Unless you marry you shall not go.' I said, 'I left my husband, what use is [another] husband to me?' They said, 'If you don't [marry] who will work to give you to eat?' I replied, 'I don't care, I will stay here eating my bread.'

Finally, an official took up her case and allowed her to go:

> While we stayed behind, those who were with us boarded the buses and left. One day another man came and said, 'These children, once they grow up, are they not capable of feeding this woman? If they eat well, are clothed well, and are healthy, they can look after her. Besides, she is young; she can work. If she is not one to go, who is? When you let in anybody, why not her? Register her, go on, write.' The other man refused, saying, 'I don't go by what you

say' . . . The first man insisted and, to prove who was in charge, he gave Ibbabaw, my son, two items of clothing instead of one!

Involuntary separations also occurred when people were forcibly resettled or when some family members entered the shelters first and left before others could join them. Such was the case of Felleqech, an elderly woman who had planned to go with her daughter:

My grandson, Ayyenew, was placed by his mother in another person's house, where he was watching their cattle until times improved. When the famine became severe, his mother sent me a message saying, 'I am about to resettle with my husband. Come quickly with my son, and let us leave together.' When I went to collect Ayyenew, I found him embroiled in a dispute. Another lad had insulted him twice, calling him the son of a slave – for he was black. Ayyenew picked up the lad's stick and hit him on the skull till the 'cheese' [i.e. the brain] showed through.

By the time the dispute was settled Felleqech's daughter had left and she eventually departed with her son and grandson.

The lad's parents took Ayyenew to court. The judge heard witnesses, who corroborated Ayyenew's version. The judge said: 'You did well to hit him when he insulted your ancestry, you should have hit him twice.' When we reached the shelter my daughter had left. People said that she was crying after her mother. I know not where she is now. A beauty, you would not have thought I gave birth to her. Her teeth alone made people kneel. At the time I was living with an old man who was well-off. When my son Yimer heard what had happened he said, 'You and Ayyenew cannot survive alone. Let us all go together, perhaps we will find her.' I simply closed the door and left.

Even settlers who came as a family left relatives behind. Separation was keenly felt and alluded to in a number of ways. Settlers spoke of being 'strewn like salt'. One woman expressed her sense of isolation by saying, 'I am single, hovering like a bird'; another exclaimed:

Times of difficulties scatter [people], they do not heap; it is good times that bring [people] together. Those to whom a mother gave birth have not gone together; we are cattle without a herdsman.

Sometimes people spoke of seeing their loved ones in dreams. Many expressed feelings of guilt and regret at having left relatives behind. Common expressions were 'It needled me' or 'It eats my innards'. General statements, such as 'mothers hated their children', seemed to be ways of emphasising the hardships of the famine and justifying the separation. A sense of guilt at abandoning relatives is reminiscent of 'survivor guilt' noted in other resettlement situations.[41] As one woman put it: 'Famine made us desert our children and parents, we came leaving them behind. *Injera* [i.e. bread] was our relative, we left the old and young and came without them.'

The costs of the programme

The resettlement programme required a greater degree of coordination between various Government Ministries and commissions than any other operation in the history of the Ethiopian State. The following ten Government bodies were responsible for different areas:[42]

Ministry of Construction: building roads.

Mapping and Geography Institute: planning site layout.

Water Development Commission: sinking wells.

Ministry of Transport: moving the settlers.

Relief and Rehabilitation Commission: providing food rations, household equipment, agricultural tools, clothing and mills.

Ministry of Agriculture: selecting sites, providing oxen, tractors, seed, fertilisers and pesticides.

Ministry of Health: building clinics, providing medicine and health care.

Ministry of Education: building schools and organising literacy classes.

Ministry of State Farms: assisting nearby settlements.

Office of the National Committee for Central Planning: preparing plans for regional integration of settlements.

The whole operation could not have been undertaken on such a scale within such a short time span without the coordinating role of the WPE, which issued directives to the various Government bodies and sent teams of cadres to coordinate the programme. Nor could resettlement have been carried out without the organisational

structure of the PAs, both in the 'sending areas' where they organised recruitment and in the 'receiving areas' where they assisted
settlers.

The costs of the resettlement programme cannot easily be estimated. Certain aspects, such as the human costs to settlers and the
local populations, are impossible to compute. The considerable
environmental impacts are likewise difficult to assess.[43] Government inputs were enormous and largely unquantifiable in monetary
terms. Since land had been nationalised, the State had the authority
to allocate areas for resettlement. Labour was mobilised in the
form of campaigns which involved a wide spectrum of society,
from local PAs to university students and staff. Centres of higher
education were closed several weeks early so that teachers and
students could spend an extended period during the long vacation
building huts.[44] Over 13,000 campaigners were sent from centres
of higher education[45] and over 25,000 personnel from Government
departments. Mass organisations were mobilised on a full-time
basis (Clarke, 1986, p. 33). Ministries were instructed to provide
extension staff and the WPE recruited cadres. Tractors were
diverted from other areas; food from relief; seed, fertilisers and
pesticides from MOA allocations; and medicine from MOH budg-
ets. Settlers thus became a favoured section of society. They were
allocated a higher proportion of extension staff in agriculture and
health than any other sector of the country. Moreover, despite
considerable State inputs, settlers, unlike the rest of the population,
were exempt from taxation, since they were initially destitute; this
anomaly was, however, rectified in 1990.

The resettlement component accounted for a quarter of the planned expenditure on emergency development in the Action Plan,
which set out a budget of 531.92 million *birr* for development,
excluding emergency daily assistance in the famine areas. This
figure was unrealistic, and actual Government expenditure for part
of the resettlement component alone far exceeded the total emergency budget. A Government study for the Council of Ministers
estimated expenditure on the new resettlement sites for the three
year period 1985–7 at 564.3 million *birr* for 176,000 households.
This does not take into account input by the Ministries of Construction, Health, Education and Water Resources. Total expenditure was therefore considerably higher. A report by the Planning
Agency suggests a figure of 471 million *birr* for the period 1986–8
(ONCCP, 1988a, p. 114). Government expenditure may be esti-

mated provisionally at some 600 million *birr* (Dessalegn, 1989, p. 77).

Foreign assistance may account for another 400 million *birr*. Total expenditure, including foreign assistance, would therefore have reached at least a billion *birr*. This would give a *per capita* figure of 1,686 *birr*, or US$814 in a country with a *per capita* income of US$123 per annum. This figure alone gives an idea of the disproportionate spending on resettlement.

Resettlement was opposed by the USA; its lead was followed by the UK, the Federal Republic of Germany and several other EC countries. Bilateral assistance was, however, provided by four foreign States: Italy, the Soviet Union, Canada and East Germany. A few aid agencies, four secular[46] and four religious,[47] were prepared to provide assistance to settlers.[48] International organisations, including FAO, UNDP, UNESCO, UNICEF, WFP and WHO, also assisted with limited aid as part of their country programmes.

The Government's orphan[49]

The resettlement programme was temporarily suspended at the end of January 1986, precisely when the famine threat was abating. The timing of the halt, it would appear, was due to internal reasons related to the stress of the famine on the economy rather than, as some commentators assumed, to external criticisms.[50] The logic of the Government response was in fact closely correlated to the intensity of famine. As the situation worsened, the Government became more anxious to be seen doing something long-term. It is therefore not surprising that resettlement was resumed at what, to foreign eyes, seemed the worst possible time, when resources were most stretched.

For almost two years after the suspension no further resettlement took place and Government efforts were directed towards extending support to existing settlements through the Ministries of Agriculture, Health and Education. Other issues, most notably villagisation, administrative reorganisation and the war in the north, came to the forefront of Government attention and resettlement received little publicity.

Later, in the last quarter of 1987, harvests were poor and the possibility of a famine of equal intensity to that of 1984–5 was recognised by the Government and by aid agencies. The resettlement programme was resumed in November 1987 amid reports of crop failure. However, the new famine did not take on the proportions of that of 1984–5 and the pace of resettlement slackened. In the six months from the end of November 1987 to the end of May 1988 some 10,000 persons were resettled. Harvests in 1988–9 were not too bad, and no further resettlement took place after June 1988. With the changes in political climate following ex-president Mengistu's reforms announced in March 1990, and the demise of the old regime and its authoritarian social policies, resettlement seems no longer to be on the cards.

In the first three years resettlement administration was carried out on a 'campaign' basis. WPE cadres were sent on three successive campaigns to organise settlements. Extension staff from the RRC and relevant Ministries were likewise despatched on successive campaigns. However, the campaign strategy presented serious disadvantages in terms of cost, efficiency and continuity. This was acknowledged at the highest level, and a new resettlement authority was due to be set up in September 1987. In his address to the Central Committee of the WPE on 23 March 1987, Mengistu stated:

> From our past experience, we have learned a lot in directing this programme. Every effort will be made from organising the settlers up to selecting suitable ones. *Since it is not possible to direct this vast and continuous programme through temporary committees and campaigns, a special government institution will be set up from next year which will lead the resettlement programme in a coordinated manner.* [Emphasis added]

Five years after this statement was made resettlement remained the orphan of the Government, without any institution mandated to take responsibility for the programme.

Conclusion

In this chapter I have argued that resettlement was perceived by the Government as a cure-all: a means of resolving the problems engendered by famine and its perceived deeper environmental roots in a durable way which would help rid the country of its dependence on external assistance. Resettlement came to be seen as the mirror-image of famine: despair and dependence transformed into a promise of prosperity and self-reliance. Further, resettlement was viewed as a means of developing areas presumed to be fertile and under-utilised. Finally, it was perceived as an opportunity to introduce economic and social change and promote socialist agrarian transformation through villagisation, mechanisation and cooperativisation.

The Action Plan formulated by the then Government was implemented with haste and little careful planning. Many settlers were influenced by propaganda in meetings at which officials urged them to leave, and presented them with a glorified view of a land of opportunity and plenty awaiting migrants. Registration criteria were not always adhered to and were sometimes in conflict. Coercion was used to further policies other than the resettling of famine victims: to 'dispose' of urban unemployed, to settle pastoralists, to move people off areas designated for development, to resolve land disputes and to evict tax evaders. Family separation occurred for a number of reasons related to famine and resettlement, coercion and the chaos of the journey.

The costs of the resettlement operation were largely borne by diverting funds, equipment and labour from other sources on a campaign basis. The human consequences cannot be quantified and remain nebulous, an enigma, upon which the rest of this work attempts to shed light.

Notes

1 Speech during a visit to settlements (*Addis Zemen*, 12 Meggabit 1977).
2 Constitutional Drafting Commission 1987, Art. 10.2 states: 'in order to create a situation that is conducive to development, the Government will make sure that the settlement of people is related to the distribution of natural resources'.
3 The Government came under criticism from Western journalists for ignoring the famine during the celebrations.
4 A cadre in Village Three once made a speech in which he stated: 'Having to beg from our enemies is worse than dying in battle.'
5 *Addis Zemen*, 12 Meggabit 1977.
6 While the Soviet Union and East Germany provided aircraft and trucks, Western countries refused to help with transporting settlers. The US Government also strictly forbade the use of food aid for settlers.
7 At the second congress of the WPE Central Committee in April 1985, Chairman Mengistu noted that, since aid for resettlement was forthcoming only from socialist countries, self-sacrifice was required on the part of the Ethiopian people (*Addis Zemen*, 1 Miyazya 1977).

8 During a visit to settlements Chairman Mengistu stated: 'The efforts ... to prevent the settlers from being exposed to penury again have upset the anti-popular forces that hope for the demise of Ethiopia, (*Addis Zemen*, 12 Meggabit 1977).

9 From 1984 to 1986 at least fifty-three aid agencies were involved in Ethiopia. These agencies spent over 1.7 billion *birr*, out of which less than 5% (75.6 million) was spent on development work (Council of Ministers, 1988a, p. 93).

10 In a speech to the Second Congress of the WPE Central Committee in April 1985, Fasika Sidelil, chief WPE economic affairs adviser, suggested that '90 per cent of the potential for agricultural expansion is in lowland regions of the fertile west of the country' (*Addis Zemen*, 4 Miyazya 1977).

11 E.g. Cerulli (1956), Bender (1975), Stauder (1971). See also Dessalegn (1988a, 1988b, 1989, pp. 84–94).

12 Villagisation was carried out in Balé during the Ogaden War (1979), and in Harer and Arsi regions in 1985; this was followed by an ongoing national campaign in most regions of the country (Cohen and Isaksson 1987).

13 The campaign, launched in December 1974, mobilised some 50,000 students to propagate the aims of the Revolution in the rural areas, and facilitate land reform and the literacy campaign (Clapham, 1988, p. 49).

14 *Ethiopian Herald*, 17 January 1985.

15 In his speech to the departing cadres Leggese Asfaw, Secretary of the WPE Central Committee Drought Relief Committee, observed that the cadres were 'emulating Lenin's programme on cadre activity' (*Ethiopian Herald*, 17 January 1985).

16 *Addis Zemen*, 12 Meggabit 1977.

17 *Ethiopian Herald*, 23 November 1984.

18 *Addis Zemen*, 1 Miyazya 1977.

19 The three *awrajjas* which received the greatest proportions of settlers had the lowest pre-resettlement densities (Gambélla 2.8, Metekkel 7.8, Asosa 15.7 per cent). Conversely the three *awrajjas* with the highest densities received less than 3 per cent of the settlers (Chebo 1.3, Jimma 2.5 and Limu 2.6 per cent).

20 E.g. Pawé in Gojjam Region (*Ethiopian Herald*, 3 November 1984).

21 Two reports were compiled, one from the 'sending areas' and the other from the 'receiving areas', by teams from different branches of Government (Council of Ministers, 1988a, pp. 72–90, 100–26; 1988b, pp. 126–62, 236–43).

22 Some mentioned figures of five or seven years.

23 Simpson (1975) distinguished between high, medium and low input schemes on the basis of the degree of extension support. The RRC made use of two sets of distinctions: first, 'low cost' as opposed to 'special' settlements, and secondly, schemes 'under budget' as opposed to those 'under technical assistance' (RRC, 1985, p. 160).

24 The Ministry of Agriculture also recognises another category, 'Lesser Settlements', with some 26,800 people (MOA, 1989b). These are larger than Integrated Settlements, but are not organised into complexes like Conventional Settlements.

25 Council of Ministers (1988b): seventy-four Conventional Settlements are sometimes also designated *sefaffi sefera*, literally 'wide [i.e. extensive] settlements, (MOA, 1989b Council of Ministers; 1988b, p. 73).

26 RRC (1987), p. 8; Council of Ministers (1988a), p. 21.

27 Taddese Wolde (1985), p. 7.

28 Tamrat Kebede, former head of the settlement section of the RRC, wrote: 'For

fear of being separated from their husbands some pregnant women falsified their delivery times thus many babies were born *en route*. In contrast, persons that were aged and infirm who insisted on joining their families also died *en route*' (RRC, 1987, p. 9). Germaine Greer also describes the desperate desire of families, including the sick themselves, to move on, and the resulting separation when ill members were left behind (1986, pp. 294–5).

29 In the aftermath of the controversy the Ethiopian Government did not initially allow foreign journalists to visit resettlement. This embargo contributed to suspicions concerning the Government's motives.

30 Niggli (1986), Médecins sans Frontières (1985), Colchester and Luling (1986).

31 In fact more people were resettled from Shewa than from Tigray, and three times as many from Wello. Recruitment from areas not under central rule was considered unwise (Council of Ministers, 1988a, p. 103).

32 This had initially been the Government's official position. Internal documents and subsequent reports acknowledged, and deplored, the use of coercion (Council of Ministers, 1988a, 1988b).

33 This is the thesis of Clay and Holcomb (1986), Niggli (1986), Colchester and Luling (1986), and Clay (1988).

34 This policy was deplored in the report to the Council of Ministers (1988a, p. 123).

35 The story was told of a PA chairman who fancied someone's wife and had him forcibly resettled. However, the man obtained his revenge, for as the bus left he saw the chairman's wife, claimed she was his and with the backing of others who had also been injured had her taken with him despite her protestations.

36 Jansson *et al.* (1987, p. 66); Dawit Wolde Giorgis (1989, p. 289).

37 Council of Ministers (1988a, p. 102).

38 Council of Ministers (1988b, p. 211).

39 Some of the 'convicts', known as the Tolpuddle Martyrs, were unwanted trade unionists (Clarke, 1971, p. 425).

40 Some settlement sites had desertion rates of over 50%, and exceptionally even up to 73% (NRCP–CPSC 1982, p. 56).

41 Scudder and Colson (1982, p. 269).

42 In addition the Ethiopian Nutrition Institute sent extension agents and financed small income-generating projects.

43 See Alemneh (1990a; 1990b, pp. 104–9) and Dessalegn (1989, p. 91). A Government report warned that the problems in the north could be replicated in resettlement areas within eight years unless conservation was accorded top priority (Council of Ministers, 1988b, p. 159).

44 In the early stages of the Revolution students were used to propogate the message of reform; a decade later they were relegated to building huts. Party cadres were sent to instil the socialist philosophy.

45 *Addis Zemen*, 27 Sené 1977.

46 The French Secours Populaire Français was the first to become involved in March 1985. It was followed by the Austrian/West German Menschen für Menschen in May 1985, and the Irish agency Concern in November 1985. The Norwegian Save the Children, Redd Barna, started a programme in January 1987.

47 Jesuit Relief Service, the Ethiopian Evangelical Church Mekane Yesus, and the Catholic and Adventist missions.

48 Jansson *et al.* wrote that the agencies 'did not want to go against the policy of the USA from which many of them got their resources' (1987, p. 67).
49 This usage was coined by Father Jack Finucane of Irish Concern.
50 This is the view of both Dawit Wolde Giorgis, former Commissioner of the RRC (1989, p. 304), and of Kurt Jansson, former Head of the United Nations Emergency Operations for Ethiopia (1987, p. 68).
51 Several Government reports called for the creation of such a body (Council of Ministers, 1988a, 1988b; MOA, 1989c).

IV

A mosaic of motives

What is this thing they call resettlement? It is chickens that
settle [to roost on a perch].   A settler's comment

The Amharic term *sefera*,[1] used for resettlement, was unfamiliar
to settlers, as suggested in the above reaction when people first
heard about the programme. The root *seffere*, 'settling in a place',
is commonly used for locusts, bees and birds, and for chickens
roosting. Although resettlement was a new venture it struck a
deep chord, and was associated with the only State-sponsored
recruitment peasants knew of, namely the call to arms.

In this chapter I seek to answer the questions 'Who were those
who resettled?' and 'Why did they leave?' The variety of motives
almost defies classification, for resettlement did not stand for one
and the same thing in the minds of those who moved. It was an
all-embracing term which encompassed such contradictory notions
as starvation and surfeit, hope and despair, nightmares of death
and dreams of prosperity.

Discussions of migration often attempt to view settler motivation
in terms of 'push' and 'pull' factors.[2] While the division may be
convenient analytically, the dichotomy is artificial, and the two
types of factors are often inextricably linked. Frustrations at being
dependent are closely related to aspirations of independence. While
attempting some classification, I try to preserve a sense of the
variety and complexity of motives. The approach adopted discusses
social categories by using individual cases to build up a picture
which conveys both the diversity and the intricacy of motivations.
Even so the reader should be aware that complex sets of factors
have been simplified and that few cases are as straightforward as
the exposition suggests.

I first consider individual and then social factors. The former
include wealth, position, occupation, age and gender. We will see
that wealth and age were the most important individual factors.
The elderly wished to remain in their homeland, and established
peasants who had not exhausted their assets were better able to

avoid resettlement; youth, on the other hand, often saw resettlement as an opportunity for self-improvement. Besides destitute
famine victims, resettlement attracted people subject to the classical
motivation of migrants the world over. Although none of the above
factors on their own can explain resettlement motivation, taken
together many of them become significant. Gender, in particular,
assumes relevance in combination with status, age and wealth.

The second part of the chapter is concerned with social factors.
Collective attributes such as language, ethnicity and religion were
insignificant in motivating settlers. The most important factor,
which has tended to be ignored in popular accounts, is the influence
of social groups, including household, family, kin, affines, peer
and community. The discussion begins at the lowest level with the
household and moves to the widest sphere of the community. In
this way the paramount importance of social pressures on individual decision-making is illustrated, and the atmosphere of mass
exodus is explained. Finally, the importance of locality and regional
difference is considered. Differences between two regions of Wello,
namely Desé and Lasta, are arguably related not simply to variations in the intensity of famine, but also to longer-term ecological
degradation and historically rooted tendencies towards conflict.

Individual factors

Attributes which may be defined as individual include wealth in
land and livestock, position and occupation, age, and gender. At
first sight it would appear that wealth was a key factor obviating
the need for resettlement. Settlers' accounts make it clear that
those who had grain reserves and/or livestock were better able to
withstand the drought than those who did not. Settlers would
often mention that richer people were able to survive without
disposing of assets, notably oxen, without which they could not
maintain their status as independent producers. The corollary
should be that those who resettled were likely to come from the
underprivileged. However, little evidence suggests that resettlement attracted landless or oxenless households. Although land
shortage and livestock losses were mentioned as factors encourag-
ing resettlement, these were, more often than not, subsidiary factors and resettlement was often conditioned by other factors, such
as power, age and gender.

Nonetheless, evidence suggests that young people living as dependants of their parents, or who had only recently separated from parental households, were more vulnerable to famine and more attracted by resettlement. Many such households were on their way to becoming independent through ox loans, small stock investments and cash crop sales when the drought reduced them to potential dependence. Resettlement also attracted young disadvantaged persons who were without means of support, who had not acquired their independence, or who were in conflict with those upon whom they were dependent.

Land and livestock

Land

A small proportion of settlers came from the densely populated regions of Kambata and Hadiyya in southern Shewa. These were the only settlers who were officially moved on grounds of land shortage. Within Wello, differences in population density existed between highlands and lowlands and from one region to another. While settlers from Desé scarcely mentioned land as an issue, those from Lasta presented it as an important factor, although their concern was less about the amount than the location of the land and the quality of the fields. Settlers spoke of hillsides that were so steep that they had to be cultivated by hand. Nonetheless they preferred small and eroded fields in the highlands to larger holdings in the lowlands. Although the prospects of plentiful and fertile lands were incentives for people to move, land shortage by itself was seldom mentioned as a reason for resettling. Rather, land issues were related to questions of power, age and gender.

Settlers mentioned choosing to resettle as a result of land disputes in two types of cases: firstly, disputes with PAs, usually over land redistribution. A few of those who resettled were former landlords and their sons. With land reform, lands belonging to rich peasants were confiscated and distributed to landless households. Some of those who were bitter about the redistribution saw resettlement as an opportunity to start afresh in new surroundings, as Yimer recalled:

I was well-off before the coming of this flag [i.e. the Revolution]. I used to have three pairs of oxen and had two labourers who ploughed for me. I used to give them three sacks of barley and good land to plant onions on. All that was taken with the land reform. I was not the richest of those who came; Seyd Chiqaw[3] had more land, and Mehammed, the chairman, used to employ twenty people to weed for him. If my land had not been taken from me, I would not have come. I still had two oxen and a cow at the beginning of the famine. But I no longer had fields in which the cattle could graze, nor fodder to give them.

It was not merely former rich people who left because of land disputes. Poorer peasants were also involved in quarrels, and in some instances complained of favouritism and corruption in their PA. Wuddiyyé, a poor peasant from Mujja, felt wronged when a former landlord took land allocated to him:

I used to supplement my income from ploughing by weaving. During the land distribution I was allocated a plot that used to belong to a rich landlord. The man regained influence in the PA, and bribed the leadership to have the land returned to him.

A second cause of disputes with PAs arose from the use of land belonging to settlers who had already left. Many had difficulties retaining their family land, unless they had influence with the PA. 'Land of those who went to resettlement' was subject to redistribution, although relatives sometimes managed to retain part of it. The case of Destaw illustrates this point:

My uncle went to resettle in Asosa with his family, leaving me in charge of his land. The [PA] leadership said, 'They have left; the land will be given to others.' There was one good piece of land which I started to plough; the chairman came, and said '[Stop] in the name of the law'. I untied the oxen, waited till he left, then yoked them and ploughed. The PA took me to the *Wereda* court, which imposed a fine of 300 *birr* on me, and forced me to relinquish the land. Rather than suffer this injustice I decided to resettle.

Land disputes were often an expression of conflict between generations. Disagreements would arise when sons wanted to build their own homesteads or share parental land, while fathers preferred to retain control over their holdings and let their offspring work for them, sometimes even after they had married and set up new homesteads. Such tensions were often brought to a head by opportunities for migration provided by resettlement. Ultimately it was a question of independence expressed as: 'My father and mother won't order me about any more.' Resettlement offered an opportunity for rebellion. Kasa, a young lad from Lasta, explained:

> We clashed on 'I will go out of the house.' 'No you won't.'[4] I said, 'Give me my third of the harvest and let us part houses.' My father replied, 'I won't give you land.' I was at the time 'eating *siso*' [receiving a third of the harvest]. I became angry and said, 'I will work alone. Does the Government not recognise me?' [i.e. Do I not have rights?] My father replied [with the proverb], 'A father cannot be taken to court, nor can the sky be reached; for he is the creator, is he not?' My mother said, 'My land will be enough for you, stay,' but I felt frustrated and left.

Land questions were also sometimes related to gender issues, as in the following case of a widow who was pressurised by her PA to resettle:

> My husband died a year before the famine, leaving me with three small children. We had an ox and a cow. I asked a neighbour to pair his ox with ours, and plough our fields in exchange for half the produce. But our ox died in the drought from lack of food and I sold the cow. The PA said to me, 'How will you manage with these small children? You had better resettle.'

PAs sometimes took the side of women, as in the following case of a man who, upon divorce, did not want to share his land:

> We quarrelled. I said to her, 'Be a wife to me.' She said, 'I won't.' I said, 'Then leave.' She replied, 'I won't let go of my right to a share of the land.' The PA wanted to give her half my best land. I said, 'How can I live if I give her half my land and have to bring in another wife?' I became angry and decided to leave, saying, 'There you are, you can have it all!'

Livestock

Ethiopian peasants usually define wealth in terms of livestock. The word *genzeb*, literally 'money', is used by settlers to denote livestock and wealth in general, as well as money.[5] The ultimate measure of wealth and social standing was celebrated through a ceremony called 'He wore tripe'. If a wealthy man had 1,000 cows which gave birth within a single calving season a ceremony was

performed at which he was covered with the tripe from several
slaughtered oxen.[6] Those who spoke of this ceremony had not
witnessed it themselves but knew of old people who had; this may
suggest that large livestock holdings have become rarer during the
present century.

Grain may be considered with livestock, since it is not a durable
commodity but one which is converted into livestock in good
years. In bad years grain plays a vital role, since, as we have
seen, the terms of trade between grain and livestock are reversed.
However, even during famine, the possession of grain prevented
peasants from having to sell livestock. Given the 'conversion strategy', few peasants were wealthy enough to maintain large grain
reserves, especially in a situation of recurrent lean years.

We have seen that settlers commonly mentioned losses of livestock, particularly oxen, as a reason for resettling. This was due
not always only to the famine and lack of fodder but also to
disease. Arragé, a man from Werre Ilu, decided to resettle when
his animals began to die of what he explained as witchcraft.

> I was a ploughman without equal; I had a cow and two oxen, a
> horse, a donkey and a mule. The animals started dying one by one.
> I had tied the horse at home one evening. The following day I
> found her dead. The donkey died the next day. The oxen spent the
> day ploughing; when the sun set one died in the field, the other at
> home. It must have been medicine from a sorcerer that killed them
> off. I did not want to use the cow to plough the land. There was a
> meeting; they said, 'There is a country called Wellegga where there
> is much forest. People who will work and eat may go; single women
> can't go, nor the weak.' I said, 'Take me with my wife and three
> children.'

The loss of livestock points to the fact that the vast majority
had cattle in the first place, but lost them in the famine. It is
impossible, in the absence of a comparative study among those
who remained behind, to provide firm figures. Resettlement seems
to have attracted poor households but not necessarily the poorest
in livestock holdings. Few in Village Three had been mere labourers
without cattle, and most tended to have left their homeland only
after losing or consuming their livestock. However, settlers who
had owned a pair of oxen were a small proportion of the total and
very few had owned three or more. A UNICEF survey of four
Integrated Settlements in Wellegga and Kefa retrospectively

showed that the average number of cattle per household had been almost five and the number of smallstock more than seven.[7] A study undertaken by a Government team reviewing resettlement suggested that oxen were the most significant determinant in resettlement motivation. Half the respondents expressed a willingness to resettle, if conditions did not improve and they had consumed their assets.[8] Over a third (39%) of those willing to resettle, but less than a fifth (17%) of those unwilling to leave, had no ox. The figures also suggest two facts which confirm assumptions made above, namely that most settlers had oxen[9] and that most of those who had not were young.[10]

As the discussion has shown, wealth on its own is not a sufficiently reliable indicator of likely resettlement, since other social factors were involved, most notably group pressure. The following account by Husén was not unusual:

> Although I was not as wealthy as some of those who came with me, I was richer than many who stayed. I had an ox, which I paired for ploughing with my cow. I had a donkey and several sheep with offspring. While others were spending the night hungry, I went in [to resettlement] still eating. What was I to do when all my kin and my wife's relatives and our friends decided to go?

Position and occupation

Thus far we have considered wealth independently of position or authority. We have seen that rich people sometimes left because of kinship and community pressure. However, people who had been in authority remained behind. This was not simply because their position usually coincided with relative wealth which enabled them to avoid having to leave. Instructions were given that persons in leadership within Associations for Peasants, Women and Youth were not to resettle, as they were needed in their homeland. This was a policy later criticised on the grounds that settlers were left without people experienced in leadership.[11]

Occupation was not a major factor influencing the decision to resettle. This was largely because settlers were peasants, and crafts,[12] trade, education, religious service and soldiery were generally part-time activities. Those with such additional occupations generally came for reasons entirely unconnected with their work.

Few artisans were exclusively engaged in crafts.[13] Only one man

was a full-time weaver, while half a dozen had sufficient skills to
earn a supplementary income from weaving. Out of four black-
smiths, only one was a professional whose forefathers had a distinct
status as workers of iron.[14] Why did artisans resettle? It might be
thought that under famine conditions, at a time when survival was
the only priority, crafts were no longer in high demand. Although
artisans did not mention a significant drop in demand, this was
not the reason why they resettled, for most of them were only
occasionally and/or seasonally engaged in crafts. For Abba Yimer,
the senior smith, the answer was clear:

> When I saw that so many friends and relatives from Gerado were
> leaving, I saw no point in remaining behind. What is life without
> your *qire* [burial ground], without the country [people] you grew
> up with? Anyway, a smith is a smith anywhere; wherever there is
> agriculture, people need smiths. So I packed my tools, gathered my
> family and joined my friends.

Abba Wedajew, the chief weaver, came out of a sense of paternal
duty, for the sake of one of his daughters. She decided to divorce
her husband, who then refused to share the land. Embittered and
unable to gain redress, she joined the resettlement.

> I had a decent income as a weaver; even if times were hard I could
> have survived. Besides, I had another daughter in town who could
> have supported me; but I felt responsible for my younger daughter,
> and wanted to make sure that she would come to no harm. People
> said to me, 'You are elderly, don't go, the Government will help
> you,' but I wanted to see where my daughter would end up.

A small number of settlers had previously been engaged in seasonal, or part-time, short-distance trade, using donkeys or mules to
transport agricultural produce, particularly irrigation-grown cash
crops, such as onions, tomatoes and peppers.[15] These they traded
in towns for salt and consumer goods, notably cloth and articles
of clothing. Prior to the Revolution, a few elderly men had been
engaged in long-distance trade with mule caravans, travelling south
as far as Ilubabor and Kefa. A few younger men reported transporting items for their PA cooperative shops. As for education,
although a number of settlers' children were at school, only five
were in secondary school and only one settler was himself in full-
time secular education at the time of his departure.

I was an eighth-grade student; I had to cut my schooling short because of rebel activity near the Tekkezé river. For a while I worked as a registrar in an aid shelter. Then I applied to resettle with hopes of completing my education. Here I became chairman of the Youth Association and later PA secretary.

Generation and gender

Age

Age was no doubt the most important indicator of resettlement motivation. In general the young were attracted by the opportunities of resettlement and registered with more enthusiasm than their elders, who wished to remain behind and so be able to die in their homeland. The proportion of people above sixty in resettlement areas represented less than half the national average and a third of the Wello average.[16] The desire of the elderly to remain behind is not surprising. Sayings attributed to them include: 'I wish to remain and die in my homestead,' and 'May the earth of my homeland clothe me.' Settlers sometimes reported their parents

Table 3: Age of settlers in Village Three, 1985

Age	Male	%	Female	%	Both	%
			Sex			
0–5	119	12.9	140	15.8	259	14.3
6–10	162	17.5	160	18.0	322	17.8
11–4	60	6.5	64	7.2	124	6.8
19–9	70	7.6	65	7.2	135	7.4
20–4	60	6.5	70	7.9	130	7.2
25–9	99	10.7	87	9.8	186	10.3
30–4	68	7.3	101	11.6	169	9.5
35–9	69	7.5	77	8.7	146	8.1
40–4	79	8.5	54	6.1	133	7.3
45–9	56	6.0	32	3.7	88	4.9
50–4	47	4.8	19	2.1	66	3.6
55–9	11	1.2	5	0.6	16	0.9
60–4	15	1.6	8	0.9	23	1.3
65 +	11	1.2	2	0.2	13	0.7
Total	*926*	*51.1*	*884*	*49.9*	*1,810*	*100.0*

Source: Village Three PA files.

expressing the customary wish to die and be buried 'where their umbilical cord was buried'.

Age was often related to other factors, such as wealth and gender. Among the elderly settlers, men were in a distinct majority (64% of those above the age of forty). This may well have been because elderly women were more reluctant to leave and because once elderly men were no longer household heads and had handed over to their sons they had little option but to abide by the latter's decision to resettle. However, in some cases mothers left while fathers remained behind, as Wendé's mother recalled: 'When my son decided to leave I went to the shelter in Lalibela to try to dissuade him. He insisted on going, so I set off with him, leaving my husband behind. A man is hard-hearted, but a woman is sensitive.'

Elderly persons who were dependent on adult children wishing to resettle were not in the same position as those who had an independent means of livelihood. If a father was still in control of production he could remain behind, as Ahmed recalled:

> When I decided to resettle my PA chairman declared that my parents should go with me as my dependants. My father did not wish to go; at the transit shelter he appealed and was allowed to remain behind, since he had a means of survival, not having sold his oxen. My mother preferred to leave him and come with me.

The reverse pattern of the young staying behind was rare. Established households usually departed with their offspring. Young children were occasionally left behind with parents or siblings who did not have children of their own; during the famine some placed children in 'other people's houses'. However, the slightly lower than average proportion of children under five is likely to be primarily due to high child mortality.[17] Older children seldom remained behind unless they had become independent.[18]

The population in the settlements was comparatively young. More than half the settlers in Village Three (53.4%) were under the age of twenty-five. A quarter (24.9%) were between the ages of fifteen and twenty-nine, as opposed to just over a fifth in Wello (20.8%).[19] What were the factors which made young people opt for resettlement? Among 'push' factors the main issue seems to have been the wish to be free from the control of parents, or stepparents, and, in the case of poor young men, from affines or those for whom they worked. Sometimes disputes were of a general nature. One young man quarrelled with his mother because he had sold some sheep for her and she suspected that he had not given her all the money. Another youngster wanted to go to market, but was told by his mother to tend to irrigation fields. He disobeyed and went to town; seeing people registering for resettlement, he did likewise.

Resettlement attracted young persons whom one might classify as marginal or disadvantaged. These included three main categories: 'orphans', young persons who suffered discrimination from step-parents, and poor young men who had married richer women and were dependent on their affines.

Famine and resettlement combined to create a category of 'orphans' who officially had lost their parents through death or separation, though, as we shall see, not all the thirty 'orphans' in the village had in fact lost their parents. In some cases children had left parents with whom they were at odds; in other cases, parents were too poor to support them. If a wealthier relative could not be found they would place their offspring in '[other] people's houses', where they often became virtual servants. If children were small, parents would receive some remuneration; older children could hire themselves out for a modest sum. A young boy would look after cattle and a young girl fetch water and help in the house. Remuneration varied considerably. Youngsters mentioned sums of between nine and fifteen *birr* a year, or one to five goatskin sacks of grain. Sometimes the renumeration was in the form of a live goat or sheep in exchange for tending herds. The opportunities were limited and, even though they received a small wage, it left them dependent. As one young woman put it, 'It had no value: we worked for out stomachs [i.e. for food].' Young people living in 'other people's houses' saw resettlement as a way of escaping such dependence. Juhar, a young man whose father had left the region while he was small, and whose mother had died, recalled: 'I had no one responsible for me; I decided I wouldn't be ruled over in some one else's house. My only regret is that I didn't bring my younger brothers with me.'

During the famine even wealthy people were reluctant to keep on extra mouths to feed, as Tsehaynesh recalled: 'They said, "We can't keep even our own children; it is no good for us, let alone you. What you eat can be for those we have given birth to. We too are about to have to be sent into exile; you go now." '

We shall see that the divorce rate was high in Amhara society;
step-parents and the 'Cinderella complex' were commonplace, as
expressed in the rhyming saying: 'A stepfather is [like] a fat
donkey, a stepmother kicks like a donkey.' Fiqadé recalled:

> My stepmother became a stepmother: she favoured her children.
> Being another person's child was unpleasant. My step-sister and I
> were looking after the pair and a half of oxen [three oxen]. I went
> to collect chaff; when I returned one ox was missing. I asked her
> where it was; she was silent and I hit her. She left for her father's
> house. Elders were sent to persuade her to return but she refused
> unless I left. My father said: 'I won't exchange my son for another
> person's child.' But my stepmother would not forgive me, so I left.

Quarrels with affines were also a cause of departure. This was
particularly the case among men living with their wife's kin and
working for them, a situation which was associated with dependence. Debbash recalled how his wife's father tried to dissuade
him from going: 'He said, "You won't go in, you must stay put,
I will help you," but I said, "I won't be forever in a someone
else's hands." '
Chekkole explained how his decision to resettle likewise resulted
from a quarrel which developed between him and his wife's
brothers, with whom he used to work:

> After my wife's father died, they did not divide the harvest equally
> as we used to do before. I was angered when they did not give me
> my share. I was not thinking of coming, but they cheated me and
> stole what was mine. When there was the meeting about resettle-
> ment, I decided to leave them and join.

Given stereotypes of settlers as victims of famine, or of coercion,
it was surprising to hear so many young people explain that they
left because they thought resettlement would offer them better
opportunities. Resettlement attracted youth, mainly young men.
Dissatisfied with their lives, they were persuaded by propaganda
offering them new opportunities. As such they conformed to the
general pattern of migrants throughout the world. To understand
their mentality let us consider the terms they use. One of the most
frequently heard statements was the expression *zim biyyé*, literally
'I came silently.' The term has lost its original sense, and has come
to mean 'I simply came,' or 'I just came.' Young settlers often

maintained at first that they came for no particular reason. Although motives gradually emerged, this initial response is significant, since it sets this category apart from those who came because famine had reduced them to destitution.

The next most common term used by these volunteers to explain their motivation, *teggebku*, means literally 'I was full,' or 'satiated'. The dominant metaphorical meaning is to be arrogant, conceited, perhaps even irresponsible and lacking in maturity and respect. This term is of central importance in Amhara culture in that it defines people who are non-conformist. It is significant that it was the term used in a famine situation because it highlights the diametric opposition between those who came because they had too little in their stomachs and those who came because, as it were, they had too much. This point was made explicit by some who said that they came 'satiated, without being hungry'. It is also revealing that this term, which has negative connotations and is used of others, is here a self-designation. It implies self-condemnation for what was seen as impetuous behaviour. With hindsight the decision to move was often considered rash or ill-advised. It was frequently referred to as 'an act of youthfulness'. Arregga added: 'If my father had been alive to advise me, I would not have rushed into the decision.'

Some even used terms which convey the notion of frivolity, irresponsibility and becoming deranged, and suggest light-headedness and rushing about. When I asked one young lad why he came he replied with the saying: 'When a lad becomes satiated, he climbs up a tree.' In addition to this impetuosity, many young settlers recalled that they took a sudden, spur-of-the-moment decision. Expressions often used were: 'I leapt up.' or 'I came suddenly without considering it.' Sometimes the imagery is one of 'plunging in'.

The decision of the young to resettle was often opposed by their relatives, who would try to prevent them from leaving. Many left without telling their parents. Common expressions were: 'I disappeared (or I escaped) and came,' 'I slipped out and came,' or 'I hid and came.' The secrecy was justified on the grounds that parents would not allow them to leave. Young men and women would go surreptitiously, as Wendé recalled: 'I didn't tell anyone; I slipped out by night without anyone seeing me. I escaped by moving a plank and squeezing through the wall so as not to be heard [opening the door].'

Some deceived their relatives by saying they were going to market, to visit relatives, or even to a church service. One young man tried to take his best clothes, claiming he wished to visit relatives, but his father guessed: 'He said, "You want to go [to resettlement] I won't let you take the clothes out [of the box]." I waited till he had forgotten the incident. Then I said I was going to wash my clothes and left.'

Dinberu recalled how his father had responded to the suggestion that they should leave together: 'We were loading our donkeys with hay, when I told him I was planning to leave. He flared up and said, "How dare you! What is wrong with you that you wish to go? What do you lack, while I am still alive?" '

Sometimes the PA or shelter workers also tried to prevent young people from leaving. Mulu, a young woman from Lasta, recalled: 'The camp guard was a priest, a neighbour; when he saw me come to resettle he became angry and said, "I won't let you in; you are not hungry. I know your parents; return home quietly before I tell them." So I went to the town and waited till I saw the bus come, and got in quickly.'

What were the 'pull' factors which attracted youth to resettlement? For most it was the prospect of new horizons and an independent way of life. Some joined under the illusion that they would be going to an easy life without drudgery, as one young man recalled: 'I thought it would be a means to becoming powerful and prosperous.'

Others had ambitions of going to lead an urban life in a town or spoke of the hope of becoming soldiers: 'We left thinking they would make us hold straps [of guns]. I thought I would spend the night boasting at the town edges. I did not intend to settle, and certainly had no idea of getting married.'

The eagerness among young men to become soldiers can be explained partly because they considered it as an opportunity to see the world, and partly because of the prestige of being an 'owner of metal', i.e. a gun, or 'belted', i.e. a soldier with a cartridge belt. Moreover, those who returned would gain the status and respect given to heroes, and were likely to receive a pension if wounded, or lighter work, such as guard duty. A deeper reason was no doubt that settlers saw themselves as much in the same vein as traditional warriors, attracted by the excitement and adventure of a campaign.

Gender

At first sight it would seem that gender was not an issue in resettlement motivation, since the imbalance in the sex ratios is only marginally in favour of men.[20] Earlier figures suggest that the difference was probably initially higher,[21] no doubt because more men left the settlements. Combined with other factors, such as age, status and kinship, gender becomes particularly significant. The traditional pattern of virilocal residence was a hidden factor which meant that women suffered more than men from separation from their families. A woman's marital status influenced her options. Girls living with parents usually left with them; married women tended to leave with their husbands, while a number of single unmarried women, like Itagegn, resettled on their own.

> Although I have had several husbands, I never lived with any one of them. I came to the town of Lalibela, where I earned a living brewing beer and as a prostitute. I retained some of my father's land in the countryside, and had it ploughed for me by a relative. My first child died, and I consumed my wealth when I had a second child. During the famine the army worm destroyed my crop, and I did not know what to do to survive from July to August. Then I heard that the Government was taking people to a swollen i.e. fertile land. I decided to go and wait till times improved. God willed that I should leave, or I would not have come. My child's father, a soldier, said, 'Stay!' but he could not help me, and I could not live for ever by borrowing. So I left with my three-month-old baby.

Women were placed in a dilemma by resettlement because of the virilocal marriage pattern. Their allegiance to their parents and husbands was often put to the test, since they tended to live away from their parents. Even if her husband and parents both decided to resettle, a woman's affinal and consanguinal relatives often lived in different PAs, and were called to leave at different times and in different buses. Inevitably separations and painful choices were forced on women when husbands decided to leave while their parents decided to remain, or vice versa. Consanguinal ties often proved stronger than marital ones. Women would remain with parents who, being elderly or infirm, needed their help, or who were well-to-do and could therefore support them. In the former case the separation was often understood if not always accepted by the husband, as Debbash explained: 'I had decided to leave, but my wife's mother was blind, she tied her down. She said to her,

"Stay behind and look after me; you will pick our coffee and sell it." How could she leave her? How could I bring her?'

When a man's affines were wealthy the latent tension between husband and wife's kin came to the forefront. Fathers sometimes admitted 'divorcing their daughters' to bring them along with them, and former husbands often suggested that their affines prevented their wives from accompanying them. Yimer recalled,

> I said, 'Get up, let us go.' Her father was well-to-do – meat was eaten like cabbage in their house – He said, 'If you wish to trail from country to country, that is up to you; we won't send our child, we will look after her.' They kept my wife back; angered, I went straight in.

The opposite pattern of women leaving husbands might partly explain the slight preponderance of women in the twenty-to-forty age group. Usually this occurred because the wife's parents or siblings decided to resettle. Aminat recalled: 'My parents decided to leave but my husband would not leave his parents behind. My parents are more important to me. Mehammed goes, Mehammed comes, you can always find another husband, not another father.'[22]

Among those women who came on their own, some had never been married and came as dependants of their parents; others had left their parents behind. Most, however, had been married previously, and were divorced or separated for a number of reasons, including remaining behind for the sake of a relative, or involuntary separation arising from wage-labour and disputes.[23] The resettlement option created tensions between spouses and provided opportunities for those wishing to separate. Just as resettlement provided a release for rebellious young people, so it enabled couples to part. Longstanding disputes came to a head and were resolved through one party leaving. Fantayé recalled: 'We did not get on, we were constantly fighting. He used to go out [to other women] and cause trouble; so when I heard of resettlement I just left him.'

The resettlement option itself created a new source of disagreement over whether the couple should leave or not. Mersha was quite explicit that it was resettlement that made him separate from his wife. 'The sun [i.e. the famine] would have been easy [to withstand], it was frustration and the conditions of the time: seeing people getting aboard [buses]. I was determined to go, so we divided our belongings but did not divorce.'

In several cases custody of the children became an important source of disagreement. One woman who decided to leave surreptitiously took her child when her husband refused to give it to her. In another case a man decided to resettle, but his wife refused to go because of her ageing mother, so he took the older child, leaving the younger one: 'I snatched the elder child. I could not be a murderer and take away the one that was breastfeeding.'

Addisu, a young man from Lasta, had an illegitimate child whose mother brought it to him during the famine; he asked his wife to accept it and bring it up, but she refused. Angered, Addisu left for resettlement with the two-year-old, who died during the journey.

Gender interacted closely with age and kinship. We have seen that elderly women tended to remain behind. Resettlement attracted more single young men who came on their own.[24] Young women, on the other hand, tended to come either with their families, or in pairs with girlfriends, as Werqnesh, recalled:

> I entered the resettlement, fearing that the children of my country people were leaving without me. A friend went, and I decided not to remain behind. My family came looking for me and tried to persuade me to stay; my brother cried and my mother begged me, but I refused. When they came looking for me I went into another tent.

Independence from parental control was an important motivating factor among young people. The tensions between fathers and sons over land had a parallel in disputes between parents and daughters over marriage, and were brought to a head by opportunities for migration provided by resettlement. Daughters often expressed a wish to make independent marital choices; disputes arose over both the right to marry and the choice of spouse. Tiringo, a young woman from Lalibela, quarrelled with her mother because she wanted to marry against her mother's wishes: 'It was not that there was a particular man, but I felt that I was ready to marry; but my mother and father said, "You are too young," so I thought I would marry a little further away from them.'

Another woman, who had returned to her parents after a dispute with her husband, resettled when they tried to pressurise her to return to him. Although fathers had more control over their daughters' marital affairs than over those of their sons, disputes sometimes also arose with the latter, revealing the latent tensions between in-laws. Ibbabu recalled:

The dispute did not even concern me. I got on well with my wife; but my stepfather quarrelled with my wife's parents, and insisted that I should divorce her. He said, 'I will marry you to another woman,' but he did not do so, and kept me at home. I felt he had not kept to his agreement, so I decided to leave.

Social pressures

We now turn to the influence of social factors. Language, ethnicity and religion do not seem to have been mobilised as salient issues. On the other hand, family, kinship, affinity, peer and community pressures were highly significant and affected individual factors, often overriding expected trends.

Settlers in Village Three included both Amhara and Oromo, as well as Christians and Muslims. The question of religion deserves further comment. Several settlers had received religious education and officiated at religious ceremonies. Among the Muslims a number of elders were religious leaders, called *qallichcha*. They comprised the head of the Muslim community, and five others who had been engaged in agricultural work, and officiated at religious ceremonies and healing sessions only on a part-time basis. Among the Christians there were three priests, two former priests and five deacons. Although the priests were also engaged in agriculture, two deacons were involved in full-time church service. What were the reasons which motivated religious functionaries to resettle? The answer is almost always family, kinship and community. Many *qallichcha* and priests did not wish to resettle but found themselves impelled to go when relatives and friends left. The case of Shéh Ali, the head of the Muslim community who subsequently left the village, illustrates the point.

> My son, Husén, had been in the militia; he became the leader of a number of families deciding to resettle together. I tried to dissuade him, but he would not listen. Then the relatives of those who remained sent me to try to stop them, but they would not be deterred. Husén said, 'Come with us and see what the place we are going to is like.' I had not been planning to go, all I had was the clothes on me and my Qur'an.

Among the Christians several young men training as deacons had no other source of income. One of these, Kasa, explained how famine conditions and his modest allowance, combined with the departure of his friends and his sister, influenced his decision:

> I was receiving fifteen *birr*, and might have been able to survive, despite the cost of food. But then all my friends were beginning to leave. Finally, when my only sister came to tell me she was leaving with her husband, I decided I could not stay behind.

Household, family and kinship

By now the reader will be aware of the importance of household, family and kinship. We have seen that the decision to resettle was usually made by male household heads, often after attending PA meetings at which they would register the rest of their family as dependants. Sometimes the decision by the family head was unexpected and even resented. Zeyneba recalled how her husband did not even consult them, and how her son refused to leave:

> My husband went to town saying he was going to talk to our son, who worked in Desé; when he came back he informed me that he had registered the family. Our other son, who was living with us, refused to go, saying, 'While I do not lack food, I won't leave.'

Household heads would often register their children, even if the latter had already set up separate homesteads in their own right. Male household heads also commonly registered their parents or their wife's parents as dependants. Parents in this position would speak of coming for the sake of their sons or daughters. Common expressions used were 'I came saying: "Let the kite that eats him eat me," ' or "Let the hyena that eats him/her eat me."

Some settlers suggested that those with several young children were obliged to resettle to save their offspring, while those without large families or small children were better able to withstand the famine. However, parents sometimes attributed their departure to their children. Umer recalled: 'Our lot was to leave our country for the sake of our children. They were starving; we couldn't bear to hear them pleading for food. We might have been able to survive without them but we had too many mouths to feed.'

The departure of a household head often affected siblings, other kin and neighbours. An older sibling usually influenced a younger one, as in the case of Yiddenequ:

My husband decided to leave, so I prepared myself too. Then my
younger brother came the following day. I sent him back to our
father. He was his only son. I could not separate them, for my
father had made a vow in order to have a son. But he returned the
following day and no amount of persuasion could induce him to
remain behind.

Sometimes an older and established sibling would leave out of
a sense of responsibility and self-sacrifice. Abba Addisé, an elder
from Desé, had a position on the local school committee. He came
with his wife and daughter because of his younger brother Adem.

I had been working for six years in the school. My brother decided
to leave and fell ill in the shelter; he couldn't get on the bus. He
said to me, 'I am relying on you. Bury me, and hand over my
children to the Government.' I felt responsible for his family and
joined them. Then my wife's sister left her husband to come with
us, saying, 'If my sister gets up I won't sit.'

Peer and community pressure

Sometimes the trend of leaving for the sake of someone else led to
a sort of 'chain reaction' which helps to explain the atmosphere of
community pressure on a larger scale. This sense of connection
was expressed by Abbay:

We came 'pulling each other'. There are so many interlocked relatives here. Fantayé left because of her mother, who left because her
son decided to leave. He was persuaded by a friend. When I entered,
my nephew came. When he came, his mother and my sister got up;
she brought with her all her children and a grandchild.

People were influenced not simply by genealogical proximity,
but also by a person's status and standing. Often a young man
would follow a respected relative who decided to leave. Ali had
been looking for work in Desé; when he returned people were
leaving: 'They said to me, So-and-so has gone, and So-and-so, and
when my mother's brother decided to leave I set off, putting my
trust in him.'
A common statement was: I came 'believing in him' [i.e. 'putting
my trust in him.'] The key person was often an elder, usually male.
In one instance a young man was influenced by a sorcerer who

told him that his destiny lay in a foreign land. His brother Fiqadé, who came because of him, gave the following account:

> When livestock started dying, people said to our elder sister it must be witchcraft. She went with my younger brother Debbash to a soothsayer, who said, 'Medicine has been buried in a black container.' You must bring in a *Debtera* [a lay priest learned in such matters]. As she was about to leave, the sorcerer turned to my brother and said, 'Young man! Your livelihood is outside [i.e. your destiny is in another land]. Debbash said to our sister, 'I must go, I won't go back with you to your house.' To gain time she said, 'You won't go without at least eating a meal.'

Fiqadé went on to explain that he felt honour-bound to accompany his brother:

> Our sister had me called, and said, 'Insult him [i.e. reprimand him], he will cool down.' She sent for relatives, he was beaten and went home; but he just got up again and left. I did not want to be left with the guilt of thinking I let my brother die in some one else's land [i.e. abroad].[25] Instead I decided to go with him. We said, 'We will go to look for work and return.' Then he said to me, 'Let us go in [to the resettlement shelter].' I said, 'Let us at least wait until our relatives come to say goodbye.' He would hear nothing of it. He went in, and I followed. In the afternoon the bus took us. When I look back it angers me; I curse him. We had no need to leave; the *belg* [short rains] crop was ready.

The person who influenced others was sometimes a younger man with experience in the wars and/or PA administration, as in the case of Husén, a literate young man who had been a militiaman and was well known for his initiative. In another case the leader was an elderly woman. Yeshi influenced a number of persons who came for a variety of reasons. She herself gave several motives for leaving:

> The famine was made worse by the army worm, which devoured the sown seeds. I had been to the meetings where they said, 'Save yourselves; don't remain like tins trodden by cattle, there is a bread-land to go to.' I came from a well-to-do family; my father was a soldier for most of his life. However, after he died, the family became impoverished. I had seen people who left come back rich, so I thought resettlement would be a way of becoming prosperous. Also, I had a daughter in Metemma and another in Jewwaha, and

I thought perhaps I might find them. I said to the others. 'The poor
man's son [goes and] comes back well dressed.' When I got up they
followed me.

About a dozen families accompanied Yeshi for a variety of
reasons. They included famine victims, people who had disputes
with their PA over land, a soldier returning from the wars who
could no longer settle down, a woman abandoned by her husband
who went looking for wage-labour and never returned, another
who divorced her husband to come with her father. One young
man, despite his parents' pleas, joined the group hoping to become
a soldier; another had divorced his first wife, quarrelled with his
second and wanted to return to his former wife, but could not
obtain his father's approval:

> When I approached my father he refused to help me, saying: 'How
> can you abandon your new wife? Where will she go?' But I loved
> my former wife and went to her father. He would not let me have
> her back unless my father stood as guarantor, which he refused to
> do. The whole affair upset me so much that I decided to leave with
> the others.

Among the young, as we have seen, peer pressure was an important motivating factor which led many to resettle, when there was
no real pressing need to do so. Mulu was influenced by her cousin,
who came from a destitute family. She looked back with regret on
what she saw as an impetuous decision.

> My uncle's daughter and I discussed and planned together. She said,
> 'We will improve ourselves and wear [nice] clothes.' We spent the
> night in a friend's house and got up early to go. We did not tell
> our relatives. Her parents had very little food left, but mine had
> enough. It was satiation and youthfulness that uprooted us. My
> father is rich. Should I tell him now he would sell a mule and come
> to look for me. But what if bandits should attack him?

Settlers often felt they had no alternative but to leave, even
though they wished to remain, since their relatives, friends and
neighbours were leaving:

> I was working on a cotton plantation when I received the message:
> 'Come quickly; people are on the move.' I hastened back with my

wages. When I reached home, I found them ready to go. What to do? How could I keep my wife and children behind when relatives and friends were leaving?

Settlers were keenly aware of the break-up of communities that resettlement entailed. Often it was not simply relatives and neigh-bours who were seen to be leaving. There was a general sense of exodus expressed in terms such as 'people were on the move' and, most vividly 'the torrent drove us'. Often the community was split. Yimam described how his relatives performed a ceremony to try to prevent him from going, but the departure of a neighbour led him to register:

> There was a serious drought but, unlike others, we were not measur-ing out our grain. All the people from the neighbourhood were getting up. I got up suddenly too. My mother and my brother had elders brought to beg me to remain. When they performed a *wedaja* [a religious ceremony] upon me, I stayed behind. Meanwhile Ali [a neighbour] had had himself written down [registered]. I broke [my agreement not to go] and had myself registered in his family as a dependant. Then my brother Yesuf came and joined us too.

Regional differences

Regional differences, noted in Chapter II, seemed to have influ-enced resettlement motivation. In Village Three differences existed between settlers from Lasta and those from Desé. The former tended to be younger, more often single; they left for a broader range of reasons. Lasta settlers included young people who felt restricted in their home environment and migrants lured by reports of fertile land who imagined opportunities for independence and prosperity. Settlers from Desé, on the other hand, tended to come in families. More households came together from a single PA. As a result peer and community pressure influenced people who were not destitute. For many resettlement was thus an anticipatory strategy, since they wanted to leave with relatives and feared things might get worse.[26]

What accounts for these different patterns? An important factor was undoubtedly variations in the intensity of famine. As we have seen, Lasta suffered more than Desé and famine resulted in more disruption, family separation and disputes. Paradoxically the people of Lasta came less because of famine than those from Desé.

Long-term historical reasons may lie at the heart of the matter. Lasta had long been subject to environmental degradation[27] and dissatisfaction had built up to a point where many youths wished for change. But it was not merely a matter of a release of built-up 'push-factors'. Resettlement had awakened a military zeal for which Amhara culture is well known (Reminick, 1973), and had struck a cord which generated a fervour reminiscent of traditional military campaigns, part of the dominant ethos. Debbash recalled: 'As for myself, I was all right; but people were getting up and setting off; seeing the others leave, the spirit took hold of me. When I heard the lads boasting, my feelings were affected; my enthusiasm awakened.'

In the past, population pressure in Lasta was relieved through spontaneous migration. Since the Revolution movement had been restricted, and resettlement offered new opportunities for those who wished to migrate.

A further factor militating in favour of resettlement from Lasta was the history of warfare and strife. The area was notorious for its feuding and banditry. The following two stories illustrate the atmosphere which encouraged resettlement. The first is by Abeba:

> My husband was killed in a feud. It started with a drunken brawl. His uncle killed Seffiw, whose brothers retaliated, killing two people. My husband heard the shooting and arrived on the scene and they killed him too. No one dared pick up the corpses. We wanted to have a funeral but the bandits prevented us. I said: 'We cannot leave three people like that; they must be buried.' We did not have a *leqso* [mourning ceremony], but held a *tezkar* [subsequent remembrance ceremony]. Five days later my son's uncles killed two brothers from among Seffiw's relatives, who killed my husband's brother's son. I feared for my children. When I left they were still killing each other; I hear that it is still going on.

The second account is by Zegeyye, who had himself been a *shifta*, or bandit, for many years.

> My relatives were murderers. Even now, those seeking revenge would be looking for me, since there are seven lives owing. I belonged to a band of outlaws for eight years after my uncle killed someone who was committing adultery with his wife, and refused to pay compensation. There were twenty-eight of us, all related to each other. Our enemies killed three of us and paid 700 *birr* blood-

price for a truce; but we broke the agreement. My younger brother killed one of them. They then killed four of our men, two at a wedding and the other two on a threshing floor. I was fed up with all the killing and wanted some peace. I did not tell the others, or they would not have let me go.

Zegeyye decided to leave the band and look for work. During the famine he quarrelled with his wife, who could no longer look after him when he was ill. He decided to leave for resettlement with his only son.

I planned to go to Begemdir to find work. After two months away I sent my wife 130 *birr* that I had saved. When I came back I fell ill. She fed me for three days, and then she left and went to her relatives, saying, 'What can I give you to eat?' I went to my brother, who looked after me and, when I recovered, I went back to look for work. When I returned my wife came with her child on her back and said, 'Let us be reconciled and bring up the child.' But she had abandoned me once before when I needed her. What use would she be to me? I am responsible for my own son. Should I fall ill and die, or be shot, who would look after him? I decided it was better to resettle so that he would be in the Government's hands.

Conclusion

This chapter has sought to convey a sense of the multitude of motivations which led to resettlement, an all-embracing term so variegated in connotation as to be almost meaningless as an analytical concept.

The discussion started with individual factors. Wealth in the form of land and oxen played an important part in resettlement motivation. Once peasants had lost their means of production by selling or consuming their oxen, they became dependent on others or on the State. Nonetheless wealth cannot be equated with remaining behind, and poverty with departure. Kinship and community pressures induced many who were well-off to leave. Moreover, property was related to power both at the PA level of land disputes, and at the family level in quarrels across generations.

Status and occupation played a minor role in influencing resettlement motivation. Those endowed with positions of authority tended to remain behind, as PA officers were not allowed to resettle. On the other hand occupations other than agriculture, such as crafts and trade, did not affect resettlement motivation, since peasants' involvement in them was part-time or seasonal. Those engaged in full-time artisan work tended to resettle for reasons unconnected with their occupation. Likewise most religious functionaries, both Muslim and Christian, spent much of their time working the land, and resettled to remain with their kin.

Age and gender, especially when combined, were the most decisive individual factors affecting the decision to leave. The elderly, notably women, usually wished to remain behind, while youths, especially men, were attracted to resettlement. Many of them were still dependent on their parents and relatives, and valued the opportunities for self-improvement which they assumed the move could offer. Resettlement thus attracted young people who were disadvantaged or disenchanted. Quarrels with parents, step-parents or affines created discontent, for which resettlement provided an outlet. Some of the youth who decided to leave were marginalised, working for non-kin, because their parents had died or were too poor to support them. Youths were also more easily lured by the hope of better opportunities, and were motivated by a sense of adventure. Many thought resettlement would lead to a more glamorous life as soldiers, and the resettlement campaign awakened a deep-seated military ethos.

Gender affected resettlement through the mediation of other factors, including wealth, age, kinship and affinity. Women suffered disproportionately from separation from kin, since they were confronted with divided loyalties when parents and husbands made opposite decisions. Under the stress of separation, consanguinal ties often proved more enduring than marital ones. Some young married women chose to stay behind, either with well-to-do parents, or to look after poor or aged and infirm ones; others divorced their husbands in order to leave with their parents. Emancipation from parental control over *marital decisions* for young women was sometimes the analogue to independence from parental control over *land* in the case of sons. Just as resettlement offered a chance for rebellious youths to leave their parents, so it allowed marital disputes to be resolved through separation.

The most pervasive factors were social pressures. These were reviewed in this chapter from the lowest level of the household to the widest of the community. Families that had separated according to the household development cycle regrouped to depart: offspring rejoined their parents, and elderly parents left as dependants of their adult children. The lines of connection, however, stretched beyond generations from close kin to more distant relatives. Siblings often travelled together, while the decisions of younger people were sometimes influenced by respected older relatives.

Neighbourhood and community also played a crucial role as the cumulative effect of individual departures began to be felt. A 'domino effect' led to escalating departures. Such social factors were described by settlers in such graphic terms as 'we came pulling each other' and 'the torrent drove us'. Individuals who opted for resettlement for a variety of quite unrelated reasons came together. To remain behind when close relatives and friends were leaving, and to be separated from people who shared the same burial groups and neighbourhood associations, became unacceptable. The individual will was subsumed under the collective spirit. This cumulative effect created an atmosphere of excitement, reminiscent of a traditional military campaign. An effervescent mood of mass exodus animated the youth; this was felt particularly keenly in Lasta, where a history of environmental degradation, combined with a tradition of feuding and migration, predisposed the young to opt for a new life.

Notes

1 Guidi (1901, cols. 198–9), Baeteman (1929, col. 231).
2 For a discussion of 'push–pull' factors among spontaneous migrants in Ethiopia see Wood (1977, 1982).
3 The nickname Chiqaw refers to the fact that Seyd was a *chiqashum*, or landowning tax collector under the imperial land tenure system.
4 The concept of 'going out of the [parental] house' was an important idiom symbolising independence.
5 Likewise, the Amharic word for cattle, *kebt*, is related to the word for wealth, *habt* (Baeteman, 1929, col. 1696). An even stronger coincidence of meaning exists with the Oromo term *horii*, cattle, money, wealth (Gragg, 1982, p. 214).
6 Lobo, a Jesuit traveller of the seventeenth century, relates a similar custom which acted as a measure of wealth (Lockhart, 1984, p. 167).
7 Some 397 households were interviewed; they had owned a total of 578 oxen (1.46 per household), 785 cows (1.97), 522 calves (1.31), 1,453 goats (3.66), 1,584 sheep (3.99) (Teshome Mulat and Tennassie Nichola, 1988, p. 54).
8 Council of Ministers (1988a, pp. 52–61). Out of the eighty-one peasants interviewed in three regions, forty-one were willing to resettle and forty were unwilling to do so.
9 Among those who were willing to resettle, more than half (60%) had one ox or more, and more than a third (39%) had two oxen or more.

10 All those under the age of thirty had no oxen. A third of those without oxen (37%) among those willing to resettle were under the age of thirty, and over a quarter (28%) were among those unwilling to do so. Of those without oxen, all except one were under the age of forty-six among the volunteers, and all except two of those unwilling to leave.

11 The problem of lack of leadership was common in other resettlement situations (Scudder and Colson, 1982, p. 270).

12 Many women among the settlers can spin and make baskets, and some can make pots; skills among men included weaving, woodwork and smithing (ITDG, 1988a).

13 Weavers and smiths cultivated and engaged in crafts mainly on saints' days, when ploughing was forbidden. Traditionally, artisans would work in exchange for having their land ploughed or for a annual sack of grain. Muslims, who used not to be allowed to own land prior to the Revolution, specialised in crafts. It is worth noting that the only two Muslims from the Christian area of Lasta now living in Village Three are weavers.

14 Although smiths were looked down upon, peasants relied on them for making and sharpening vital agricultural implements, particularly ploughshares, and could therefore not afford to antagonise them.

15 The production of cash crops was particularly developed around the Desé area; settlers from Lasta tended to be much more subsistence-oriented.

16 According to RRC figures for 1987 those above sixty in Conventional Settlements represented 2.91%. The proportion was 4.06% in Qéto, and 1.99 in Village Three. The national proportion was 6.25% and that for Wello was 9.0%, according to 1985 projections (CSO, 1985b, pp. 167, 348).

17 Children under the age of six represented 15.5% of the Conventional Settlement population in 1987. Those under five represented 14.2% of the Qéto population and 14.3% of settlers in Village Three. The national proportion of under-fives was 17.7%, and that of Wello 15.9% (CSO, 1985b, pp. 167, 348).

18 For instance, when a son was employed in town, or held a position in the Youth Association, or when a daughter remained with her husband.

19 CSO (1985b, p. 348).

20 Women represented 49.7% of the national population and 50.1% of the Wello population (CSO, 1985b; pp. 4, 137). In contrast women represented 46.9% of settlers on Conventional Sites in 1987, 48.1% of settlers in Qéto, and 48.9% of settlers in Village Three.

21 RRC figures for 1986 show that women represented 44.8% of settlers on Conventional Sites, and the first census of Village Three in September 1985 reveals a proportion of 43.6%.

22 Aminat married a man on the way who died shortly after arriving in Village Three.

23 In 1985 one woman in five was registered as divorced, as opposed to one in ten men.

24 There were slightly more men than women in the fifteen-to-nineteen age group (seventy as opposed to sixty-five).

25 The concept *yesew ager*, 'someone else's land', denotes what is alien, and is opposed to one's own land and people.

26 Many also mentioned rumours that resettlement would 'close' after a while, and felt that they should leave while they could.

27 McCann (1987, pp. 173–80).

PART TWO

Settling for a new world

V

Starting from scratch

Having eaten the Commission's [RRC] wheat, I came to
Wellegga, invited to the return banquet.[1]

A settler's comment

In this chapter I describe preparations for the settlers' arrival in
Qéto after the misguided initial choice of another settlement
location. Settlers' accounts portray a picture of disease among
plenty in the crowded transit shelter at Bakko; an administrator
describes the shelter by the Qéto river where the influx of settlers
turned into a crisis. Social norms seemed to disintegrate, and
settlers fled into individual shelters.

Resettlement is described with reference to Village Three and
constraints on the administration of assistance are discussed.
Finally, settler responses to an aid environment are considered in
household strategies, formation of teams, and the creation of an
orphanage.

Gurra Ferda and the journey west

The settlers living in the Qéto area were originally destined to be
sent to the Gurra Ferda *Wereda* of Gimira *Awrajja* in Kefa. At
the last minute the site was abandoned owing to lack of water.[2]
The area had seemed fertile to prominent officials who inspected
it by helicopter[3] but was chosen without surveys to assess soil
fertility, and the availability of land and water.[4] After the initial
decision the pace of activity increased rapidly: 177 cadres from
the WPE were assigned to the area; the Ethiopian Transport and
Construction Authority built 60 km of road from Bebbeqa to the
Dima river. Surveyors from the Mapping and Geography Institute
planted stakes for houses in seven sites near rivers. Workers from
the Bebbeqa coffee plantation and a thousand Youth Association
members from Jimma were assigned to build temporary huts.[5]

In one site huts were erected on land already occupied by fifteen
households of people who call themselves Menit, and were known

by outsiders as Shuro.[6] They practise shifting hoe agriculture, collect honey and pan for gold, which they exchange for grain. When the Menit burnt the grass to clear the land a number of new huts caught fire. This was interpreted by some as an expression of resentment at an act of expropriation and a deliberate attempt to prevent resettlement taking place.

As plans advanced it became clear that the area was unsuitable. The Water Authority sent a team to bore wells but no water could be located and the rainy-season streams began to dry up. The MOA discovered that the soil was shallow and the sloping land unsuitable for mechanised agriculture. By this stage preparations for resettlement were already advanced: the RRC had built a store and had stockpiled agricultural hand tools, household equipment, mills and food for four months. Health workers were on stand-by. However, the MOA and WPE at the local level were opposed to the plan. Their views were communicated to Chairman Mengistu, who visited the area at the beginning of March 1985.[7] Within a fortnight the operation was cancelled, and a new location was sought.

Selection of Qéto and preparations

The initial choice of Qéto followed a familiar pattern. In October 1984 the regional WPE issued a directive to the Qéllem *Awrajja* WPE first secretary to look for suitable sites. He went on a helicopter tour with a team comprising a Soviet agricultural expert, and chose three potential sites: Anfillo, Koya and Qéto. After assessments by agriculturalists, Qéto was selected in February 1985. The campaigners allocated to Gurra Ferda were instructed to move to Qéto. After some delay they were sent, at the end of March, to Neqemté, the capital of Wellegga. The cadres were then divided into three groups.

The 158 cadres assigned to Qéto arrived on 8 April 1985, in Chanqa, a small roadside town in Qéllem *Awrajja*, 600 km west of Addis Ababa. Chanqa became the centre of the Qéto resettlement complex.[8] Twenty settlements are situated mainly along the Qéto river and its tributaries, the Chebel and the Indina. The settlement area lies in a semi-lowland region, at an altitude ranging between 1,200 and 1,600 m, spanning some 60 km. The land gradually rises towards Mount Tullu Welel.[9] The southernmost villages are on the banks of the Birbir river.

The countryside presents two contrasting types of vegetation due to varying availability of water. On the one hand savanna, with occasional acacia trees and tall elephant grass; on the other, riverine forests, with dense, lush vegetation, the habitat of a variety of wildlife. The population was made up almost exclusively of Oromo farmers, belonging to the Seyo or Leqa Seyo section of the Macha Oromo, who had moved into the area in the eighteenth century.[10] The Oromo had displaced or assimilated the earlier inhabitants, the Mao, through conquest, slavery and marriage.[11] A couple of families designated as Mao lived by the Qéto river and a few remained near Jarso settlement.[12] Some lived alongside

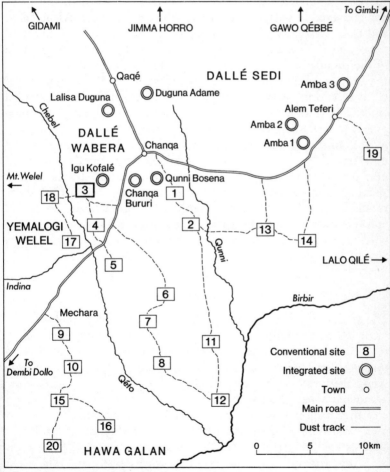

The Qéto resettlement complex

Oromo with whom they traded, selling maize, sorghum and chickens to buy salt and clothing; others fled to the lowland marshes
as the Oromo expanded. Near the banks of the Qéto river there
were also a couple of Anuak families who, following the Baro and
Birbir rivers, had arrived there ten years previously. They lived
among settlers in Village Four. Further to the south and west are
small groups of Majangir,[13] who walk to Dembi Dollo on market
days to sell pots and honey.

With an average density of seventy-two people per square kilometer, the three *weredas* including the Qéto settlements were not
sparsely populated. People were concentrated in the highland areas,
and clustered in villages and the small towns of Qaqé, Alem Teferi
and Rob Gebeya. With the coming of settlers the density increased
to around 100 persons per square kilometer. The settler proportion
of the population was just over a quarter of the total.

Land on which the settlements were located was not under
cultivation. However, in some areas Oromo landlords had farmed
land using tractors and established themselves in areas since taken
over for settlements. At the time of the Revolution their guns
were confiscated, and, fearing wild animals, they returned to the
outskirts of local towns. Two elders from Iggu Kofalé once lived
near the present entrance to Village Three; the only traces of their
abandoned homesteads are a couple of mango trees. One elder
recalled: 'I used to live near the settlement. I grew beans, sorghum,
maize, a little *téf*, and chickpeas. At the time of the Revolution the
wild animals became a nuisance. The others left and when I was
alone I too decided to leave.'

The journey west

The settlers travelled at least 1,000 km from their homeland. For
most it was the longest journey they had ever undertaken. They
recalled being amazed as the countryside rolled by. As they passed
through fertile lands, crossed lowland regions and large valleys,
rising again into highlands, travelling through forested areas, they
wondered when they would arrive. Some observed they had no
idea that Ethiopia was so vast. Not all, however, had remained in
their homeland all their lives. Among the elderly, many had travelled extensively prior to the Revolution to visit relatives, to look
for work, for trade, as soldiers, or to litigate over land. They had
seen big towns such as Desé, Asmara and Addis Ababa.

Two patterns emerge from settlers' accounts of the journey.[14] Some hardly stopped on the way, while others spent several weeks in roadside shelters. The former completed the journey in as little as four days, stopping only at night, and arrived without too many hardships. The latter spent a month or two *en route*. Many became ill and death was rife.

The bottleneck in the relocation operation occurred at the town of Bakko, on the border between Shewa and Wellegga. The place is engraved in the memory of hundreds of settlers living in Village Three. The Bakko episode presents a paradox: settlers had more food than they could remember seeing in months yet people died like 'falling leaves'. For famine victims used to measuring out food and rationing themselves, Bakko is recalled as a time of plenty. However, as one man put it: 'Disease swept us away like a broomstick.'

During the famine, settlers had lived off food aid, including wheat flour, oil and milk; in Bakko they were given food with which they were less familiar, such as biscuits and pasta, and things they had never even seen, such as rice, tinned meat and reconstituted egg:

> It was [like] 'a mother's house'; there were not enough people to eat the food. They gave *injera* [bread] to the children and *tiré* [grain] to the adults. One day they gave us food called *ruz* [rice]. It was tasteless but we became used to it. When tinned meat was brought some people worried that it might be pork and the more devout would not eat it but most of us did not ask questions; not for nothing had we been through famine! When I fell ill I was taken to the tent with electric lights. They took spoonfuls of powder from a tin and told us it was egg. I became very ill; after they put me on a 'food injection' [i.e. a drip], I recovered.

Another account retains a touch of humour while emphasising the same points: plenty of food, disease and death:

> We stayed in Bakko for a month. At first they gave us [unground] wheat; the children fell ill [since they could not digest it]; when the 'higher authorities' visited they became angry. After that we were given flour and much besides: oil, rice, meat. My stomach became massive, I was looking like a *Mislené*.[15] Ashagre was about to explode [from too much food]. One man became so fat that he broke the hospital bed! Several among our group fell ill . . . Don't ask me about death!

Addisu described the quarantine imposed on the sick. He did not fall ill at the time, possibly because, as a guard, he was able to go to town, find other food, and escape the crowded shelters; but he attributed his poor health ever since to his stay in Bakko

> The sick were separated from the healthy. We guards were told to stop people from defecating near the river. I saw a Qallichcha [a Muslim religious leader] relieving himself. I forced him to pick up his faeces and he cursed me. I have not felt well ever since, and have been looking out for him on market days to ask forgiveness.

Addisu went on to describe the reticence concerning death.

> We did not talk about it. Even the word was avoided. We used to go round asking, 'Is there any one who has "slipped out"?' Corpses were carried off like sacks of maize; they were piled on a trailer and taken to mass graves, Christians alongside Muslims. Children were placed between the feet of adults. Grave diggers received extra rations.

The ghost-like wooden structures of the former shelters in Bakko, now devoid of thatch, still stood five years later as a grim reminder of settler suffering. The poles were falling; soon this chapter in the history of resettlement will have left no visible physical trace. But Bakko has left a deep wound in people's consciousness. For many couples, two or three years went by before they had another child to compensate for the loss of the loved one. Like many, Indris will never forget his daughter:

> She was so beautiful that you would not have thought she was my child. She used to be so cheerful and goodhumoured, with an endearing smile, revealing brilliant white teeth. Zemu [his wife] is now pregnant, but no child will ever be quite like her.

Husén was perhaps the worst afflicted. He lost seven family members out of ten, including his wife, a child, his sister and all four of her children. Understandably, it was not something he wanted to talk about. Ansha, a young woman from Kombolcha, summed up the sense of loss in a pun on the word Bakko, 'We remained wasted [like empty] packets.'[16]

The settlers' arrival

The quota set for Qéto Conventional Sites was 10,000 households. According to the Wellegga Region Environmental Rehabilitation

Aerial view of Qéto. Village Three is the pale shape in the centre, surrounded by darker fields and black forest area, encircling the fields to the north. To the west, across the river, is Village Eighteen. To the south are three villages: Seventeen (lower left), Four (lower middle) and part of Five (lower right, across the Chanqa-Dembi Dollo road, seen as a white line)

Committee 1985 report, 49,202 settlers in 13,232 households were received in Qéto by September 1985. Preparations were inadequate to cope with the influx, and the situation turned into an emergency. Surveyors from the Mapping and Geography Institute arrived in February 1985 and determined village layouts according to a grid model. Two bulldozers were used to clear tracks and land on sites nearest the road. Away from the riverine forests tall elephant grass was removed by lighting fires. Nearer the rivers clearance work was more difficult and took longer. From March onwards the rains impeded work. It took four months to complete site preparation. In the meantime most settlers had arrived.

Health workers began to arrive two weeks after the first settlers, and WPE cadres and agriculturalists a fortnight later. There were chronic shortages of medicine. Feeder roads had not been cleared and in most villages site preparation had not started. Tractors, few in number, arrived late and agricultural hand tools were in short supply. There were also extreme shortages of cooking implements and water containers, clothing and blankets; this resulted in much hardship during the rainy season. Finally, there were only four trucks to transport weak and ill settlers, their goods, grain supplies and household equipment. In short, the Qéto area was simply not ready to receive the enormous influx of almost 50,000 people.

The local people were organised to assist settlers in various ways. The local WPE Committees mobilised PAs and Youth Associations to build a shelter for 10,000 people by the river as well as some 2,000 huts in seven sites in three areas. The campaigns imposed on the local population placed a strain on the peasants' labour when they were beginning to plough their fields. The local people also ploughed land for Integrated Site settlers, who were the first to arrive in the area. Abba Tarreqe, now living on Qunni Bosena Integrated Site, recalled the settlers' fears and the local people's generosity as they arrived in January 1985:

We arrived in Qaqé by night on 16 January, having travelled five days from Korem; our people feared we would be thrown in the sea, or in a desert, but I reassured them: 'Don't worry, why should the Government toil to bring petrol? Why should it labour unless it was so that people should not die? When the local people brought us *injera* made from *téf* our people [almost] died of happiness. The local people said to us: 'Don't worry, your place is only one hour's walk [from here].' The area appeared one immense forest. People said: 'This is not a land we have entered, but a wilderness. However, there was a church, and though they don't speak our language, they are Christians.'

Most settlers now in the twenty villages arrived between March and May 1985. Two phases may be distinguished. The first began in early March, a month before the cadres' arrival. The local WPE Committee organised the movement of settlers to seven villages for which an average of 300 huts per village had been built. These settlers stayed only a few days in the shelter. The second phase began with increasing numbers towards the end of April and continued throughout May. The influx soon exceeded expectations and the administration was overwhelmed with thousands of extra people. Most remained in the shelter for at least two weeks waiting for the site preparation to be completed. They suffered in crowded and insalubrious conditions; many fell ill and died. Others moved out of the main shelter into small individual shelters. The emergency reached such proportions that the move had to be rushed, without adequate preparations.

Crisis in the riverside shelter

When the cadres arrived they were told that settlers refused to remain in the shelter and would not use the trench dug by the bulldozer as a latrine. The settlers left the large shelter, which they disliked and feared, and began building small individual shelters on both banks of the river. In no time dozens of little temporary wigwam-like shelters appeared away from the crowded mass shelter. These hutlets were called *huddu gela*, an Oromo term signifying 'enter with your back first'. Settlers preferred these hutlets, which afforded privacy in a way totally lacking in the shelter, which consisted of long corridors without partitions. The hutlets also provided slightly better protection from the rain. Most importantly they offered a means to escape appalling sanitary conditions in the shelter, which became infested with sickness and death. Taddese Wolde, one of the cadres involved in the shelter administration, wrote in his diary:

The new place I have been assigned to, Qéto, is ten minutes away [from Chanqa] by car. Qéto is a river; 70 m downstream from the bridge is a pleasing waterfall . . . to the left and right, in front and

A *huddu gela* shelter as reconstructed later to recall the hardships of the early days

behind, [the area] is splattered with settlers' faeces. You are at pains to find a place to tread. With the intense heat, the stench which emanates from this 'wrath of the earth' suffocates you. Beyond the bridge, to the right and left, the land is covered with *huddu gela* hutlets. These amazing people even light fires inside them!

Cadres recruited the fittest settlers to build another 200 m long shelter. However, it was too late in the year to find thatch. The roof was therefore covered with wet grass. Settlers began to arrive in alarming numbers at the beginning of May and the situation began to get out of hand. They came by the busload. On some days as many as ten buses off-loaded their 'cargoes'. The crisis reached a peak on 10 May, when ninety buses with some 5,000 settlers arrived, enough to fill two or three villages. The bus drivers would dump the settlers, requiring only a signature that the 'consignment' had been handed over. As settlers were dispatched to villages new batches arrived. In the words of Taddese: 'The settlers' arrival was like a river; as people were reduced from below, more came to be added from above.'

Before long both banks of the Qéto river were covered by a mass of settlers. A census at the end of May revealed that there were still some 14,000 people in the shelter areas although fifteen villages had already been settled with some 550 households each. This meant that five new sites were required.

Medical and administrative staff were swamped and a delegation went to the Qéllem *Awrajja* WPE first secretary, to try to halt the influx. Sanitary conditions were appalling and diarrhoea was common. The rains washed waste into the river, which was the only source of water. Taddese confides to his diary:

> Should you come to visit our shelter and enter suddenly, in the middle of many ill persons, you would be saddened to see two young beauties sitting, one dressing the other's hair. Perhaps they might be the ones you see tomorrow lying down groaning. As they say to you, smiling, 'Come in!' you pity their state.

To reduce contamination, the cadres organised the preparation of food for children and the sick. Six empty barrels were provided by the RRC and a mixture of semolina, oil and salt was served several times a day. Oral rehydration mixtures provided by UNICEF were used, and the medical staff of the French aid agency, Secours Populaire Français (SPF), and the health centre staff worked night and day.

The little hill to the right of the bridge turned into a large graveyard. Taddese wrote:[17]

> I do not know how many died. Before you cross the Qéto river, there are numerous graves at the site where there was a quarry. From morning till sunset you can see as many people as in Chanqa's market, digging graves. From the bridge to the road, you can hardly pass because of the stench. You see settlers, who care not as they relieve themselves, cover their noses with cloth when they walk past. Beyond the river the road is full of people. Apart from the dirt and the people's race the multitude of people resembles the crowds you see around Moscow's Gum [department store].

There is a growing literature about human responses under stress, much of it speculative and emotive.[18] Some have argued that societies disintegrate and individuals retreat by instinct into self-centred survival.[19] Others have emphasised the retention of societal norms, the appearance of inventive responses, and an intense will to find ways to survive. To some extent both perspectives seem true; Sorokin once noted that famine brought out the best and the worst in people.[20]

Taddese's account portrays behaviour which shows signs of anomie: a deterioration in human relations as evinced by apathy, increased individualism, a refusal to help others, theft and marital instability. At the same time one can find indications of a determination to struggle on, as demonstrated by the construction of individual shelters and frenetic trading activity. Taddese recalled that it soon became impossible to find people to bury the dead. The cadres used the militia to search for helpers:

> The healthy, fed up with burying, hide all over the place. You send those who have been to the war front, to look for people to bury [others]. The living carry the dead on stretchers along the avenue of death to the slope of the graveyard hill. Five or six mourners climb the hill in single file, carrying the corpse in turn . . . Thus the dead make the living follow them . . . under the bridge of the river of death, the healthy and the sick, women and men, wash the sickness from themselves. Lest you think of telling them to wash their garments soiled by bedbugs, diarrhoea and dirt, they have nothing else to wear; they have to put their clothes out, waiting naked for them to dry.

People became numb to death. They no longer mourned. They slept, ate and drank coffee next to corpses. They no longer had the strength to dig proper graves. There were even occasions when these were so shallow that the toes of corpses stuck out and hyenas dug up the bodies. The shelter gave off the acrid stench of death:

> Twenty-four people were found dead on 24 May 1985. You might have been surprised not to hear the sound of mourning. Well, those who weep are those who have buried only their first dead; the rest have buried relatives repeatedly, and their tears have dried up. Then, when they cross the 'Bridge of Death' it is in single file, silently.

Some were buried in blankets, until blankets became too valuable to be spared. Even the grain sacks in which aid had come could not be wasted:

Many brave youths, many beauties fell; children and old women too were carted to the 'Hill of Death'. Since we lacked cloth for shrouds there were also those who were buried with grass and leaves. Neither grain nor fertiliser sacks could be found for shrouds. The times turned cruel. The lad who takes the sick to hospital and buries the dead is groaning the next day; the following day you see his body withered. Let me not tell you the end. No mourners, no tears for the unfortunate corpses; when you see them go by on stretchers you are only reminded of your own futility.

The shelters became places for those who had no will to leave, to build their hutlets, or go to the villages. Some people even refused to go to the health centre; on one occasion about a hundred ill persons were forcibly removed from the shelter by settler militia who took them to the health centre. Under the stress of the journey and shelter life people's probity was affected. Theft, even from the dead, was reported. People could steal easily, for there was nothing to distinguish one person's belongings from another's: 'The people were illiterate, the blankets similar, and the flour was [all] white.'

It is clear from Taddese's account that people were quick to find ways of obtaining aid while shirking demands for labour.

When settlers are sent to the new sites the team leaders abandon the sick without leaving them their share of rations . . . the healthy don't pity the sick, they unload their own things from the trucks and vanish. You see that in times of hardship people are cruel to each other . . . It is these ill ones who lack mourners. Some team leaders hide their people so as not to be asked to do the burying; others say they have many more in order to obtain more food. When you want to clean the dirt you don't find them, but on food distribution days they suddenly all turn up.

There were two persons who became deranged: a teenager refused to talk and a woman started eating grass; her husband tied her hands and sent her to the health centre. There was also much pairing of couples. Women would say: 'I married him so as not to be alone.' Men displayed jealousy when their wives cooked for others:

While complaining that the food they receive is insufficient, while crying as disease pains them, you see these people upsetting their marriages; there is much intercourse. A man may leave the mother of his three children and marry the friend of his first daughter. When he marries her he tells his former wife he has divorced her.

His children's mother then accuses him. This is what life in Qéto is like.

Husbands and wives were seemingly no longer tied by previous bonds of mutual obligation, rooted in the sexual division of labour. Subsistence was a gift from the State and a spouse could therefore obtain sustenance independently of a particular partner. Taddese addressed this issue in a report:

> Since food rations are provided by the government and are not obtained by people striving and toiling, and since the economic relations between husband and wife are therefore marked by a considerable degree of freedom, a wife knows that she can be certain of obtaining anywhere the 500 g of wheat she wants. She may leave her husband and marry another; and a husband likewise.

The most dramatic example of settler determination to struggle was the propensity to engage in trade. When the cadres first arrived in Chanqa they were amazed to see crowds travelling for miles along the roads to market. They did so partly out of necessity but also to search for lost relatives, to exchange information, to enjoy a change of routine, and to partake in the main social occasion during the arduous early days. Roadside markets began to spring up near the shelter and on the way to Chanqa. Taddese recalled:

> Whether on a work day or a holiday, you see settlers crowding the roads . . . The people flooding the market and going to the mill would lead someone who did not know better to assume that settlers were deserting the shelters and the villages . . . In the market a section for the sale of blankets has been established. Perhaps for the first time in the history of Chanqa a flour quarter has been set up . . . The local people sold all manner of things: spices, bread, mangoes, butter, cloth, pots for cooking and carrying water. The settlers' 'produce' was flour and blankets which they sold to obtain salt and chillies. You see men, women and even girls drinking spirits, coming out [of the bars] cackling heatedly.

The cadres tried to restrain the sale of aid items which 'had come from so many countries abroad for famine victims'. The settlers, it was also said, were behaving like 'tied dogs let loose'. The cadres went round with loudspeakers issuing warnings to try to stop the sales. Needless to say, this had little lasting effect. The cadres also saw settlers selling jewellery, including ornaments made from Maria Theresa dollars, for fifteen *birr* or less. They needed salt and money to pay for grinding the aid wheat received.

An enterprising person rented a room from a Mao man for ten *birr*, and set up a bar selling tea, alcohol and food; the place became a centre for relaxation, gossip and some wheeling and dealing. The cadres debated whether this should be seen as profiteering from innocent famine victims; they decided that anything boosting morale could only be beneficial.

Settlers from Village Three did not recount quite such atrocious stories as those recounted above. This may be partly because they stayed only a few days in the shelter. A comparison with the situation in Bakko may be apt. Qéto was, to the later phase of settlers, what Bakko was to many settlers who spoke of their tragic experiences. Another reason may have been that settlers were loath to talk of things best left to rest. As an elder from Qallu put it: 'Qéto should not be mentioned, nor can it be forgotten.'

This epitomises settler attitudes to the tragic suffering at the Qéto river: people did not want to speak about the hardships and deaths but what happened could never be entirely forgotten. This sentiment was echoed by many settlers in the village, who referred to death in Bakko with expressions such as 'What can you say about it?' or 'Don't bring it up!'

Most settlers in the village arrived at the Qéto shelter in March and April 1985. Those who arrived first had to construct shelters, as Abba Demisé recalled:

> Our bus stopped to help another, so we were separated from the convoy; the bus dropped us at the Qéto river at night on 9 March 1985. It was pouring with rain; we put our blankets over our heads, holding our children close, but water trickled under the blankets. In the morning we were told to build shelters and given flour. We had brought a few pans with us and made pancakes.

Abba Teferi arrived with a group of settlers a month later, again at night, in the rain, carrying a child, who had died on the way.

> We arrived in Qéto on 8 April. A large shelter was awaiting us: long live the Government! They had given us blankets. We slept; it was raining, but luckily this country throws it down with all its might and then it stops. Ashagré's daughter had died on the bus.

Since it was dark when we arrived we could not bury her till the morning and slept with the corpse. The following morning we buried her on the hill by the river.

In the history of resettlement the Qéto shelter remains a chapter filled with unforgettable and unmentionable memories. On 29 June, after the last settlers had been evacuated, two cadres burnt down the thatched shelters to reduce the risk to sanitation and to exorcise the memory and stench of death. Taddese reflected: 'The burning seemed to have its own logic. Even if only for a while, men suffered there, and it seemed like [an act of] revenge.'

The 'Hill of Death' by the river is overgrown with grass, beneath which circles of stones bear witness to this tragic episode.

Settling the villages

By the time the campaigners arrived, seven villages had been settled. For the rest, roads had not been built, land had not been cleared, and huts had not been constructed. The directive had been to settle 500 families per village, but most villages received at least 550. Many more were dispatched to the nearest roadside villages. The strong and healthy settlers were then sent ahead to build temporary shelters on sites further from the roads. Weaker relatives with their belongings were taken by truck to join them. Four trucks were used by the RRC to bring grain from Dembi Dollo to Chanqa and, once stores had been built, into the villages. Food distribution was delayed, as trucks had to alternate between ferrying people and food. Sometimes people and their belongings were moved after nightfall; once the rains came several villages were cut off. The hasty pace resulted in family separation; sick people were left behind in the shelter and family relocation took time.

In the villages a repetition of the Qéto shelter conditions occurred on a smaller scale; people rapidly moved out of collective shelters into individual *huddu gela*. Having arrived in the rain, settlers had to make do with wet grass for thatching; however, there was a desperate shortage of sickles. One eye-witness commented: 'What is the point of food without tools? You can't cut grass with your teeth!' Some villages borrowed sickles from integrated settlers or locals. More hand tools were distributed in June, but even these did not suffice. Settlers from already established nearby villages, and local peasants, were mobilised to build shelters for the new villages.

The cadres placed much emphasis on building a shelter, then a grain store and a clinic for two paired villages. By July, three months after the settlers arrived, half the villages had clinics, and eight had a grain store. Within a few months half the villages had also built offices for the cadres and a literacy teaching hall. A quarter had built offices for Mass Associations. Seven villages had built model houses, six had reading rooms, four meeting halls and two kindergartens.

In aid agency circles the RRC has an international reputation for efficiency. In the case of Qéto, however, the programme was poorly managed, partly owing to the last-minute decision to establish the new settlement. The food supply operation was costly and wasteful. Soviet trucks transporting the grain used excessive fuel and the food was not protected from the rain. The RRC store in Chanqa was completed only in July 1985. Until then food was stored in Dembi Dollo. Trucks went past Chanqa to Dembi Dollo and returned empty. Others had later to be hired to transport grain back to Chanqa, also returning empty. This added two return journeys, more than 250 km, to transport costs. Fuel shortages at times threatened to interrupt the vital supply of grain. In Dembi Dollo the stores were overcrowded. Even the regional administrative buildings were brimming with wheat, some of which had to be stored on verandas, subject to damp, which resulted in losses. By mid-July eight villages had built stores and trucks could deliver food directly; but the rains rendered access to villages far from the road almost impossible. Settlers had to spend much time and effort walking to the main road, in some cases as much as 10 km away.

Another major constraint was the dire shortage of water carriers and cooking implements. People could be seen carrying leaking plastic bags and small tins to the river to collect water. Women even lugged their baking pans filled with flour to the river to prepare dough there. By the end of July the situation had improved and almost all households had received a cooking pan, bucket, plate and cup, although three families had to share a cooking pot.

The agricultural operation in Qéto was slow to get off the ground, and, owing to the late arrival of the tractors, most work was done by hand. Two bulldozer's prepared some 60 ha of agricultural land in forested areas. The first three tractors arrived in mid-May, two months after the first settlers. By mid-July thirteen of

the twenty three tractors were inoperative, and the rest had
ploughed only 404 ha of land.

Given the amount of construction work carried out, there was
little time left for agricultural activities. Despite the shortage of
tools, settlers worked on their household plots in their spare time
with tremendous energy. They cultivated 1,100 ha, almost three
times as much as the tractors. The MOA distributed several kinds
of seeds[21] notably maize and sorghum. The latter was preferred,
since it was late in the season for maize. Results in the first year
were poor and some areas received insufficient rain.

Health workers were few and supplies of medicine had not been
allocated for Qéto so that they had to be diverted from Dembi
Dollo hospital. A doctor and two nurses from SPF arrived with a
lorryload of medicine on 19 April 1985. They set up a health
centre with forty five beds, which were filled immediately. Health
workers were sent out to the villages with small boxes of medicine
which were soon exhausted. The Government was alerted to the
critical health situation; in June seven health workers were added
to the first thirteen, and another lorry of medicine arrived. However, it was not till September that the health crisis began to subside
and preventive care was considered.[22]

One of the initial concerns was to improve sanitation. Health
Assistants gave teaching at Association meetings; the Youth
Association mobilised youngsters to build latrines and dig rubbish
pits. Once a year settlers were mobilised for a 'Sanitation Day'.
An average of seventy latrines per village were built.[23] However,
settlers were not accustomed to them and few were used or maintained, with the result that diseases could spread in the closely
built settlement habitat.

When a second aid agency, Irish Concern, arrived in 1986 a
division of labour was worked out whereby SPF concentrated on
curative and Concern on preventive care. Successive teams of doctors and nurses from SPF came on short assignments and worked
alongside MOH health agents, with weekly village visits. Urgent
cases were taken to the health centre in Chanqa, and serious cases
to Ayra or Dembi Dollo hospitals. Concern introduced antenatal
and mother-and-child health programmes, and trained community
health agents and traditional birth attendants.

Health aspects of resettlement were reviewed by Kloos (1990).
He concluded that settler health had not improved, that new health
problems arose, and that preventive health care needed more

emphasis. The settlers in Qéto encountered new diseases, notably malaria, the jigger flea (*tunga penetrans*) and podoconiosis, involving a swelling of the feet (Kloos, 1990, pp. 646, 662). Undoubtedly the crisis in the shelters meant that settlers' health was worse than their pre-famine condition. However, later on, the main difference was one of diet, notably the lack of milk and scarcity of pulses and vegetables. As for mental health I was struck by the paucity of visible trauma. We heard of two cases in the Qéto shelter. One woman in Village Three lost much of her memory and vocabulary after the death of her husband.

However, access to health care became an area where settlers became better-off than before resettlement. Conventional villages had two health assistants and were provided with free medical services for the first five years. For several years they became a privileged section of society, especially in comparison with the local population and settlers in Integrated Sites. The health centre in Chanqa was open to locals and settlers from Integrated Sites, but they did not receive care in their villages. It was only in 1988 that both aid agencies began to take an interest in them and in 1989 vaccinated against meningitis in their villages. Comparisons between local and settler health is an area of debate. A study of children under five carried out in Qéto suggests that there was little difference in nutritional status between settlers and locals (Adane Mekonnen, 1988). However, information from other settlements suggests that settlers were often worse-off (Kloos, 1990, pp. 650–1). Certainly in Qéto Conventional settlers were initially worse-off; subsequently their lot improved and their access to health care was better than that of locals. It remains to be seen whether differences will even out in the future.

Settlers were grateful for the health care, although they retained their belief in traditional healing practices. In 1988 SPF concluded that the crisis was over and that it should hand over the programme to the Ministry of Health. Visits to village clinics were gradually reduced, and, before leaving, SPF doctors concentrated on training village Health Assistants to diagnose and treat common diseases. In 1989 the last SPF doctor left, and the building of the permanent health centre was completed out of reinforced mud bricks. In 1990 payments were introduced for medicines supplied by the MOH to the Chanqa health centre, which distributes them to clinics. The question of provision of basic drugs for villages without clinics has not been resolved.

Since careful records were not initially kept, we cannot tell how many people perished, or how many left the settlements in the early days. According to statistics in Neqemté 49,202 people were sent to Qéto. The first census in July 1985 gave a figure of 48,395 people, almost a thousand less. Official RRC sources for the first year give a figure of 38,340, a difference of some 10,000 people. Assuming the figures are accurate, a fifth of the population either left or died in the initial stages.

Village Three

Settlement sites in Qéto were numbered in the order in which they were cleared. Village Three was thus one of the first to be settled. This took place in several stages over a period of six months from March to October 1985. The first group, who arrived in early March, were Muslim Oromo-speakers from the Harbu and Kemisé areas of Qallu, southern Wello. Forty-nine household heads, with a total of 162 people, came in two teams. Abba Demisé, an elder in charge of twenty-five household heads, or eighty-four people, perceived himself as the man who pioneered the land. He was the only one who had brought matches, and several settlers recall lighting their fires from his. Adem, the other team leader, was the first to be taken by officials to see the location: 'They said, "Come, get in." ' The white car followed the track cleared by the bulldozer. We could hardly see anything because of the tall grass. They showed us hutlets that the local people had built for us. Beyond was the forest.'

The next day the two groups were instructed to make their way to the village site, carrying grain for a week. Settlers had never seen such lush forest; they moved in groups for fear of wild animals, as Abba Demise recalled:

We searched for the hutlets among the tall grasses; you could not see from one hut to the other. We cut the wet grass and piled it on the makeshift roofs. We set ourselves up, two families in one hut, huddled like chickens. For about a week we did not even realise that there was a river close by, so dense was the forest. We drew water from the spring, and several people went in single file together for fear of wild animals; we could hear lions roaring at night. We were told not to let the women walk alone. After a week we returned to the Qéto shelter to collect more grain. A fortnight later the cadres came; then we built a store and a shelter.

Settlers were struck by the wildlife: they saw buffaloes, wild pigs, gazelles and large snakes which they had only heard about in tales. What was strangely missing were birds. Seyd, an elderly settler, recalled that he knew he would settle down when, shortly after arriving, he saw a bird that he recognised from Wello. After his death a friend commented: 'Seyd was right; at first we saw no birds, then only one kind, which followed us; it came looking for people.' A similar quest for the familiar went on in the forest. Although most trees were new to the settlers, they expressed pleasure at finding several known species.

The majority of settlers arrived more or less simultaneously in April. They came from two main regions within Wello: Desé Zurya and Lasta. By then the Qallu people had already planted their crops; they recall with amusement the fears of the wilderness expressed by the newcomers, fears that they themselves had conquered. People from Lasta were frightened by the Qallu settlers, as one woman recalled:

> When we arrived we were alarmed at the forest and thought we were going to be attacked by wild animals. Then we saw people coming from afar. They were the Qallu settlers who were returning from near the river where they had buried one of their number. We heard them speaking in Oromo and were suspicious, until we discovered that they too were settlers from Wello. We lit our fires from theirs.

By the beginning of May the population was estimated at 395 households. Another 195 household heads arrived the same month. At this stage the population was entirely from Wello. However, the village already included people of two religions, Muslims and Christian, and speakers of two languages, Amharic and Oromo.

In August 1985 the composition changed once more, with the introduction of two groups of settlers who did not come from Wello, but from Wellegga, the very *awrajja* in which resettlement was taking place. Some forty families came from two PAs in Lalo Qilé *wereda*, 50 km eastward. A couple of months later a report noted that thirteen had died within three weeks, and that eighteen households had left. A few days later fourteen persons were brought from Dembi Dollo, 60 km to the west. Four left immediately, and by January 1986 there were only eight left. A year later only one remained and had become an asset to the community.

The last settler group arrived in October 1985, after the first settlers had harvested a meagre first crop. This group consisted of thirty families from Werre Ilu *Wereda* in southern Wello. They were settled in a row of huts to the north, where they suffered from an epidemic resulting in many deaths in the first few weeks.[24]

The heterogeneous composition of the village was accentuated by its spatial organisation within a grid of huts in rows. The first settlers moved into some 100 hutlets built by the local people. As more people arrived the village had to expand. Settlers, following the stakes laid out by the mapping surveyors, started building makeshift huts. At first two households lived in one hutlet. Later 'excess' households were told to move and form new rows at the bottom of the hill. As additional settlers arrived existing rows were extended or new ones added. Earlier settlers were therefore generally located near the centre, while later arrivals were on the outside and lower down.

The allocation of land for household plots was haphazard. Team leaders were assigned strips of land. The principle of building in rows was rigidly imposed but settlers from one area tried, as much as possible, to build close to each other. The following account by Teferi, a settler from Meqét, described a dispute between teams, illustrating competition in the settlement process:

> When we came, part of the village was built but from Ali's house this way it was forest; not even a path, no entrance, no exit. We first crammed into some houses at the bottom of the hill. Then Mehammed [a team leader] claimed he had been allocated that area. We had been allotted the area near the centre, but Taddese's lot had already moved in there. Who was going to leave, and who come in? We said, 'See if you dare try to evict us!'

The matter was about to be taken to the cadres when another team leader suggested pioneering a new area to the north.

> We sent our leaders to discuss the matter with the cadres. On the way they met Haylu [another leader], who said, 'Let me reconcile you; come with me and I will show you where you can settle.' We began building along this row the following day, one house each day. After we had built eight huts Seyd [another leader] claimed he had received that area; we refused to move and went on building. Three of our men had remained where we first settled. Haylu said to Ashagré [one of the three]: 'Leave my house!'

When this further dispute was taken to the cadres they favoured retaining the *status quo*.

> Ashagré complained to the cadres, saying he had been there since the start. They said: 'If you received it first, keep it. Who made the others leave?' Haylu was angry and said: 'My God eat you for having done this, you have sold me; I showed you a good place and now you refuse to go there.' So when the cadres said, 'Each to his den,' we stayed put.

Although teams that came together were allocated a single strip of land, this did not resolve how the huts were to be allotted within the team. In some cases the cadres read out names, in others team leaders assigned houses; in the case mentioned above, lots were drawn:

> We cut pieces of straw and drew lots. Mesay and I got the last huts in the row; beyond us was the forest. We used to come to each other in the evening to comfort each other. Those above the path could not even see us. Then Gelaw and Aligaz came and built beyond us. Finally, Masre, who did not have a place, wanted to build below me, in between two huts, but the cadres stopped us, saying: 'This won't do, this is a road,' Siménesh, who had been allocated a plot in the draw, said to him: 'I have no husband, you build on it.'

When this group of settlers asked for help to clear the forest they were told to move to an already cleared area, but they insisted on staying together.

> We struggled, chopping wood and burning the bush until the sun became visible above. We asked for help, either that the 'ox machine' [i.e. the bulldozer] should plough for us, or that other people should help us. They said, 'This won't do. Leave that area. What if the animals or serpents do something to you, who is responsible?' They tried to stop us, but we said, 'We won't be separated.' We cleared the land, sowed maize in the month of May. It became enormous and plentiful, thanks to the Lord it bore fruit. I measured a cob, it was a full arm's length. I was amazed. What an incredible land! We've never since had cobs that size.

The forty settlers from Lalo Qilé arrived after the others and were told to build a row of houses at the bottom of the hill beyond the last existing row, near the river. Many fell ill in the first weeks.

Malaria was suspected, owing to the riverine location. The PA and cadres were also concerned at the refusal of these settlers to partake in collective work. They decided to split the group and place households at the end of existing rows upon which work teams were based. Most settlers from Lalo Qilé therefore lived on the outskirts. The only place where they formed a group was in Team One at the eastern end of the village, which gained the name 'Oromo village'.[25]

Since the initial settlement layout there has been much movement, and some settlers have changed location three or four times in as many years, owing to settlers leaving, marrying or separating. People have moved to come closer to relatives, to avoid people they did not like, and occasionally because of PA policy. Gradually the two bottom rows nearest the river have become depleted and the village has moved uphill.

Language and ethnicity

Although most settlers came from Wello, they differed in language, religion and local traditions. Historically, Wello was the scene of much mixing of races, languages and religions, and the diversity in Village Three is partially a reflection of this past. Although the majority speak Amharic, there are notable regional variations, particularly between Desé and Lasta dialects. The former bears many traces of Oromo and Arabic influence,[26] while the latter presents pecularities which occasionally resulted in confusion.

A man from Lasta came to one of the cadres and said what the

Table 4: Village Three settlers by language and sex

Language	Male	%	Female	%	Both	%
			Sex			
Amharic	781	84.4	765	74.0	1,546	85.4
Afan Oromo	143	15.4	119	26.0	262	14.5
Tigrigna	2	0.2	884	0.0	2	0.1
Total	*926*	*100.0*	*884*	*100.0*	*1,810*	*100.0*

Source: PA files, Village Survey (1985).

latter understood as 'Come quickly, twenty people are dying over there.' It turned out that one man was lying on the ground panting, whereupon the cadre said, 'What has happened to the other nineteen?' In fact the word *haya*, which the cadre mistook for 'twenty', meant 'there' in Lastan Amharic.

A fifth of the settlers speak Oromo. Most of them came from Wello, but some were from Wellegga. Slight variations did not impede communication, although misunderstandings sometimes occurred, as in the following case involving a Wello Oromo: 'I went to Chanqa and asked for *kosho* [tobacco]. They did not know the word and insulted me, thinking that I was looking for a prostitute, for they have a word which is similar in Wellegga Oromo, meaning "vagina".'[27]

Language did not present an insuperable barrier, since quite a few Oromo from northern Qallu are bilingual. Among the Oromo from Wellegga two men spoke Amharic well; one was a priest who learnt Amharic through the scriptures, the other an ex-soldier. Five settlers from northern Lasta spoke Tigrigna as well as Amharic;[28] two women also spoke Agew.

Religion

The majority of the settlers from Wello, notably most of those from Desé, Qallu and Werre Ilu were Muslim. Those from Lasta were Christian. However, these regional distinctions were not hard-and-fast and there were many exceptions.

Conversions were not infrequent, for three reasons: marriage, illness and migration. Several Muslim men had married and converted Christian women, and at least two Christian men converted

Table 5: Village Three adults by religion and sex

Religion	Male	%	Female	%	Both
			Sex		
Muslim	268	54.0	293	60.4	561
Christian	228	46.0	192	39.6	420
Total	*496*	*100.1*	*485*	*100.0*	*981*

Source: Author's census (1988).

upon marrying Muslim women. A priest from Werre Ilu had married a Muslim woman and had her baptised. Conversions on account of illness occurred when people went to religious leaders who promised them health if they changed religion. Migration was as important as marriage as a source of conversion. Abba Demisé, an elder from Qallu, recalled:

> My family were Christian *neftegna* [soldier-settlers of imperial days]. My father and grandfather were priests; I too, trained as a deacon. After the Revolution people stopped paying the tithe to our church and the *tabot* [representation of the Arc of the Covenant] moved into the town. Some seven years back I decided to convert rather than leave my community.

Likewise Abba Yimer, a former Christian elder from Desé, recalled:

> Christians started to move away from the countryside to the town of Desé. I felt I could not remain a Christian when my 'burial group' was Muslim. At a feast some one said that those whose godfather had died should take another. I said that I would not take another. One man said, 'Then you are not a Christian!' I replied: 'So be it!' and I converted to Islam.

In Wello, Christianity tended to predominate in the towns and Islam in the countryside. On moving to the towns some Muslims converted to Christianity. Most of those from Lalo Qilé in Wellegga were Christian, although three families were Muslim.

Regional background

Apart from 5% who were from Wellegga, the rest came from Wello. The largest category were from Desé Zurya. These were Muslim Amharic-speakers, though there were also a few Christians. The next largest group came from Lasta in Northern Wello, and except for a couple of Muslim weavers were Christian Amharic-speakers. The third largest group, from Qallu in south-eastern Wello, were Muslim Oromo-speakers, though there were a few Christians and a number bilingual in Oromo and Amharic. The smallest group were from Were Ilu in south-western Wello, and, apart from a Christian priest, were Muslim Amharic-speakers.

Even within regions considerable variations in local traditions

Table 6: Village Three adults by sex, region and *awrajja*

	Sex					
Awrajja	*Male*	*%*	*Female*	*%*	*Both*	*%*
Wello						
Desé Zurya	224	46.0	255	51.9	479	49.0
Lasta (Labibela)	152	31.2	128	26.1	280	28.7
Lasta (Meqét)	50	10.2	43	8.8	93	9.5
Qallu	23	4.7	37	7.5	60	6.1
Werre Ilu	10	2.1	6	1.2	16	1.6
Wellegga						
Qéllem (Lalo Qilé)	27	5.6	22	4.5	49	5.0
Qéllem (Dembi Dollo)	1	0.2	0		1	0.1
Total	*487*	*100.0*	*491*	*100.0*	*978*	*100.0*

Source: Author's survey (1988).

existed. These were particularly marked among the two largest groups from Desé and Lasta. Settlers from Desé came from its two *weredas*, Desé Zurya and Kuta Berr, and from three areas, Gerado to the west of the town, Kombolcha to the south, and Kuta to the north-west. Most came from west of the town, and the older people consider themselves as part of the Were Himeno tradition farther west. Settlers from Lasta came from all three *weredas* – Bugna, Gidan and Meqét – and from numerous areas. Most came from east of Lalibela town, from Mujja, a few came from the south, near the Tekkezé river, and the rest from further west, from Meqét. The last of these groups were from near the border with Gonder and in speech and traditions resemble the Gonderé with whom they have close links.

Peasants' Associations

Table 7 shows that 546 households from Wello came from no fewer than sixty-seven different PAs, i.e. an average of just over eight households per PA. Just over half the PAs (51%) provided fewer than five households, and only three PAs more than twenty-five. Over one in ten households (12.5%) came with fewer than five other households, over one in five (23.1%) with fewer than ten. The table also reveals differences between Lasta and Desé;

Table 7: Households by Peasants' Association and *awrajja*

| | Number of Peasants' Associations | | | | | | | | | | | | |
| | 1–4 | | 5–9 | | 10–14 | | 15–19 | | 20–24 | | 25–55 | | Total | |
Awrajja	C	N	C	N	C	N	C	N	C	N	C	N	C	N
Lasta	15	33	7	42	4	41	8	121	1	24			35	261
Desé	12	20	2	15			4	52	1	21	3	118	22	226
Qallu	3	4					1	17	1	22			5	43
Werre Ilu	4	11	1	5									5	16
Total	34	68	10	62	4	41	13	190	3	67	3	118	67	546

C stands for cases, i.e. the number of Peasant Associations within a category, e.g. 1–4 households, and N stands for the number, i.e. the total number of households within a category.
Source: Adapted from PA Village Census (1985).

settlers from the latter tended to arrive in larger groups than from the former.[29]

The aid environment

The RRC was responsible for three kinds of aid distribution: food, household equipment and clothes. The hand-outs created an 'aid environment' to which settlers responded by altering their house-hold structure and increasing household fission. Moreover, the 'ration economy' led to the strengthening of the team structure which began to develop in importance as a primary neighbourhood unit.

Over the first four years RRC involvement in resettlement, both at national and village level, was gradually scaled down. Settlers remember the first two years as the time of *rashin*, when they relied almost exclusively on fortnightly food rations. Initially they received grain (usually wheat) and sometimes a little oil, milk and occasionally salt, *berberé* or chillies, and pulses, such as peas or beans. By the third year, grain had become the main staple ration, while other items turned into occasional luxuries.

Apart from food the RRC was also responsible for distributing household equipment, including buckets, pans, plates, cups and agricultural tools, such as picks, hoes and spades. At first settlers tended to sell some of these to meet other needs. However, the price of aid items was low and their sale resulted in hardship, since they were all vitally important. After the first year the main settler strategy was to sell grain and livestock rather than permanent assets. The RRC also distributed blankets and clothes, including shirts, shorts and dresses made in the country to a standard design, as well as clothes provided by aid agencies.

Over the first four years the RRC gradually withdrew; rations were stopped. In the third year the RRC campaigners left, RRC business being handed over to a settler in each village. After 1989 the RRC played only a minor role, maintaining a Settlement Co-ordination Office. However, the Commission was still responsible for orphans, a family reunification programme and the flour mills.

Over the years aid distribution had a distinct impact on settler adaptation. Since distribution was organised on a household basis through the team structure, the household and team became the most important units of resettlement administration.

Abba Werra *and* béteseb: *household fission*

The *béteseb* or household in Amhara society is a fairly elastic concept. Since most aid was given on the basis of household heads, the important notion for the administration was the *abba werra*, or household head, an Oromo word imported into Amharic. The Word *béteseb* in the new context came to denote dependants rather than household members. Sometimes numbers of *abba werra* and *béteseb* were mentioned separately, without stating the total population.

Resettlement started by reversing the fission inherent in the domestic cycle. Families that had split to live in separate homesteads, sometimes in different locations, came together and travelled as one unit. Moreover, settlers who went as individuals were under pressure to pair up. However, in the new villages resettlement had the opposite effect of speeding up household fission. The household was in theory supposed to be composed of a household head, spouse and dependants. In may instances where whole families came as one unit, children rapidly separated to form their own households so that the family could receive more than one private plot and aid allocation, both distributed to households irrespective of their size. Moreover, the change from a ration regime to one where points were earned had important consequences. It was no longer advantageous to have a large family. During the ration era household heads received rations according to the number of their household members; subsequently a household head received only what he earned. This provided an additional incentive for household fission. Young sons able to work began to register as separate household heads. Yimer came with his wife, Arreggash, two sons, Ibrahim and Yesuf, and a daughter, Aminat, with her son Ahmed.

Within a short time the family split into three households. Aminat married a man at Bakko shelter. They built a hut next to her father's, in the same row.[30] Ibrahim had his eye on a woman called Ansha in Bakko but her father refused to give her to him till they had reached their destination. Shortly after arriving in Village Three, Ibrahim built his house, to the right of his father's, and moved in with his new wife.[31] Yesuf, the youngest son, was not envisaging marriage; however, one of the first-year cadres persuaded him to marry Toyba, whose parents had died and whose brother had left her. By then all the plots had been allocated. Yesuf obtained permission to build a house at the end of the same row as his father at the outer perimeter.

It was also not unusual for brothers and sisters who came as one unit to separate shortly after arriving. Likewise children would leave parents to establish separate households earlier than they would have done in their homeland. Elderly parents who came with their children often set up independent households, sometimes marrying other elderly persons or a younger one unable to find a spouse.

Menen, an elderly woman from Desé, followed her grown-up daughter and son. As she put it: 'How could I live away from my children?' In Village Three she became a woman household head; a year later she married Yesuf, whose wife had died. They lived together for about a year, but she fell ill and they quarrelled. Finally, she left him and went to live with her daughter and the latter's husband.

It was also not uncommon for unexpected household arrangements to be worked out. For instance, an elderly mother left her adult son to form a household together with her grandson, as happened with Felleqech, whose grandson, aged ten, was registered as the official head.

In some cases nominal households were set up when families split up to obtain aid and land. The family would assemble for meals and in some cases slept in the same hut, even though a separate one had been built. There were also at least two cases of spouses who 'divorced' in order to have access to two plots but were later 'reconciled'. Occasionally a plot was allocated but no hut was built on it for a long time. For instance, Ahmed was allocated a plot in the first year, but only built his hut in the fourth.

The budin *or team unit*

As we have seen, settlers travelled in teams, some formed in the shelters and others during the journey. When people arrived in the village, teams built huts together. The team structure was thus mapped out according to the grid layout. The village was divided into teams on a residential basis. The team was the smallest unit above the household and was usually composed of dwellers from two rows of houses facing each other, with a track between.

The teams were given numbers. Settlers tended to refer to them by their leaders, and even in the third year there were some, especially elderly women less in contact with the work teams, who knew the name of their leader but not their team number. The ration system favoured the strengthening of the team structure. Whenever rations, equipment or clothes were distributed they were handed over to the team leader and secretary, who were responsible for distribution. Village social life beyond the household thus took place largely within the setting of the team.

The team developed beyond its formal role to become what may be termed a 'primary neighbourhood unit'. Most disputes were resolved at the team level by neighbourhood elders. Only if no solution could be found locally was a dispute taken by the team leader to the PA chairman, who might refer it to the Law Court. In cases of theft elders called team members together, on the assumption that the culprit was likely to be a neighbour of the victim, and hence another team member, rather than someone living farther away. Occasionally a *belé* would be held to determine who was responsible. According to this procedure elders call team members individually and cross-examine them. If need be they make them swear on oath that they are not guilty. There was even the possibility not used – to my knowledge – of holding a ceremony to curse the criminal. The team also acted as a burial group, for only members of a team were expected to contribute towards *qiré*, the payment in kind for funerals. Rotating credit associations, known as *qub*, were often based on teams. Since food distribution was carried out every fortnight, this was a suitable occasion to pool a certain amount of the grain which a person could use in one go, to sell or prepare a feast.

The *budin* became a unit to which settlers related in daily life. Unlike other positions of authority, that of team leader was not coveted, for the responsibilities were great and the likelihood of antagonising members ever-present. Although team leaders were responsible to the PA leadership they were also accountable to team members, who could and sometimes did accuse and depose them.

The tim: the orphan dilemma

Forty orphans were taken from Qéto shelter to be cared for separately. Those under five, except ones with elder siblings, were later sent to Dembi Dollo by the Qéllem *Awrajja* Natural Disasters Committee, and were taken in charge by the Catholic mission. Some thirty children lived in Village Three without families. They were referred to as *tim*, but did not form a homogenous category. Some had parents who were poor and had placed them as servants in 'other people's houses'. During the famine they were either expelled or chose to depart. Others chose to leave parents (or step-parents) with whom they had quarrelled. Others again were separated from parents during the journey. Finally, a few were genuine orphans, both of whose parents had died.

In a sense the orphan issue was a microcosm of the problem of assistance in general: how to help without creating dependence on structures which perpetuate the need for institutionalised assistance. The question of the orphans was first raised by the cadres at a PA meeting in February 1986. A list of orphans was drawn up, and it was decided that the Youth Association should build them five houses and that three women allocated by the Women's Association should look after them.[32]

The destiny of the 'orphans' and their numbers depended on the vagaries of concern for them. Initially they had survived as best they could with relatives or people from the same region. Then a cadre called Alemneh took a personal interest in them. He ensured they had adequate food, received the pick of the clothes, and went to school. The orphans remembered this as a golden age. Report has it that other children became envious of the orphans, since they were fat and, 'unlike settlers', wore new clothes. Later, when the third round of cadres came, the orphans were neglected and their condition deteriorated. The amount of food given for them would run out before the specified time, allegedly because the cooks did not ration it adequately; towards the end of the fortnight the orphans sometimes went hungry.

One of the old men was supposed to ensure that they were well looked after[33] but the PA was not interested in these 'children of nobody', perhaps because of resentment stemming from their previous privileged status. The leadership felt that all orphans should work like the eldest, who was a weaver; another became a messenger boy. Many of the orphans wished to go to school but the PA was not keen to subsidise them or give them exercise books and pens. Some who had relatives went back to them. One, named Imru, was whisked away by a relative who came to find him on behalf of his father, who had earlier left the village. Several older girls sought employment in nearby towns. One worked at the RRC headquarters in Chanqa, fetching water; another left with a teacher living in Dembi Dollo. Concern and SPF occasionally gave them soap, utensils and school equipment.

In 1988 the RRC Family Reunion Programme registered all the 'orphans' to see whether their families could be traced. In the meantime a few were taken to Dembi Dollo by Church missions willing to support them. The RRC planned to regroup all orphans in one site. Aid agencies were sceptical about the benefits of this and were against institutionalisation. However, a degree of regroupment had already occurred, and the condition of orphans in the village left much to be desired. In 1989 the RRC plan was put into effect. The new orphanage received support from Concern. By April 1989 the orphans' huts in the village had collapsed. Mehammed, the eldest, had become a household head with his own plot. Three others had gone to mission schools. Eventually the RRC traced the relatives of a few, among whom were two sisters, Alem and Hawwa:

> Their father was a militiaman who had gone to fight in Eritrea. The sisters left for resettlement with their mother, who died in the village. The two girls lived with their uncle until the orphanage was

established. After a while the girls were taken into the care of successive agricultural and health workers. The eldest, Alem, was very bright and worked her way up the sixth grade. Her younger sister worked as a servant to the Government workers.

In 1988 an RRC worker who was leaving persuaded the younger sister to go with her. Hawwa was therefore separated from her elder sister, much to the latter's chagrin.

Through the help of Concern, Alem obtained a place in a school in Dembi Dollo, with mission support. Her younger sister eventually left the RRC worker and returned to join her sister. In 1989 the RRC family reunion programme traced an uncle living in Wello. Alem had to interrupt her schooling and the sisters were taken back to their homeland. Alem wrote a letter to her uncle in the village in April 1989 saying that she was hoping to resume her schooling the following academic year.

In 1989 twelve of the orphans were in the Village Nine orphanage. One of them came to visit relatives in April. He looked well fed and dressed, and reported that the others were also well looked after, and going to school. During my visit in January 1990 I met a brother and sister living in the orphanage. However by August it had apparently been closed down.

Conclusion

This chapter provided a transition between the background to the settlers' departure from their homeland in the north and their new life in the west. The experience of moving settlers to Qéto was plagued by a series of avoidable mistakes, resulting in crowded and insanitary shelters, a site which had to be abandoned, and a rushed and overloaded assistance programme. The journey west was less arduous for those who completed the voyage in a few days than for those who spent over a month in transit shelters, such as Bakko, the scene of plenty of food but serious epidemics. Similarly, those who left the shelter at the Qéto river promptly suffered less than those who spent weeks there.

The nightmare of Qéto shelter, so vividly portrayed by one of its administrators, could have been prevented if fewer settlers had been sent, and more time available for preparation. The difficulties were largely due to the initial ill-advised and hasty choice of Gurra Ferda, which proved unsuitable and had to be abandoned at the last minute after much waste of resources, labour and time.

The influx of far more settlers than initially expected strained the settlement administration, and resulted in a crisis in the provision of assistance and much hardship due to insufficient supplies. The campaigners arrived late after settlers had begun to arrive. The local population was mobilised to build shelters and houses and ploughed land for the Integrated Sites. The move to the villages was rushed, though sites had not been prepared. Stocks of household equipment, blankets and clothes proved inadequate. Shortages of hand tools delayed land clearing and reduced agricultural productivity. Tractors arrived late and in insufficient numbers. With the construction of houses, stores, clinics and offices taking priority, little time was left for agricultural activities before the rainy season. However in spite of shortages settlers worked diligently.

Resettlement and the aid environment prompted families to split into several households. The provision of assistance led to the development of teams as primary neighbourhood units. Finally, the creation of an orphanage highlighted the issue of dependence on external inputs.

Notes

1 The *mels*, literally 'return', is the feast at the bride's family's house after the wedding at the groom's.
2 The WPE First Secretary told journalists that the 'non-avalability of large rivers' could be overcome by digging wells (*Ethiopian Herald*, 12 February 1985).
3 The RRC commissioner described the site as 'a densely forested area, reminiscent of the African jungle in Hollywood's Tarzan films. It was vast, green and dense – completely virgin and inaccessible' (Dawit Wolde Giorgis, 1989, p. 295).
4 The lack of permanent water sources was noted by Montandon, who visited the area in 1910, and remarked 'all this greenery is but for the eyes' (1913, p. 248).
5 *Ethiopian Herald*, 6 March 1985.
6 Shuro is probably a general term (Bender, 1975, pp. 36, 46) rather than a reference to people who live further south, the Chouro (Montandon, 1913, p. 125) or Me'en, known as Shuro by the Kefa (Cerulli 1956, p. 39; Bender 1975, p. 39). Gurra Ferda itself is said to be inhabited by Shakko (Cerulli, 1956, p. 89); Montandon, 1913, p. 232).
7 The visit took place on 3 March 1985.

8 Chanqa was transformed into a flourishing market town owing to the settler influx and Government and aid agency personnel.

9 This highest mountain in Wellegga (3,300m was a sacred Oromo site (Trimingham, 1952 p. 94).

10 Hungingford (1955, p. 12); Bartels (1983, pp. 20, 78); Negaso Gidada (1984, p. 47).

11 Two groups are referred to by the name Mao: the southern Mao, inhabiting the Anfillo Forest some 50 km to the south-west of Qéto, and a northern group some 50 km to the north-west (Grottanelli, 1940, p. 27; Cerulli, 1956, p. 13; Bender, 1975, p. 71; Bartels, 1983, pp. 21, 71).

12 The presence of 'Mao' outside areas in which they would be expected to be found fits James's theory that the term Mao was not an ethnic but an ascriptive term, used to cover non-Oromo living in close proximity to them, as opposed to the 'Shangalla', with whom they had little contact (James, 1980, pp. 38–9, 60–4).

13 Cerulli (1956, p. 39); Stauder (1971, p. 1); Bender (1975, p. 22).

14 For accounts of transit shelters at the time see Germaine Greer (1986, pp. 289–92).

15 An official under the old regime (with a reputation for a proclivity towards obesity).

16 The name is identical to the loan-word for 'packet' *bakko*, and also resembles the verb *bakkene*, 'to be wasted'.

17 He vividly described the sight of the hill as resembling 'a sea of *Timqet*' – referring to the multitude of white *shemmas*, or togas, of settlers burying their dead, reminiscent of the sea of white robes visible during the annual procession at Epiphany.

18 For reviews see Dirks (1980) and Torry (1984).

19 Such was the controversial description by Turnbull of the Ik under famine conditions (1972).

20 'If starvation provokes anti-social and brutal behaviour in one part of the population it engenders an opposite reaction in another part. The demoralisation of the one is counterbalanced by the ennoblement of the other' (1975, p. 80).

21 These included haricot beans, groundnuts and cotton, as well as small quantities of vegetables, including potatoes, cabbages, carrots, chillies, tomatoes and beetroot.

22 The MOH sent a team to spray against malaria and give settlers training in marlaria control.

23 The *History of Villages Three and Four* notes that 166 pits were dug, but only eight were in use (1987, p. 39).

24 Eighteen people died out of fifty belonging to seventeen families who came from five PAs.

25 In spite of the unpopular policy of deliberately placing this group within other teams, these settlers have maintained strong links among themselves.

26 Habte Mariam Marcos (1973, pp. 113–29).

27 *Kokoo* (Gragg, 1982, p. 248).

28 Three of these were not recorded, since they spoke Amharic as a first language.

29 Some 61.5% of the households from Desé came with more than twenty other households, as opposed to 9.2% from Lasta. Some 28.7% of the Lastan households came with less than ten others, as opposed to 15.5% of those from Desé.

30 Her former husband would not accompany them. Her new husband died shortly afterwards and she retained her own plot.

31 He left the village in 1988 and returned to Wello. His wife and his son now live with her father.

32 A report in May 1986 stated that there were twenty two boys and twelve girls in the huts (Village Three WPE Notes, 30 May 86).

33 Abba Yimer spent a lot of time with those he fondly called 'my soldiers', singing to them and playing his harp, made of an oil tin inscribed with the words 'Gift of the People of the United States of America'.

VI

Production and exchange

We are now the oxen who are yoked. A settler's comment

In this chapter I consider the relationship between the State and the village. Settlement life in the period under discussion, I suggest, can be understood only in relation to the State's pervasive influence on production and exchange. I examine the roles and activities of the intermediaries who translated Government policy into practice and created ties of allegiance with settlers. Although the latter started with equal endowments of food, tools and land, differences emerged; these were not based primarily on property or wealth in livestock, but on the types of work performed. A distinct hierarchy was instituted by State agents, based on literacy and military experience.

The structure of production from the outset introduced dependence on mechanisation; the imposition of collectivisation, and in particular the incorporation of women's labour into the collective domain, was resented and initially resisted. The concentration on cultivating maize and sorghum involved a change in diet, which settlers tried to spice rather than alter. State agents also tried to control exchange and limit the role of the market. The Service Cooperative provided a shop, with cheap but insufficient goods. The marketing of produce, however, was carried out mainly by individual settlers who sold grain principally to invest in livestock, the single area of production outside collective control.

Changes in the structure of production and exchange highlighted the paramount importance of external forces in the settlers' lives. Liberalisation of trade resulted in increased grain prices and ensured better terms of exchange for smallstock, which settlers sought to acquire. The introduction of oxen by Concern confirmed the social hierarchy, and a gradual decollectivisation of land paved the way for private initiative.

The intermediaries

A glance at the number of Government workers in Village Three over the first four years gives an impression of the magnitude of the extension operation. The village on average hosted over twenty. Their number has, however, decreased and their composition has changed. Most significantly the WPE presence was gradually phased out. Conversely the number of agricultural advisers increased until the fourth year, when they were stationed on a permanent basis. Numbers since 1990 have, however, declined since the health post was moved and agricultural personnel were reduced.

Table 8: Government workers in Village Three

Year	Round	WPE M	F	+	MOA M	F	+	RRC M	F	+	MOH M	F	+	MOE M	F	+	Total M	F	+
85–6	1	19	1	20	1	1	2	2	0	2	3	1	4	0	2	2	25	5	30
86–7	2	10	1	11	4	1	5	1	0	1	2	0	2	4	0	4	21	2	23
87–8	3	3	1	3	5	1	6	1	0	1	1	1	2	6	2	8	15	4	19
88–9	4	0	0	0	3	3	6	0	1	1	2	0	2	4	0	4	9	4	13
Total	+	32	2	34	13	6	19	4	1	5	8	2	10	14	4	18	70	15	85

Main source: History of Villages Three and Four (1987), p. 43.

The cadres were initially the most influential intermediaries between the State and the settlers, and were sent on three successive annual campaigns, called rounds, to implement WPE policies. Throughout the country, organisations in all areas of public service were required to select WPE members. The main criterion was the person's record of political awareness and activity. Those seconded on earlier Government campaigns were usually exempt; however, institutions tended to choose people who could be spared, and there was scope for victimisation.

The cadres were seen as 'vanguard campaigners' entrusted with the task of leading the people. In his message to the second round, Chairman Mengistu stated:

In your field work, while living the life of the people, assisting them in their troubles, show them all that is good; do not draw back from finding out their wishes and participating through experience.

Since your favourable example is expected, certify repeatedly in the overall task of building a new life in which you have enlisted that you are standing for the people truthfully.[1]

Cadres were divided into units called *zerfs*, each composed of twenty cadres. Each *zerf* comprised a leader or secretary and a person in charge of each of the following: ideology, economic and social affairs, cooperative organisation and women's affairs, as well as five teams called *budin*. Teams were made up of a secretary, an 'organiser' and an 'awakener'.[2] In the first round 158 out of 2,259 cadres were sent to Qéto in seven *zerfs*. In the first round *Zerf* Five was quartered in Village Three and organised the establishment of Village Eighteen across the river.

The twenty cadres came from the following institutions: nine from Ministries (five from Agriculture, and two each from Health and Education), eight from trade and industry (five from factories, two from banks and one each from the Domestic Distribution Corporation and the Small Industries Development Agency) and three from administration (two from regional PA offices and one from Addis Ababa municipality). The cadres thus came mainly from urban backgrounds and few had knowledge of agriculture.

During the second year the village was twinned with Village Four. Eleven cadres were placed in Village Three – six for the site, five for the *zerf* – and nine in Village Four.[3] The number of cadres was again reduced in the third year; the three assigned to the village were workers from soap, tyre and textile factories.

For some their campaign was a fulfilling experience. Taddese felt that it was one of the most useful services he had performed for his country. Haile Mikaél, the leader of the first round, wrote:

We felt a deep pride in being vanguard cadres campaigning on account of our people's suffering and in being the first to put into practice the rehabilitation plan of our Party's political office; entering a village where forests abounded and the sound of many wild animals reigned; experiencing our compatriots' troubles along-side them, eating the same food, suffering from the same illnesses, tasting of the chalice of death from which they died.[4]

Most found their service trying. In the countryside they felt isolated from family and friends. Some were frustrated at what they considered a waste of time, which prevented them from furthering their careers or continuing their studies. The cadres had, however, a sense of the historic nature of their mission. One of the first activities was to set up a History Committee. The first round tape-recorded the settlers' voices; the second took photographs, and the third wrote a *History of Villages Three and Four*. They portrayed themselves as fulfilling their 'national duty' and standing by their 'oath of allegiance' to the Party.[5] They saw their role as supervising the provision of assistance and organising settlers into 'Popular Associations' for peasants, women and youth. The cadres set up an administration, wrote reports on a weekly, monthly, quarterly and annual basis, and introduced a filing system. They organised the registration of births, deaths and marriages, and compiled statistics. They instituted regular meetings for the three 'Mass Associations', team leaders, and the whole PA.

The cadres' most important mission was to foster collective spirit and instil values of cooperative work. They tried to discourage trade and private enterprise. They organised the purchase of looms from individual weavers to work for the collective. They also sought to forbid women from selling beer but their attempts to clamp down on brewing were ineffectual. Cadres suggested that the Women's Association should brew as a source of collective income but the idea never took off.

Cadres expressed an ambiguous attitude towards 'culture'. On the one hand they were keen to preserve 'cultures' as a heritage for display in museums; 'cultural halls' exhibited jewellery and artefacts from settler areas of origin. On the other hand 'culture' was seen as an impediment to changing what was perceived as settlers' custom-bound mentality. Cadres saw their mission as freeing the peasants from 'harmful customs'. The practices of traditional healing rituals, credit associations and early marriages came under attack. This dual attitude to culture was reflected in the early establishment of a dance troupe, which, in addition to traditional themes of love and bravery, sang revolutionary songs extolling the virtues of resettlement and cooperation. The troupe was called upon to perform on special occasions, such as May Day celebrations, and took part in competitions with other troupes.

First-year cadres concentrated on the construction of communal buildings, such as offices for campaigners and 'Mass Associations', grain stores, a meeting hall, a clinic, a model house, and classrooms. They also started classes before the literacy campaigners arrived. The second round stressed the need to increase cultivated land. They also organised a select group of advanced readers to discuss

The Village Three dance troupe. Performing a play about literacy
(above) and (below) a performance in front of the grain store

what was termed *Ma-le*, an abbreviation for 'Marxism–Leninism' to 'nurture communists', and 'to free settlers from non-scientific views'.[6] They established a village library named after Lenin and well stocked with translated Marxist tracts. Five settlers were sent on a course to become 'settler cadres'. When they returned, they were entrusted with key positions in the PA. Towards the end of the second year, cadres were asked whether they thought a third round was required. Those from Village Three answered that the programme should continue because the Associations were still weak, settlers came from different backgrounds and customs, there was much divorce and there were signs of individualism. In the third year some cadres privately expressed doubts as to whether they had much to contribute, and felt that they could be dispensed with.

Cadres organised the referendum for the 1987 Constitution and the elections to the National Parliament, for which three settler candidates were voted for, in each village. They also chose the new name of the village: 'Fruit of the Struggle', which encapsulated the way in which they saw resettlement as an achievement of the ongoing Revolution. The name was painted at the entrance of the village and was used in official correspondence, although settlers refer to their home as Village Three.

Relations between cadres and other Government workers were often strained, if not hostile. Cadres had overall authority and supervised the activities of other workers. There were often disagreements about priorities, notably the allocation of labour. Agricultural workers complained that cadres gave too much importance to construction and literacy work, to the detriment of production goals. They resented the fact that cadres, without knowledge of agriculture and with little education, were placed above them and could overrule their decisions. Cadres often found fault with RRC staff, in one instance accusing an RRC worker of favouritism. In one village cadres were accused of diverting aid, which led to a clash in which an MOA agent was murdered.

MOA allocations of personnel to Qéto doubled over five years. In the first year fourteen extension agents were allocated; by 1989 the twenty Qéto villages had some seventy-six agricultural advisers. During the first four years MOA agents were sent on campaigns; they received their salary plus rations provided by the RRC. The campaign approach was criticised in internal documents as ineffective, since it did not make for continuity. From the fifth year agricultural extension workers were assigned to the village on a semi-permanent basis but in 1990 their numbers were reduced. A *zerf* of MOA agents served two villages and comprised a head, an 'all rounder', and agents for livestock, conservation, cooperative development and home economics.

RRC staff organised the distribution of food, household equipment and clothing. They monitored changes in population so as to assess assistance needs. Unlike the agricultural agents and cadres, MOH-trained Health Assistants were not sent out on a campaign basis. This had the advantage of maintaining some continuity. However, the health workers tended to be moved from time to time, and the frustration of not knowing when they would be relieved, or seeing any means of furthering their careers, led some of the most dedicated to leave. In 1990 the health post was closed and settlers thereafter have to go to the one in Village Five.

The literacy campaigners were the least permanent Government workers, since they came for three-month spells. Literacy campaigns followed national campaigns from the thirteenth round onwards. In 1989 the campaign was in its tenth year and twenty-first round. Campaigners were local students, who had completed or were about to complete higher education and were assisted by young settlers with several years' education.

Relationships and power

Cadres were responsible for the creation of a distinct hierarchy. One of their first priorities was organising a leadership for Mass Associations: twenty-three members for the PA, twenty-two for the Youth, and fifteen for Women. Cadres also supervised the militia, and controlled the distribution of bullets for the village's seven rifles.

Cadres had the authority to select and depose PA leaders and militia. Members of the leadership were told to move from the plots they first settled and build plots close to the centre. In this way the social structure of the village was mapped out, with the Government workers in the centre surrounded by the leadership.

The cadres instituted a system whereby privileges accrued to the leadership and militia. Those who obtained positions of authority did so partly by showing personal allegiance to cadres in a way reminiscent of the traditional patron-client system. Changes in leadership occurred after the first round of cadres had left and again after the second. Each new group of cadres were suspicious of the power base established by their predecessors and attempted to create their own ties of allegiance. A team leader was once taken to court by a peasant who accused him of having obtained his position by 'getting close' to cadres. Establishment of individual allegiances can be seen from the fact that settlers did not express the same preferences and dislikes with regard to individual cadres. One respected by some would be loathed by others. Settlers spoke highly of the first round, who worked with the people, while they had little regard for subsequent rounds.

Cadres were responsible to the leader of their *zerf* and then to the WPE Committee at the settlement level. Settlers who had grievances against particular cadres could, and on a couple of occasions did, take the matter to the *wereda* party committee.[7] The separate status of cadres as outsiders and as rulers was keenly felt, as expressed in the following couplet:

> One of the nice things about Amakkelech [the jigger flea]
> Is that she does not distinguish between cadres and settlers.[8]

Several settlers served Government workers and received work points for doing so. Two women cooked, two men cut wood, several 'orphans' cleaned and performed small chores, one man gave his son to them, a disabled man gardened and an elderly man made wall coverings and pillows out of aid sacks. Collection of water was assigned to women household heads; teams took turns each day.

Relationships of quasi-clientage were established between certain cadres or Government workers and individual settlers. For instance the latter might perform errands at market or offer fruit from their gardens, or honey from their hives. Government workers were in a position to do small favours or even give individuals jobs which involved lighter or more interesting work. A clinic worker could offer prized empty bottles and tins from the stores, or allow a family to jump a queue; a MOA agent could offer vegetable seeds or allocate easier tasks. An RRC worker could offer old food sacks. The result was not large-scale corruption but minor favours in exchange for small rewards. Several Government workers developed friendships with settlers, and there were cases of relations between them and settler women resulting in the birth of at least two children.

Differentiation

In theory resettlement should have acted as a leveller. All households received equal amounts of assistance: 500 g of grain per
person per day, private household plots of 1,000 sq. m, the same
kind and quantity of household implements and agricultural tools,
clothing and blankets. The cooperative mode of production was
based on a vision of equality; settlers were all required to work
the same hours and initially received the same daily number of
points.

Former wealth was not a means to success. We have seen that
settlers were not all destitute. Some wealthy persons came because
of community pressure. Several were able to buy a chicken or a
sheep when they arrived. However, most had exhausted their
money in shelters on the way.[9] Many formerly wealthy persons
thus found themselves no better off than their neighbours.

The most conspicuous difference between settlers was in relation
to their work. The division of labour was partly a function of the
large size of the cooperative. With over 500 households and around
1,800 people, leadership roles had to be defined and specialised
tasks needed performing. However, the establishment of a hierarchy was not primarily a matter of size. The PA and cooperative
structure were modelled on guidelines for the whole country, and
differentiation was much more a function of the relationship
between settlers and the State. Three factors were paramount in
determining the village hierarchy: knowledge of writing, or fighting, and relationships with State representatives. These factors bear
a striking resemblance to the means of achieving power in traditional Ethiopian society, where ecclesiastical and military elites
were differentiated from the rest of the peasantry through patronage relationships with representatives of the State.

Most of those who obtained key positions in the PA knew how
to wield either a pen or a gun, preferably both. When they arrived
the cadres registered 'those who had been to the battlefield'. Out of
the ten men with military experience, four held key posts in the PA
and three others were team leaders. Out of twenty-one members
of the PA leadership committee, eleven knew how to use guns.

Gradually the literacy factor prevailed. The first chairman and
his deputy had both been in the militia but one was elderly and
both could hardly write. They were deposed in favour of younger,
more literate people. The last chairman had not been to the

Table 9: Level of education in Village Three, 1986

			Sex			
Level	M	%	F	%	+	%
7–11 grade	3	0.4	2	0.4	5	0.4
1–6 grade	37	5.4	7	1.2	44	3.3
Read	10	1.4	3	0.5	13	0.9
Illiterate	640	92.8	580	97.9	1,220	95.4
Total	690	100.0	592	100.0	1,282	100.0

Source: PA survey (1986).

battlefield. He and the secretary were the most educated settlers, having completed eighth and eleventh grades respectively. The general level of education was low. Less than 5% of the settlers could read and less than 1% had attended secondary school. Literacy classes were compulsory and defaulters liable to fines, though elderly and disabled people were exempt. Settlers were divided into three groups – men, women and children – and four grades teaching four subjects: Amharic, politics, maths and health care.

Table 10: Literacy in Village Three, 1987–8

	Beginners			Improving			Advanced			Reading			Total		
Year	M	F	+	M	F	+	M	F	+	M	F	+	M	F	+
1987	401	146	547	69	74	143	29	1	30	10	21	31	509	242	751
1988	119	110	229	50	56	106	66	58	124	72	39	111	307	263	570

Source: History of Villages Three and Four (1987, p. 42).

Despite optimistic statistics, the literacy programme was plagued by shortages of textbooks, and successive rounds of teachers found that they were covering the same ground with little progress. Although many settlers enjoyed the rest from agricultural work, and children were eager to learn, literacy was not seen as a means of advancement among adults. Those who had obtained positions because of education had already been able to read and write when they came. However, settlers were eager to encourage their children to go to school in Village Five and thence to the secondary school in Chanqa, which two children attended.

The leadership and militia were privileged in several ways. They did not have to take part in continual agricultural toil. The leadership spent much time on administrative and office work, meetings and committees. The militia played a supervisory role, were off duty after guarding at night, or were seconded to the regional or even national army. They were given preference in clothes and blanket distribution. Militia away on military service were, moreover, issued with full points, while others lost points when they absented themselves. Last, but not least, they had their private plots dug by communal labour.

Just as cadres and Government workers were able to create ties of patronage, so those with power in the PA were able to dispense favours. They made decisions about allocating people to jobs requiring specialisation. However, the scope for abusing power was limited. Private land holdings were of almost the same size, but when the chairman remarried he was allowed, with cadre approval, to build a new house on a plot more than twice the average size near the centre, while his former wife retained his old plot. There were a few isolated cases of the use of communal labour by PA leaders for private purposes.

In the first five years, differences in wealth as expressed in livestock were also negligible, as a survey carried out in January 1988 suggests (Table 11). The figures are underestimates, since settlers feared that the registration of livestock holdings might be a first step towards collectivisation, though the relative ratios are probably fairly accurate. More than half the households had at

Table 11: Village Three household livestock holdings

Range	Chickens		Sheep		Goats		Hives	
	No.	*	No.	*	No.	*	No.	*
>0	287	54.0	210	7.0	81	15.3	68	12.8
>1	197	37.2	122	23.0	40	7.5	41	7.7
>2	116	21.9	65	12.3	14	2.6	15	2.8
>3	89	16.8	31	5.8	4	0.7	10	1.9
>4	53	10.0	10	1.9	0		7	1.3
>5	37	7.0	7	1.3	0		2	0.4

* Percentage of households by number of livestock, calculated on the basis of a population of 530 households, in 1988.
Source: Adapted from PA survey (1988).

least a sheep, goat or chicken but only 7% had more than five chickens, and only 1% more than five sheep or goats.

If one considers livestock by settler occupation, the militia and leadership were undoubtedly in an advantageous position, as Table 12 suggests. As much as a fifth of the households with three or more animals were militiamen, who represent about 10% of households. Fifteen per cent were in leadership positions, representing less than 5% of the householders.

Table 12: Village Three sheep and goats by householder occupation

Range	Total No.	Total %	Leaders No.	Leaders %	Militia No.	Militia %	Artisans No.	Artisans %	Peasants No.	Peasants %	Women No.	Women %
>5	4	100	2	50.0			1	25.0	1	25.0		
5	8	100			3	37.5			5	65.5		
4	27	100	6	12.7	5	10.6	1	2.1	13	48.1	2	7.4
3	45	100	5	11.1	9	20.5			29	64.4	2	4.4
Total	84	100.0	13	15.5	17	20.2	2	2.4	48	57.1	4	4.8

Source: Adapted from PA survey (1988).

The structure of production

Two aspects of production in the settlements introduced complete changes in the settlers' life-styles: mechanisation and cooperativisation. The Government's decision to introduce tractors in large settlements was not determined by environmental considerations but was part of a vision of progress. In Qéto, side by side with high-input Conventional Settlements, there were smaller Integrated Sites where settlers used oxen for draught. Dependence on State inputs was therefore built into the structure of production. Reliance on tractors proved a problem from the outset. In the first year there were insufficient tractors and harrows; most cultivation was done by hand. Subsequently, since the tractors had to cover twenty villages, individual sites had no control as to when they would have access to them. Delays were a common complaint in the reports of cadres and agricultural extension workers.

Little forethought went into the long-term viability of tractors in either ecological or economic terms. Damage to frail topsoil through deep ploughing was particularly acute in villages which

had sloping fields. The aid agency Concern encouraged the building of bunds to control erosion and campaigned to prevent tractors
from destroying them. The fleet of 149 tractors provided free
service for the first five years, although the level of assistance was
gradually reduced. MOA inputs of seeds, fertiliser and pesticides
were also reduced.[10] Faced with the task of trying to make the
operation viable, the MOA introduced fees for tractor services.
With the collapse of collective agriculture, many villages decided
against requesting tractors. Moreover, the precedent of schemes
started by the RRC in the late 1970s does not augur well. After
more than a decade they cannot be considered self-sufficient. In
Qéto, after four years, only thirty-six out of 149 tractors were
operational.[11] The low price of the maize and sorghum produced
offers little prospect of meeting the costs. Another option may be
to produce crops with a higher market value, such as groundnuts
and cotton.[12] Experience has shown that such schemes require
much capital and appropriate skills. Transport costs and fluctu-
ations in the market price raise doubts about the economic viability
of this option.

From the settlers' viewpoint mechanisation did not spare them
from digging fields for subsequent ploughing, or from sowing and
considerable weeding. The tractors, which many believed would
do away with drudgery, did not reduce the need for manual labour.
Settlers had become dependent on a technology over which they
had no control. Peasants were proud of this watchword, 'I
ploughed and ate.' Instead, a settler confided: 'Now we are the
oxen who are yoked.'

Collectivisation

> What sort of a life is it to be counted like sheep in the
> morning and evening?
>
> A settler commenting on the daily roll call

Production in the settlement was largely determined by the imposition of a collectivist model. Conventional settlements were destined to become PCs, with minimal private holdings of 0.1 ha.
Once autonomous peasants were being turned into virtual wage-
labourers. One young man recalled: 'During the famine I went
looking for wage-labour; then I joined the resettlement, wanting
to work the land. I did not know I was coming to more wage
labour.' The alienation of labour for collective use represented a

Work in the fields, 1988. (Above) clearing for planting, and
(below) threshing the harvest, two teams at work

dramatic loss of independence for the peasant, whose ambition and ethos were emotively charged towards the ideal of becoming a self-reliant household head with his own pair of oxen.

The imposition of collectivisation did not occur without resistance. Records of cadres and agricultural workers note that the number of people coming to work was not commensurate with the village population. People refusing to take part in collective work were fined by the PA Law Court and obliged to work extra hours. The second round of cadres decided to allocate two persons to check that people were not absenting themselves from work. Absconders were fetched by the militiamen. Gradually the system of collective work was grudgingly accepted. However, on 3 March 1987 an incident occurred in which settlers revolted when food was brought to them in the field, a measure which represented an intrusion of the State into the domestic sphere.

> It was during the harvest; the settlers were out threshing, one group at the sorghum stack and the other at the *téf* piles. The Women's Association was instructed to boil sorghum and bring it to settlers in the field. The cadres and PA leadership arrived and explained that the measure was an experiment, initiated because some single men had complained that they did not have time to prepare food before work and could not do a good job on an empty stomach.[13]

The settlers were suspicious, and several teams refused to eat the food.

> Some argued that they could not eat until they had washed their hands. Others privately expressed fears that the food would be subtracted from their share of the harvests. The PA deputy chairman argued that it was traditional for women to take food to men in the fields. Cadres tried to root out gang leaders. In the end only one team refused to eat; the leadership seemed to have scored a victory. However, the attempt at providing food in the fields was quietly abandoned in recognition of the peasants' opposition. In contrast, a post-harvest feast organised by the PA was well attended, perhaps because it involved the whole village, including the women and children, and did not threaten domestic rights and privileges.

The incorporation of artisans into the collective posed problems in estimating the contribution of their labour. Disputes arose between the weavers and the PA as to how much could be produced by one person. It was alleged that weavers were making cloth for private sale. Their produce was handed to the Women's Association, which sold it to settlers at fixed rates. The income was then entrusted to the PA treasurer.[14] Since the collapse of the cooperative, weavers and smiths have not been working for the PA. Shortage of cotton has brought weaving to a virtual standstill, and the main smith only recently regained his tools, which were bought by the PA.

The allocations of tasks was organised by the PA initially with directives and supervision from WPE cadres and MOA extension workers. Work was organised through team units called *budin*. Each team had a leader and a secretary who met the PA leadership once a week. Four teams formed a *birgéd* (i.e. brigade) and one of the team leaders was appointed leader. The brigades rarely worked together, since the PA realised that they were unmanageable units and that more work was achieved by smaller units. The teams were composed of members who knew each other and worked better together than the brigades. If someone was not working hard enough other team members would chastise him. In the third year the PA and MOA extension workers experimented with giving teams 'piecework'. A team was allocated a specific task after which members were free to go home. Work was completed faster and settlers had more time to devote to their private plots.

The netib points system

Remuneration was worked out according to a points system devised for producers' cooperatives. A daily routine was established. At 6.00 or 7.00 a.m., depending on the season and work load, a bell was rung at the PA office, the flag was hoisted, settlers assembled in teams and a roll call was taken by each team secretary. At the end of the day each man was allocated eight points, one for each hour worked. The number of points earned by an individual was added up on a monthly and annual basis. At the end of the harvest, the total number of points earned was calculated and the value of one point was worked out for each crop, in money and in kind. Thirty per cent of the produce was kept aside for sale, seed and reserves. The rest was distributed to householders according to the number of points earned.

The points system had three grave weaknesses: its administration was cumbersome and required complicated reckoning; it lacked incentives to encourage productivity; and the system was poorly understood and mistrusted by the peasants. In the first year registration of points was not systematic. Women's points were not recorded. Some men were occasionally omitted by mistake and there was much confusion as to whether days off, market days and days spent on house repair should be counted. Team secretaries pursued different policies and some were so poorly literate that their handwriting could hardly be deciphered. Occasionally quarrels due to errors occurred and discrepancies between work teams existed. Those who registered the points wielded considerable power and accusations were sometimes levelled by settlers, who would complain, 'I was given a zero' (i.e. registered as absent).

Peasants could see no obvious immediate incentive to work hard, since all received the same number of points irrespective of their work. When it came to distribution in the second year settlers received their own produce as rations distributed by the RRC. There was therefore little difference from the earlier ration system except that the type of food changed. Fortnightly distribution did not allow peasants to plan how to use their grain and thus perpetuated a sense of dependence.

In the third year the points system took effect. The complicated accounting required completing the assessment of produce and adding up all the points before grain could be distributed. This resulted in a long wait after the harvest. The points system therefore engendered dependence on agricultural advisers and confused most settlers. Delays in a decision 'from above' as to how the produce should be distributed further undermined the peasants' confidence and there were rumours that the grain would be taken away. It was finally decided that 30% of the produce would be put aside and the rest distributed in two lots. This gave settlers more control over their grain, and many started selling it to invest in livestock.

In the fourth year an attempt was made by an enterprising agricultural extension worker to introduce a more elaborate points system which would take into consideration the following criteria: physical difficulty, degree of skill, usefulness to production and danger. Different types of work were graded and points worked out on an hourly basis, using four categories, ranging from 0.11 to 0.2 points per hour. This resulted in such a complicated system that few understood it properly. The next MOA team had a difficult task unravelling the outcome. Both points systems ended up favouring the militia and the PA administration. Militiamen on duty outside the village received maximum points and those in the village received points for night duty.[15]

Settlers had just begun to understand the old system when it was changed.[16] Most peasants could see no justification in going to such trouble to keep records and disliked the system intensely. One man composed the following couplet, in which the points are blamed for the settlers' woes:

> A man's death used to be [caused] by a *minishir* [gun],
> A man's death used to be by an *albin* [another gun]
> What they call 'points' won't let us eat our lunch [i.e. the points
>   won't let us live in peace].

There was great relief and no regret in 1990 when the points system was abandoned.

Women's labour

Women were brought into collective work mainly at peak agricultural times, for weeding and harvesting. They started work a little later than men, and finished earlier. Women received five points instead of eight. Female household heads worked longer hours and obtained full points. This partial alienation of women's labour provoked resentment. In March 1987 the issue came to a head. Women argued that they were not accustomed to communal labour and did not spend much time in the fields in Wello. They claimed that working in the fields would 'break up our marriages'. This pointed to the fact that it was the invasion of the domestic domain which was at issue. Reactions among men were even more virulent. They complained that their food was not ready when they returned from work and saw the use of women's work for collective purposes as an infringement of their rights as household heads. One man declared: 'Now we are no longer household heads. It is the judges [i.e. the PA leadership] who order our women; they no longer listen to us. We come home and find that the food is not ready, but we cannot complain, for the women have been out in the fields.'

Women with young children were allocated lighter work such as taking maize off cobs during the harvest. In the weeding season women complained, since they had to take their youngsters with

them. The first-round cadres spoke of setting up a kindergarten.
The idea was favoured by the second and third rounds but the
kindergarten did not materialise until the fourth year, when Concern set up a scheme, training two women in each village in nursery
management and providing milk, toys and learning material, such
as blackboards. At first the kindergarten met with resistance from
mothers, who did not want to part with their children, and attendance was low. But the distribution of milk and the children's
enjoyment led to an upsurge in attendance.

Women's labour was taken for granted and only gradually recognised in its own right. In the first year of the points system no
one bothered to register their points. In the second year these were
recorded but, except for female-headed households, were added to
those of their husbands. In 1989 the agriculturalists declared that
women should 'come to sign for taking their own share'. Since the
collapse of the cooperative women have no longer been called out
to work collectively. However, until 1991 female household heads
had to work on the two days during which men work for the
leadership, the militia and the disadvantaged.

**A woman prepares the threshing ground with dung brought from a
nearby Oromo village**

Land, crops and diet

The resettlement areas specialised in the production of maize and sorghum, which account for 75% of land sown and 96% of the produce. Although altitude places some restrictions on what can be grown, the decision to opt for the virtual monoculture of the two cereals was not entirely dictated by the environment, as the fields of the Oromo peasants bear witness. The latter grow a variety of cereals, including maize, sorghum, millet, *téf* and pulses, such as lentils, several kinds of beans, chickpeas and chickling peas, besides small quantities of vegetables, oil-producing plants and cash crops, including coffee, cotton, tobacco and *chat*.

Table 13: Village Three crops by hectare and produce in quintals

Crop	1986		1987		1988		1989	
Crop	Ha	Q	Ha	Q	Ha	Q	Ha	Q
Maize	31.0	175.0	116.0	2,519.0	170.0	3,448.0	142.0	1,881.0
Sorghum	5.0	142.0	112.0	3,350.0	111.0	849.0	112.0	1,300.0
Téf	0.1		17.0	31.0	3.0		2.0	7.0
Haricot	25.0	37.0	5.5	27.0	24.0	18.0	30.0	20.0
Soya					19.5	7.0	26.5	55.0
Chickpea	6.0	1.8					2.5	5.0
Peanuts	0.2	2.5	0.6	0.7	1.0	2.4	4.0	1.5
Sunflower					5.0	3.5	2.0	22.0
Niger seed					1.0	6.0	3.0	1.5
Sesame							5.0	11.0
Cotton					4.0	2.8	3.0	?
Chillies			0.1	15.7	3.3	5.5	4.0	9.0
Sweet Potato				12.7		10.0	0.5	?
Potato					0.3	27.8		
Onion					0.4	4.3		
Total	67.3	358.3	251.2	5,956.1	332.5	4,384.3	336.5	3,313.0

Source: PA data (1989).

The main reason for the prevalence of maize and sorghum was MOA policy in providing seed and imposing quotas. The two crops were considered easy to manage and monoculture simplified the reckoning of total produce. This emphasis presented a number of difficulties. It resulted in labour shortages, since crops had to be sown, weeded and harvested within a short period of time. Crops were prone to serious pest damage. There was also a danger of reducing soil fertility by not employing crop rotation.[17] Settlers also noted that the size of cobs decreased. The market price of these crops was also very low. Last, and most important, maize and sorghum were not preferred foods, and one of the chief settler complaints concerned diet, as expressed in the couplet:

> The bread is maize; the sauce, beans.
> Will one [ever] get used to life in Wellegga?

Lack of protein was a crucial aspect of diet in which settlers were worse-off than before the famine, and were at a disadvantage compared to locals. Settlers only gradually began to start eating some meat, at first only for special occasions. Given the trypanosomiasis threat, settlers did not until recently have cattle, and children did not benefit from milk. Eggs tended to be sold for cash.

Spicing the diet

The diet of central Ethiopians to which settlers had been accustomed consists in the main of two items: a pancake-like bread called *injera*, ideally made from *téf*, and a stew called *wet*, made with meat, pulses or vegetables, salt and *berberé*, a mixture of spices of which chilli is the principal component. This binary combination of bread and stew is made in a variety of ways, depending *inter alia* on region, season, occasion and wealth.

Central Ethiopians are able to grow a considerable range of crops. This variety decreases at high and low altitudes. In the highest areas, above 3,000 m, referred to as the *wirch*, or frost zone, the only crops which will grow are barley, wheat and some kinds of beans. In the lowland areas, named *qolla*, below 1,500 m, the main cereals are maize and sorghum. Most Ethiopians, however, live in the agriculturally optimal zones, *weyna dega* from 1,500 m to 2,000 m and *dega* from 2,000 m to 3,000 m, where the range of crops is considerable. Most settlers came from the *weyna dega* zone, where they used to grow the following crops:

Cereals: *téf*, barley, oats, wheat, millet, sorghum.
Pulses: lentils, beans, peas, chick and chikling peas.

Oil-producing seeds: sunflower, niger seed and linseed.
Vegetables: cabbages, potatoes, onions and carrots.
Spices: chillies, fenugreek, cumin and bishop's weed.
Fruit: lemons, oranges and citrons.[18]
Cash crops: eucalyptus, cotton, *chat* and *gésho*.[19]

Maize and sorghum were not staples for any settlers before they came[20] although some grew a little of the former for its 'freshness' value. Some of those from the lowland areas of Lasta and Qallu used to eat some sorghum but only as one of a number of cereals. The type of bean grown locally in this part of Wellegga, called *adengwarré*, was unknown to settlers before they came. Experiments at growing other crops were not very successful, partly because those imported by the MOA were not always suitable and partly because settlers and agriculturalists were unfamiliar with local rainfall patterns. An experiment in 1987 at growing the preferred cereal, *téf*, yielded poor results and this crop was not subsequently sown.

Diversification

Given the variety of produce to which settlers were accustomed, and the marked dislike for maize,[21] one might have expected settlers to grow other crops on their private plots or to sell some maize to buy preferred foods. Neither strategy was evident on a significant scale, at least not in the first five years. Most settlers grew almost exclusively maize and beans. Several reported failed attempts to grow peas and onions. They argued that private plots were too small to risk experimenting. As one man put it: 'We know vegetables would be good for the children but we need the bulk maize provides.' However, a number of enterprising settlers have been growing chillies, sweet potatoes and small quantities of coffee, *chat* and tobacco.

Grains, pulses and vegetables were available in the markets but were expensive. For special occasions and healing rituals, settlers bought a little barley or chickpeas. A mother would buy her children a banana or mango[22] as a treat. Settlers also bought potatoes, tomatoes and onions. There was some effort to promote pulses, such as soya and haricot beans, chick and pigeon peas, groundnuts, sesame, sunflower, cotton and vegetables, including sweet potatoes, onions and chillies. In 1987 the MOA provided carrot, potato and beetroot seeds. The following year tomatoes and cabbages were added. Sweet potatoes were very successful, though settlers had never tasted them, and did not at first express much enthusiasm for them. The Women's Association was responsible for 6,000 sq. m devoted to cotton and the Youth Association planted 1 ha of land with haricot beans and chillies.

Concern encouraged diversification of crop types by providing a variety of vegetable seeds, and pigeon peas for soil conservation bunds. The agency also promoted fruit production by giving seeds or seedlings of mangoes, bananas, papayas and citrus trees. Papayas did particularly well, and some settlers who planted them in the first year have harvested several annual crops. They became quite common on private plots and act as a symbol of commitment to remain in the village. Though mangoes take at least five years to grow to maturity, a few settlers harvested their first crop in 1990.

Forestry

Village Three is surrounded on two sides by an estimated 30 ha of riverine forest where coffee grows wild. In 1987 the MOA tried to encourage coffee production by planting 1,500 seedlings. In 1989 Concern provided seedlings for 'contact farmers'[23] in each village. Attention was also paid to protecting riverine forests, and guards were appointed to prevent people from cutting trees in protected areas. The chairman of the Law Court explained the rationale to culprits in the following terms:

> We left Wello because of deforestation, an enemy we cannot fight with guns. This is not a punishment, but advice. You know that you are not allowed to cut trees in the restricted area. We must not create a second Wello; the Government cannot move us like freight loads from Wellegga elsewhere. The life of the trees is the life of the people.

Reforestation suffered from the campaign approach, with much effort put into planting trees which were then not looked after. With the increase in livestock, notably goats, seedlings stand little chances of success unless protection measures are enhanced. The PA agreed to peasant demands for one person in each team to be allowed to obtain points as a shepherd. Settlers acknowledge that there is a certain danger of deforestation. They point out that because of termites houses have to be rebuilt after a couple of years. Some anticipate that after five to ten years wood shortages will become acute. During a visit in 1989 I was with some elders when we heard a commotion. Women were authorised to take wood from the old clinic building. The ensuing scuffle would have been inconceivable when I first arrived in the village; at that time there was still plenty of wood left in the fields after the bulldozer had cleared the land. The favourable contrast between the dense riverine forest and the shortage of trees in the landscape settlers were used to was still fresh in people's minds. A project to make huts out of compressed mud bricks, initiated late in 1990 by SPF in Village Eleven, was not taken up wholeheartedly. Villagers are reluctant to work in large groups now that private enterprise is the rule.

The Service Cooperative and the market

The shop

According to national policy several PAs were to be linked in Service Cooperatives (SCs) which provide goods and market produce. In Qéto two villages formed an SC; one named 'Qéto Waterfall Service Cooperative', linking Villages Three and Four, was established in August 1986. An SC shop was established at the beginning of August 1987, with an initial capital of 4,000 *birr*, 2,000 from each village. Each household had to contribute ten *birr* over two years although initial payment was set at six *birr*. The shop stocked basic items such as salt, soap, exercise books, paper, pens, razor-blades, cotton thread and cloth. Gradually the SC was able to increase the variety of items, introducing batteries, boots and umbrellas.

The SC encountered a number of problems. It could only obtain certain goods in limited amounts which were allocated by the Ethiopian Domestic Distribution Corporation. Since resettlement was not incorporated in its planned quota, the Qéllem branch was unwilling to allocate scarce commodities. Settlements could not obtain sugar, and salt quotas ran out within days. A ration system was established, in line with SCs throughout the country. Settlers had to produce their official exercise book and have it stamped

each time they bought salt, or paraffin, required for grinding at
the mill.

The price differential between the SC shop and the market value
was such that it paid settlers to sell some of their meagre salt ration,
though this was illegal. Although commodities were sold at well
below market prices, the range and quantity were limited. For
instance, the SC was on one occasion allocated sixteen pairs of
boots (for a population of over 3,500 in the two villages). Another
problem resulted from high transport costs. The SC had to hire
private lorries to transport goods at six *birr* per quintal. Nonetheless, the shop was much appreciated by settlers, some of whom
suggested that, were it not for its cheap goods, many more would
have left. Owing to fuel shortages and difficulties with the quota
system, items provided were down to a bare minimum at the time
of my visit in January 1991.

The second function of the SC, to market PA produce, was
slow to develop. The Agricultural Marketing Corporation was not
geared to thinking of settlers as producers. From 1987 it began to
buy some 1,000 q of maize, about a fifth of the production of each
of the two villages, at twenty *birr* per quintal. In 1987 the AMC
bought grain from the settlement SCs and sold it to the RRC. In
this way the food was not moved but redistributed free and the
proceeds were deposited in the PA's bank account in Dembi Dollo.
Some money, over 42,500 *birr* for the three years 1987–9, was used
to purchase cattle in a scheme in which Concern paid half the cost.

The role of the market

About 70% of agricultural production was distributed direct to
settlers, who then sold most of what they could spare. They became
involved in the market even before they had any surplus, as a way
to satisfy basic needs, invest and buy luxuries. Cadres considered
trade a 'harmful practice' for several reasons. They believed that
time spent at market was counter-productive, diverting labour
from vital agricultural activities. Sale of food and aid items was
also seen as evidence of a lack of foresight, for it would leave
settlers hungry and destitute during the lean season. Cadres argued
that 'exploitative traders' would profiteer at settlers' expense. Aid
items they felt were 'Government goods', donated from abroad
and allocated for the settlers' exclusive use. Finally, it was thought

Settlers at Nejjo market, 1987

that sales were a preparation for, and therefore a sign of, settlers planning to leave.

Cadres tried to control time spent at market. We heard about the unsuccessful attempt to stop the sale of aid items when settlers first arrived. Later, cadres synchronised market days in different locations to prevent settlers from going to market on different days. They also tried to discourage roadside fairs, which had sprung up on the routes to the main markets. At these middlemen bought grain from settlers unable to carry their load all the way.[24] Finally, a more effective form of control was instituted. Market days during peak agricultural seasons were sometimes defined as work days so that settlers lost work points for not attending. During peak harvest seasons settlers were not allowed to go to market for two or even three weeks, or only women were given permission.

Settlers resented these restrictions. Days when they were free to go to market were referred to as ones when they were 'untied', or 'let go'. Settlers who went to market all the same were liable not only to lose points for that day but also for an additional day as a punishment. From the settler viewpoint opposition to trade made no sense. They sold food and aid items for three main reasons: to meet basic food needs and vary their diet, to buy luxuries and to obtain cash for other purposes, notably investment in livestock.

Finally, settlers went to market for the occasion. They would don their 'put away' clothes and much enjoyed the change from the routine of agricultural labour. People exchanged news about their homeland. Those separated from relatives hoped to find them or hear news of their lost ones. Many would go even if they had nothing to sell or buy. Others would spend a little money on drink and return somewhat tipsy. The market and the journey there were also occasions for intrigue and flirting. There were even cases of people 'finding' spouses at market.

Settlers were less concerned with supplementing their diet than with spicing their food. Three items seldom provided through aid were essential components of their diet: salt, *berberé* (chillies) and coffee. Salt, the most important of the three, was used with both the other two. Its price was extremely high because of transport costs.[25] *Berberé* is a vital component of Ethiopian cuisine, without which any dish tastes bland. It is as much a staple as grain, so much so that, should a guest appear before food has been prepared, s/he is given *berberé* to eat with the *injera* (bread). Chilli was especially important in view of the poor taste of maize bread.

While salt was scarce and expensive, coffee, which locally grows
wild, was incredibly cheap.[26] Its beans were often ground with the
husks to make it go further as a cheap drink. Coffee has been the
greatest, perhaps even the only, culinary benefit of resettlement.
For coffee, an indigenous plant, is so much part of the culture that
it is a symbol of sociability, a metaphor for social relations and a
vehicle for spiritual blessings.

In addition to necessities settlers occasionally bought luxuries.
Women wanted butter for beautifying their bodies and especially
their hair, elderly men tobacco powder for snuff, and Muslims of
both sexes occasionally *chat*, which plays a role complementary to
that of coffee. *Chat* is used for blessings and chanting sessions, in
healing practices, and is deemed essential for Muslim festivities.
Chat was also the standard esteemed gift from devout Muslims to
religious elders. Settlers also sold food and aid items to meet special
occasional needs. For instance, when planning a marriage families
need cash for a wedding. However, the single most important
reason for settlers selling aid items, and later their own produce,
was to invest in livestock. Although central Ethiopians are thought
of largely as *crop* producers, their own view places considerably
more emphasis on livestock than is commonly recognised. Agriculture is dependent on livestock: oxen are essential for ploughing,
treading in *téf*, and threshing. Dung is used as a fertiliser, for
construction and fuel.[27] Live animals, hides and milk products are
important sources of disposable income. Although meat is a luxury,
except in rich households, it is nonetheless the most prized food
and is prepared on special occasions when guests are invited to
celebrate births, baptisms and marriages or to commemorate
deaths.

In the settlement environment emphasis on livestock, for several
reasons, was even greater. The first and most important was that
it was almost the only domain not under collective control. Most
agriculture, apiculture and crafts were under PA control. Rearing
small stock (chickens, sheep and goats) was in the hands of private
enterprise. Livestock was therefore not simply the reproductive
form of investment settlers had been used to previously but also
represented almost the only area of private initiative until the
reforms instituted in 1990.

Another reason for the importance of small stock had to do with
grain production. Cereals were susceptible to attack from pests
such as weevils and rats. The earth was not suitable for the type

of storage grain holes used by Wello peasants. Settlers were not familiar with the local Oromo type of grain store on 'stilts' but gradually adapted to local ways. Losses to pests were recalled in the following couplet.

> The Commission [the RRC] gave us our rations
> Then we shared them with rats and weevils.

Rats were referred to as 'the lady of the house' who took her due. According to a team of experts brought in by Concern, these rodents reached epidemic proportions because of the disturbance to the ecosystem caused by the settler influx. Rats attacked not only grain but also plastic water carriers and even the tails and feet of livestock. Settlers expressed the fear that the rodents would enter children's mouths at night and suffocate them. One man had his calf tendon bitten, for several months hampering his ability to walk. When a lamb was born the family would hold all-night vigils to prevent rats 'from eating the umbilical cord'. The problem became so acute that settlers bought cats from Qaqé and Dembi Dollo, and one even from Asosa, 700 km away. Concern also imported a few cats and later rat traps and poison.

Changes in production and exchange

Liberalisation

Radical changes in the settlers' lives came about over the years, owing to changes in Government policy. The most important factor in settler prosperity was grain prices. Initially settlers sold aid grain. Later since they were not self-sufficient, they bought grain by selling aid items and the price of grain was fairly high. As production increased in the third year, grain prices dropped, local markets were swamped and the grain trade was controlled. Settlers were then selling their grain at half the AMC set price.[28]

In April 1988 the UN World Food Programme bought grain on behalf of the UNHCR to distribute in refugee camps in Gambélla. After a deduction for freight and a charge of two *birr* for the SC, settlers received 23.25 *birr*. However, by then many had already sold most of their maize. Liberalisation of markets from late 1988 allowed traders to buy produce in settlement areas. In 1989

Table 14: Price of maize in Chanqa market*

Date	Price (tins/birr)**	Price (q/birr)
March 1987	8–9	26–28
March 1988	12–14	16–20
April 1988	9–10	20–25
March 1989	6–7	30–36
January 1990	7–8	28–32
March 1990	4–6	35–40
February 1991	5–6	34–37

* These are post-harvest prices; later in the year when supplies are low
prices rise sharply, sometimes reaching double the harvest price.
** These tins, called 'settlers' tins', hold some 450 g. The 'Oromo's
cups' hold about twice as much.
Source: Author's diary; Concern.

private traders came in large numbers, and prices rose. Settlers
were therefore reluctant to sell at a fixed price and several villages
turned down requests to sell full quotas to the AMC. The quota
system was abandoned in 1990; since then prices have remained
steady, although shortages of fuel and transport have prevented
settlers from benefiting as much as they could otherwise have
done.[29]

A second shift in policy was the decision to decollectivise
initially up to half settlement land holdings and later the entire
area. We have seen how even before this families were able to
pursue strategies for obtaining more than one plot. In 1987 the PA
allocated small additional private plots on the edge of the communal fields, the rationale being that settlers working on them would
guard the collective fields from baboons and wild pigs. A few
settlers also cleared small illegal plots in a forest clearing where
they grew mainly beans and chillies.

In 1988 the MOA decided to allocate half a hectare of communal
land per household for private use, provided this did not exceed
half the settlement's holdings.[30] As Village Three had less land than
average, the MOA extension workers decided to allocate only 0.25
ha per household for private use. Since the decision came after the
sowing season there was difficulty in deciding which crops should
be allocated for private care. Most settlers were pleased with the
change, though it had negative consequences for some. A few had
their patch destroyed by wild pigs and others suffered losses due to

hail and wind. Elderly and weak persons had difficulty persuading neighbours and relatives to help them. One elderly man actually left for this reason.

In 1989 the privatisation measure seemed about to have serious consequences. The MOA decided that the only way to provide households with half a hectare of private land and retain half the land under collective ownership was to move 'excess' settlers across the river to Village Eighteen, where there was plenty of land. Since Village Three had only 333 ha and a population of 498 households, the relocation of 165 households was proposed. The move was vehemently resisted, and fortunately never implemented. Ironically the village's harvest from much less land was greater than that of Village Eighteen. The problem, as settlers were well aware, was not so much a shortage of land as of labour, especially at the peak times of weeding and harvesting. Village Three had higher than average yields of 20–30 q maize and sorghum per hectare in good years. The produce per household was, however, below the Qéto average. After 30% had been put aside in the PA store this left hardly any surplus above the minimum 6.4 q required for a household of 3.5 people. This partly explains why settlers concentrated on growing maize on their private plots, small as they were, and preferred to convert grain into animals, the numbers of which increased rapidly, as Table 15 shows.

In 1990 collectivisation was totally abandoned and all the land distributed to households, much to the delight of most settlers. However, some in privileged leadership positions, and some of the

Table 15: Livestock increases in Village Three

Date	Chickens	Sheep	Goats	Oxen*	Hives**
August 1985	104	11			5
October 1985	223	28			27
March 1986	364	56			
July 1986	438	93			45
March 1987	516	184	6		
July 1987	725	244	41		
March 1988	876	445	142	32	78
March 1989	923	644	299	25	86

* These were oxen donated by Concern, seven of which died.
** These were PA hives and did not include hives held privately.
Sources: MOA, WPE, and PA files.

most vulnerable, were less enthusiastic. Moreover, many felt that the oppressive burden of the former system had not been entirely lifted. Until mid-1991 settlers still had to work two mornings a week to cultivate the plots of the leadership and militia. The privileges built up during the collective period were thus largely untouched. Settlers were also faced with the new burden of taxation. Nonetheless, yields have reportedly increased significantly and, now that people are working for themselves, there is for the first time a sense of optimism about the future.

The oxen programme

In 1988 Concern began a programme to provide oxen and counter the tsetse-fly challenge in Qéto. Despite a trypanosomiasis threat local people keep oxen but they must have them vaccinated regularly or suffer heavy losses. The programme was running fairly successfully, and had adapted to the changes brought about by decollectivisation. In 1989 over 1,000 oxen were bought for the twenty villages. In 1990 the settler villages agreed to match Concern funds and pay for half the cost, using funds obtained from sales of collective grain, and over 1,000 further oxen were purchased. However, a number of problems raise grave questions regarding long-term viability. These include a high incidence of fatality[31] despite treatment, the paucity of oxen, the difficulty of overcoming the tsetse challenge and that of obtaining vaccine, currently provided by Concern. Moreover, the programme has to date only considered oxen, and not cows, so that no means for the programme to perpetuate itself has been thought through. Unless the settlement villages decide to use more PA capital to buy cows, and unless a means of purchasing medicine is devised, the future of ox-plough cultivation in Qéto may be uncertain. Yet this is the settlers' only hope, since they do not see mechanisation as a viable option.

From the settler perspective, the introduction of oxen was an immense boost to morale. There was great excitement at their arrival. Settlers vied to be selected to plough. One saw them competing and heard onlookers commenting on the skill displayed, and the quality of the oxen. Even members of the PA leadership, usually reluctant to do manual labour, took a token turn at the plough. The sight of oxen made settlers reminisce about their

homeland. They invariably commented that weak Wellegga oxen
were no match for the northern breeds.

The oxen provided by Concern were initially under collective
control of the PA, which decided to use them partly to plough
private plots. The way they were used revealed and confirmed
the social structure. The oxen first ploughed the plots of absent
militiamen, then the PA leadership's, then the ploughmen's themselves and finally those of female-headed households and a few
elders. The rest had to dig their plots by hand.

The oxen were first herded and stabled collectively. Settlers
attributed the mortality of 11% in the first year to poor management. The animals were then distributed to teams, of twenty to
thirty households, improving the management of a small number
of oxen (four or five). However, mortality in 1989 and 1990
remained at almost 15%. At the end of 1990 the option of moving
to private ownership, in which several households would manage
an ox, was mooted. During the first half of 1991 most villages
divided the oxen; in Village Three the resulting ratio was one ox
for five households. Each group of five then clubbed together to
buy a second ox in order to have a plough team. Given the high
risk of disease, very few individuals bought cattle on their own.
Some resorted to the strategy of buying oxen for the ploughing
season and selling them thereafter.

During the period of unrest at the time of the change in government in April, Concern was unable to supply veterinary drugs; by
August cattle morbidity and mortality had become a cause for
anxiety. Unless attempts to link this area into the national veterinary and trypanosomiasis control programmes succeed, the likelihood of cultivation with oxen becoming sustainable seems remote;
should the oxen die, the settlers, many of whom left their homeland
when their cattle died in the famine, may once again find themselves refugees.

Conclusion

This chapter has shown how, for the first four years, settlement
life was largely determined by the imposition of a collective structure of production. State policy was translated by outsiders who
established ties of allegiance of a quasi-clientage nature and instituted a hierarchy based on literacy and military skills.

A household plot in Village Three

Mechanisation introduced an alien technology over which settlers had no control and perpetuated dependence on the State. Collectivisation was resented and resisted. Former peasants were transformed into virtual wage-labourers, rewarded according to a cumbersome and disliked points system. The emphasis on cultivating maize and sorghum required an unpopular change of diet, which settlers sought to spice rather than alter.

State agents sought to limit the role of the market. The SC shop provided consumer goods; however, the range was limited. The price differential on salt resulted in settlers selling their quota on the open market. The SC also sold part of the collective harvest, some of which was used to purchase oxen. Settlers pursued a strategy of selling grain, principally to invest in livestock.

Changes in the structure of production and exchange highlighted the pervasive influence of external forces on settlement life. Liberalisation of markets attracted merchants and resulted in higher grain prices, which benefited settlers, who then bought smallstock. The welcome introduction of oxen by Concern reflected the changing social structure. However, unless settlements are integrated in the national veterinary structure and use income from grain sales to purchase more cattle and vaccines, the tsetse challenge, paucity of oxen and lack of cows render the long-term future uncertain. Finally, the gradual decollectivisation of communal land has resulted in a completely new life-style in which settlers have more say in running their own lives. It remains to be seen how they will make use of this newly gained freedom.

Notes

1 Speech to the second-round cadres, 9 Meskerem 1978, quoted in a letter from the Chanqa WPE resettlement headquarters to the Village Three WPE Committee, 21 March 1986.

2 These three roles were jokingly referred to as 'boss, mason and drum'.

3 The two villages shared services. The cooperative shop was located in Village Three and the mill in Village Four.

4 Letter, 22 August 1989.

5 *History* (1987, p. 9).

6 *History* (1987, p. 11).

7 In one instance a settler claimed to have been beaten by a cadre and in another a settler accused a cadre of taking his wife.

8 For a treatment of jigger-flea poems see A. Pankhurst (1990b).

9 Five months after the settlers arrived there were fewer than a dozen sheep in the village and just over 100 chickens.

10 From 1987 the tractors completed only the first ploughing; in 1988 they did not help with transporting the harvest to the stores. In the first two years the MOA covered all seed, fertiliser and pesticide costs for the settlements. In the third year fertilisers and pesticides were still provided, but only 50% of settlement seed requirements were supplied. The fourth-year seed support was maintained at 50% but fertiliser and pesticide assistance was reduced to 25% of requirements, a level which was being maintained in the fifth year while seed assistance was being cut.

11 MOA (1989b, Table 6).

12 This was the tenor of the section on resettlement in Chairman Mengistu's speech to the Sixth Plenum of the WPE Central Committee in March 1987.

13 Diary, III, p. 68.

14 The produce of artisans brought the Peasants' Association an income of 718 *birr* in 1988. *History* (1988, p. 29).

15 Eighteen of fifty settlers who received more than 300 points in 1989 were militia.

16 I recall a peasant running up to me with a notebook. He opened it at a page and asked me to read the number. He said: 'Good, now I know my points for this quarter; I will add them up to check if I get my full share.'

17 Maize yields in Village Three dropped from twenty quintals per hectare in 1987–8 to thirteen in 1988–9, although yields remained well above the Qéto average.

18 Only in a few lowland areas such as the Tekkezé valley.

19 *Rhamnus principoides*, used like hops, to ferment beer.

20 Older settlers sometimes called maize *bahr mashilla*, 'sea sorghum', which reveals its foreign origin.

21 This is not simply a matter of taste but reflects the increased labour time required in grinding and the fact that maize *injera* dries rapidly, becoming brittle and unsavoury.

22 Settlers did not know what mangoes were. A settler recalled going to market, where he saw a man eating a mango: 'The juice trickled down the man's beard; I was so disgusted that I swore never to touch this unknown fruit.'

23 Ten settlers were selected in each village; the idea, common in developing countries, was that innovation could be introduced more effectively if scarce resources were concentrated on a few individuals who could serve as models. It is too early to assess the impact of this policy in Qéto.

24 Settlers from the nearest Integrated village have thus prospered as intermediaries.

25 The contents of a small lid of an oil bottle weighing 50 g cost between seventy-five cents and one *birr*, i.e. up to twenty *birr* for a kilogram. In northern Ethiopia salt costs about ten times less.

26 A kilo could be bought for a couple of *birr* in season, and coffee with the husks was even cheaper. In northern Ethiopia coffee can cost up to ten times as much.

27 H. Pankhurst (1989).

28 Maize in some settlement areas, such as Gambélla, was apparently sold for as little as five *birr* per quintal.

29 Some traders from integrated villages have been making large profits. A quintal bought for thirty-three *birr* is sold for fifty-seven in Inango, with a profit of twelve *birr* once transport costs have been met.

30 Government reports acknowledged that settlers did not have a sense of 'ownership' in the cooperatives, and that this was a crucial reason for the settlements' poor performance (Council of Ministers 1988b, pp. 145–50; MOA 1989b, pp. 3–4).

31 From 1988 to 1990 the rate of mortality was almost 20%. Of 2,318 oxen purchased, 1,862 were alive in January 1991 (Concern, February 1991). However, trypanosomiasis was not the only cause. Anthrax has resulted in numerous deaths, and when an ox was unable to plough, e.g. if it broke its leg, it would be slaughtered and eaten by the villagers.

VII

Social life

Now we are in a country of refuge; since we are living
together, we must agree so that we can become relatives.
An elder during a dispute
between Muslims and Christians

In this chapter I consider forms of social life which developed
within the constraints imposed by the collective mode of production. Ritual and ceremony were initially simplified, partly
because of the settlers' indigence, but also because of objections to
traditional practices voiced by the administration. As settlers began
to establish themselves, so ritual was elaborated and accommodation with the new power structure was sought. First, I examine
the life cycle, starting with death, which figured prominently in
settler consciousness; then birth, child naming and the resurgence
of wedding rituals.

The second part focuses on religious life in an environment in
which places of worship and time for religious activities were
restricted. Different forms of religious expression are considered,
from individual adherence to prayer and fasting, and neighbourhood religious associations, to larger-scale annual events, which
gradually involved increasing numbers and greater expense. Lastly,
I discuss the role of gatherings centred around coffee, and the *qub*,
a rotating credit association.

The third part reviews relations with the world beyond, starting
with the nearest settlements, moving to relationships with the local
population and settlements further afield. Finally, relations with
the homeland and other regions are examined. Despite the frustrat-
ing and counterproductive restrictions placed on travel, close contacts with relatives were maintained through official and informal
correspondence, as well as through visits to and from other settlements, the homeland and other regions.

The life cycle

In the story of resettlement the natural chronological order was in
a sense reversed: death came before birth. We have heard accounts
of the famine and of communities left desolate by mass out-
migration. There were cases where those who remained were wary
of burying the dead for fear of disease. The horror of the worst
cases was expressed in the suggestion that hyenas dragged corpses
from houses. We also heard of people who left for resettlement
because of the death of a parent, spouse, sibling or child, without
whom life in the homeland became impossible or meaningless. The
trail of death pursued the famine victims to the shelters, where
crowded conditions and poor sanitation increased contagion and
mortality. We saw how death remained the settlers' companion on
their journey westward and in the transit and reception shelters.
We heard of the 'Hill of Death', an epitaph to the tragic and partly
avoidable loss of life at the Qéto shelter. During the first four
years official figures for Qéto record 4,700 deaths, i.e. 12%, or an
annual rate of 3%. PA figures suggest that the rate was perhaps
even higher.[1]

Death, qiré and merdo

Death

Death was initially a prominent feature of life, and memories of
the early days were replete with images of bereavement. We heard
the story of Ashagré, whose daughter died the evening before they
reached Qéto, and whose family slept with the corpse. Though
most were spared the tragedy of the Qéto shelter, early impressions
are loaded with recollections of loss. We heard Itagegn's account
of her first sight of the village: the earlier Qallu settlers returning
from burying one of their number. Bereavement was so frequent
that there were occasions when some became almost numb to loss
and did not appear to grieve, culturally a surprising occurrence,
given the importance of displays of grief, as expressed in the literal
meaning of the word for funeral: *leqso*, from the verb 'to cry'.

Each new batch experienced death in the first few weeks, as
poor sanitation resulted in the spread of contagious diseases.
Tuberculosis and malaria later became the most important causes
of mortality. Infant mortality was also high. If a child died before
it had been named, it was referred to as 'a child of blood', and was

hardly mourned except by parents. The event was usually not a public affair but conducted on the quiet.

Despite and perhaps even because of its pervasiveness, death was not spoken of; the word was avoided. Death was sometimes personified and referred to indirectly as 'The one who is never replete'. Women spoke of 'paying tribute' to death. In the case of children death was often attributed to the 'evil eye', which 'ate' the child. To protect a child, particularly if the mother had lost several children, its gender was sometimes socially reversed. A boy was thus addressed in the feminine and a girl in the masculine. Other forms of protection included shaving the child's hair down one side, tying its hair round its wrist and, among Christians, hanging around its neck an amulet or charm made from a piece of parchment with sacred writing.

Settlers recalled with horror the mass graves in the transit shelter at Bakko. They remembered the deceased being carted off by the trailer-load, children placed between the legs of adults. What most disturbed them was that Muslims and Christians were buried together. One settler recalled: 'When we objected they said they would sort out the corpses once they reached the graveyard, but we did not believe them. How can you tell a Muslim from a Christian once he is dead?'

Given the mixed population, the question of burial was one of the first that needed resolving. The initial Muslims from Qallu buried their dead near their settlement to the south. Muslim leaders recall being worried about finding the *Qibla*, the direction of Mecca, but relied on the sun to orient themselves towards the holy city. As Shéh Ibré put it: 'We had been travelling for so long that we lost our way and entered darkness; but the sun guided us until we could enquire and make sure we were right.'

When Christians arrived they requested separate graveyards. A new cemetery area was therefore allocated to the east. The areas set aside for the two religious communities were distinguished by a large *warqa* tree, marking the border between two otherwise undefined areas. However, from 1990, Christians started taking their dead to the Church of Mary at the Integrated Site half an hour's walk away.

Settlers were disturbed not to find stones, with which they used to build graves in their homeland. One Lastan commented: 'Where we come from there is no earth to plough, it is all stones; here there is not a stone in sight.' However, some, notably those from

Qallu, had recently started going to a distant location to bring stones for the purpose.

Settlers were amazed at each other's burial customs. Lastans were astonished at the amount of effort that went into digging Muslim graves,[2] while those from Desé derided the former for their simple graves, which, they implied, showed lack of respect for the dead. Lastans would sometimes retort by saying, 'What is the use of all this effort once the person has died!' There was much jesting on the subject, as well as mock theological discussions between members of the two religions.

Even among Christians there was not always agreement. Those from Lalo Qilé dug much deeper graves, as the Lastans discovered when Nemerra's wife, Ayantu, died on 9 March 1988.

> The family was the only one from Wellegga in Team Thirteen, otherwise composed of Lastans, who went on ahead to dig the grave. When the Lalo Qilé priest arrived he reprimanded them on their poor work, and urged them to dig deeper and wider. He then instructed them to prepare a ledge and a deeper area the size of the corpse. The body was then brought on a reed cover. The deceased was placed in the narrow part at the bottom of the grave, and the cover was rested on the ledge thus protecting the body. Straw was then placed on top of the reeds to keep out the earth, which was piled in after the priest's blessing. He commented, '[Even customs between] Amhara[3] don't fit together.'

For the Muslims the construction of graves required much effort, as became apparent at the burial of Seyd Muhé in November 1987:

> A group of *qallichcha* stood in a clearing apart from the rest. Team members dug a wide rectangle to a depth of more than 1.5 m, before excavating a side chamber. While some dug and removed the earth with shovels, others brought water to prepare mud. The *qallichcha* were called to inspect the work. Elders and PA leaders also gave their opinions. Then logs were lowered into the grave to form a wall; the position of the logs was marked before they were removed. A cloth was held over the grave, while the corpse was carefully lowered, and positioned sideways towards Mecca. The *qallichcha* recited prayers and sprinkled a little earth under the shroud. The logs were put into place, and mud was plastered on the wood to seal the gaps before the grave was filled with earth, and was protected with thorns.

The qiré *institution*

Death is no doubt the most important social event in highland Ethiopian society, forming the link between the individual and society through the burial community to which s/he belonged. Funerals were usually large-scale events lasting for several days. Far more people attended funerals than marriages, and obligations incumbent on the community for them were greater and more rigorously defined. Indeed, the social definition and commemoration of death were arguably some of the main markers of community.

The term *qiré* has a range of connotations. The semantic ambiguities emphasise the importance of burial associations in Amhara life. The primary connotation is the burial association itself. A secondary sense is the occasion and gathering. Thirdly, the word refers to the contributions expected for the funeral. People thus spoke about 'measuring out the *qiré*', since each contributor had to bring specified amounts of grain. Finally, the term designated the sense of belonging to a community. When Abba Yimer, who used to be a Christian, converted he commented: 'I wanted to resemble my *qiré*,' i.e. he converted in order to be like his burial partners.[4]

Membership of a burial association, called *iddir* in some Amhara areas and *qiré* in rural Wello, was thus the definition *par excellence* of belonging to a community. Attendance at funerals and the payment of regular contributions were compulsory. Failure to comply resulted in fines and even possibly excommunication, or a boycott. Men were expected to make donations of wood and women of water. Each *qiré* had a leadership, referred to as 'judges', who ensured that donations were made and fines paid. *Qiré* judges were powerful persons whom no one wanted to cross. The burial association was thus a central institution with its own rules, regulations and leadership.

Given its importance in pre-resettlement society, the *qiré* provides an important way of understanding settler adaptation. During the famine, people noted the breakdown of the *qiré* mechanism of community help. In the new context initially there was no community. We have seen that Village Three was made up of a number of different groups who suddenly found themselves thrown together. As elder Abba Addisé put it: 'Desé Zurya and Lasta were brought together by the car.' The *qiré* was the first

autonomous organisation set up by settlers. Yet it was organised
on the basis of the PA team structure, an artificial creation resulting
from the accident of geography, grid layout and division of the
PA into smaller units.

On the journey to resettlement there was no *qiré*. In Bakko only
a few settlers were allowed to accompany the dead to the graveyard. In the village, settlers initially had little to offer the deceased's
relatives except their labour in helping them with the burial. From
early days it became the custom for each household to bring a tin
of grain. In the first years this was almost invariably aid wheat;
later, maize or sorghum became standard payment. Gradually the
required contributions increased. Teams set their own rules. Some
included a ten-cent payment to purchase coffee. Others decided
that households should prepare *injera* instead or as well as grain.

> In Team Five at the funeral of Melkamu's wife in May 1986 only
> a small cup of grain was expected. After the harvest, this amount
> changed to a larger tin of maize. In 1987 the *qiré* decided that one
> *injera* should be added, and in 1988 a small contribution of coffee.
> By the time Hasen's wife died in April 1989 the contribution had
> been set at two tins of maize, two *injera* and some coffee. Two
> households contributed a pot of *wet*. In addition team members,
> except for the female household heads, had to contribute a piece of
> wood. The two men without wives were allowed to provide four
> tins of grain instead of two prepared *injera*.
> Burial became the team's responsibility. The PA chairman and
> his deputy would often come and bow in front of the mourners
> before returning to work. The emergence of the *qiré* as a unit
> independent of the PA became evident in a case when an infant
> died. The PA tried to suggest that only four people should bury
> the child and the rest should go to work. Team members argued
> that they all wanted to attend the funeral. The PA sought to enforce
> its decision by allowing only four people to receive points for the
> burial work, but the whole team insisted on taking part. One of the
> MOA agents indignantly remarked: 'They are turning the cooperat-
> ive into a burial association!'

The merdo *mourning*

Two terms are commonly used for funeral ceremonies: *leqso* and
merdo. The former term, coming from the verb 'to cry', is mourning proper. The latter is literally the 'announcement of death' but
also refers to cases where a person died away from home and had

to be mourned without a burial. In the settlement context *merdo*
was an important occasion which gave rise to tensions.

As settlers began to receive letters from their relatives in Wello
and other settlements they would hear of deaths which had to be
mourned. Because of the distance news could take over a year to
come. The arrival of messengers was therefore feared. Some said:
'We would rather not receive letters from our relatives, for they
will contain bad news.' Death was not announced straight away.[5]
When travellers came from Wello, they always started claiming
that everyone was well. Often several days would elapse before
they revealed news of a death, and settlers, even after being told,
waited till the guest had left before starting mourning. Loud wail-
ing would alert neighbours and relatives. In some cases there would
be more than one *merdo* simultaneously, since a visitor would
bring several letters.

Debates arose concerning the degree of relationship which justified contributions for a *merdo*. In one case this led to what the
Lastans called an *imbidadé*, a boycott of someone who does not
comply with *qiré* rules. When asked about the consequences of an
imbidadé, an elder replied:

> It means that you cannot obtain any help. If your ox falls down a
> ravine no one will help you pull it out. If you want to rebuild your
> house no one will come. If your fire goes out no one will let you
> take embers from their hearth; you are totally outside your *qiré*,
> and must send elders to beg for a truce.

Others referred to an *imbidadé* with the phrase 'They won't
light fires in each others' houses'. Lighting fires from someone's
hearth symbolises neighbourliness and stood for sociability in general. The *imbidadé* case in the village concerned Abba Alemu, a
respected Lastan elder, well known for his enthusiasm for the new
life, his skill at thatching and his unforgettable high-pitched voice,
with which he excelled at traditional boasting during weddings.

> In early March 1988 Abba Alemu went to the *merdo* of a woman
> in his team; he enquired about the degree of relationship between
> the deceased and the mourning woman. On learning that her cousin
> had died, Abba Alemu expressed the opinion that contributions
> should not be made for such distant relatives. Two prominent PA
> members were called to the reconciliation session. Alemu was
> accused of not accepting the authority of the *qiré* judges. He in

turn accused the team of bringing matters concerning only team members to the attention of the PA, but conceded that he was at fault; the judges, as custom dictates, punished both parties. Alemu was, however, to present two rubber containers of beer, while other *qiré* members were to offer one. Abba Alemu later suggested that an *imbidadé* was less serious in the settlement, since all were under the Government, and if one team ostracised someone he could join another.

Among Christians, problems occurred when the deceased was not in a state of religious purity. The priests would refuse to perform the last rites, the *fitat*, literally 'untying' or 'releasing', in this sense referring to the absolution. The cases of two men raised moral problems for the Christian community. The first was a respected carpenter, named Abba Gelaw, who committed suicide in 1987 after a dispute with his wife. His body, hanging from a rope, was discovered by his twelve-year-old son. The priests would not give him a Christian burial, since he had taken his own life. The second man died a natural death in 1989:

> Shortly after he arrived he had married a Muslim woman. They quarrelled and he later married a Christian. The priests refused to perform the *fitat*, because he had not been rebaptised. His relatives sent a letter to a brother of his, who is a priest at a church in Addis Ababa, requesting that the *fitat* be performed for him in his own country.

As we have seen, most teams comprised Muslims and Christians, resulting in a need for accommodation. An interesting situation developed when two rows of huts, which at first formed separated teams, were regrouped in 1986 to form one. The upper row was composed of Muslims except for three Christian households; the lower, of Christians except for two Muslim households. The Muslims had formed a *qiré* with contributions of one cup of ground maize, while the Christians opted for one cup of unground maize plus one *injera*. When a death occurred in the upper row after the merger it became necessary to reconcile the two different ways of contributing to what had become one *qiré*. After much debate the team decided to opt for the Lastan way, a compromise which did not last, as Abba Addisé, an elder from Desé, recalled:

> At first we were two teams. Then the cadres said, 'Be one, you are

too small on your own.' We had been burying separately. At the time of the Ahmed's death, they [the Christians] said they would enter [our *qiré*]. We agreed. We wanted things the way it was done in our country, but they went back on the agreement. When Tesfaye's mother died we measured out grain [for them]. They fled, saying, 'It will be too much. We are enough by ourselves.' They destroyed the agreement and sent us a message. So we formed a separate *qiré* again.

Birth, perinatal care and child naming

Birth and perinatal care

Settlers recall that in the early days there were few births, but frequent stillbirths and miscarriages,[6] no doubt largely owing to poor nutritional conditions and psycho-social stress. The first child to survive was born on 20 January 1986, more than ten months after the settlers arrived. Births increased dramatically thereafter. By the second year the number of pregnant women began to alarm the cadres, who feared the potential reduction in the labour force.[7] When she gives birth a woman is provided with her own secluded bed, which the husband is expected to build off the ground, and a screen made of sticks or a blanket hung from the roof.

The role of midwives is customarily filled by elderly women. In the settlements midwives were trained in modern forms of delivery, and courses for 'Traditional Birth Attendants' were organised by Concern. The TBAs' role as mediators between tradition and development was ambiguous. They were provided with kits from UNICEF and learnt about modern means of sanitation. Many did not accept all they were taught. For instance, Simegn was convinced that delivery was easier if a woman squatted rather than lay back. Settlers also believed in putting a pat of butter in the newborn baby's mouth, a practice they were taught was harmful. Recognition of the TBAs' contribution was also not immediate or straightforward. At one point a dispute arose because the two TBAs were not given full points like men, but only 'women's points'. They complained, pointing out that their work kept them up at night, and were supported by Concern, which argued that they had received training. The TBAs won their case. Although the cooperative system has since been disbanded, the plot of one TBA continued to be cultivated for her by the PA.

The period of pregnancy was a time when marital disputes were frequent. Elders stressed the need for husbands to show special care and insisted that a husband could on no account obtain a divorce until his wife 'had become two safely'. Shortly before a woman delivered, Muslim relatives, notably among the Qallu Oromo, gathered for prayer and chanting. A woman's wish to give birth in her mother's house was always respected if it was her first delivery. Men often kept their distance while the birth was taking place and manifested a degree of embarrassment.

The death of babies during childbirth or shortly afterwards was not uncommon. This probably explains the caution with which a birth is greeted and the fact that fathers do not at first seem particularly interested in the child or its gender.[8] Settlers believed that the new land promoted fertility; as Indris once put it: 'The country is conducive to women and sheep [giving birth].' As evidence he cited the fact that sheep almost invariably delivered two lambs, that women considered infertile had given birth and that many twins were born. Yesuf, who overheard the comment, added: 'Look at Mehammed Hasen. His first wife had never had a child, so he had married a second before he came here. Now they have both given birth within a week!'

Having twins is traditionally considered unfortunate,[9] as expressed in a saying, often used metaphorically, 'the mother of twins dies [i.e. suffers] lying backwards', i.e. she lies on her back so each child can suckle at one breast. Although at least five twins were born, only in one case did a pair survive. Asrebib lost one twin immediately; the other survived for only a few months. People commented: 'If only she had died before we got to know and love it, it was such a beautiful child.'

Mother and baby are secluded for a period of two weeks to one month. The couple are sometimes referred to as 'the newly married', for they are secluded like a newly wedded couple. The designation of mother and child together is reflected in the Amharic word *aras*, used to refer to the infant and the mother during the initial seclusion period. Traditionally another woman, called *arrash*, perhaps a close relative, would look after her.

A problem arose in the resettlement village when female labour was incorporated into the cooperative work system. The responsibility for providing an *arrash* was transferred from the family to the PA. A compromise between traditional and modern systems was reached. The mother could nominate an *arrash*, who, with PA approval, would obtain points. If the woman could not find

someone, the PA delegated the Women's Association to find a
volunteer. The arrangement seemed to work fairly well, although
the PA decided they would provide an *arrash* for only fifteen days,
whereas the period was traditionally twice as long.

Child naming

Names in highland Christian society are often imbued with meaning, revealing parents' experiences and aspirations. Muslims tend
to adhere to traditional names. In Village Three the Lastans showed
ingenuity in choosing names which reflected their past experience,
present circumstances or future aspirations. Some of the most
common names which served as reminders of lost children were
Kasa, ie. 'compensation', and Debbash or Masreshsha, 'The one
who helps one to forget'. Parents who lost children chose names
suggesting that the infant would outwit death, such as Attalel,
'May s/he trick [death]', or hoping that it would grow up, such as
Biyadgillign, 'If [only] he would grow [up] for me'. A number of
names are connected with the idea of moistness, symbolic of life,
such as Irtiban, 'Moisture'; and light and renewal: Negga, 'It
dawned'; Tsehay, 'The Sun'; or Addis, 'The New One'.

A few names recalled what the settlers had been through, such
as Sintayyehu, 'I have seen so much [i.e. been through so much]';
Allefnew, 'We passed [through] it [i.e. the bad times]'; and Min
ayyen, 'What have we seen'. Several children were given names
which referred to relatives, such as the popular name Bayyush, 'If
[only] they [i.e. your relatives left behind in Wello] had seen you'.
An unusual name, which was given to no fewer than seven children,
was Ageritu, 'The Little Country'. This name was ambiguous. It
could recall the land the settlers had left, or the new one they had
came to. One man tried to get the best of both worlds by calling
his daughter Hull Agerish, 'Everywhere is your land'. Some settlers
did not hedge their bets, with names such as Nur Addis, 'New
Life'; Meseret, 'Foundation', i.e. of a new life; and Zemachu, 'The
Campaigner'. One man called his son Socialist, but altered it to
Tesfaye, 'My hope', after the economic liberalisation policy.

Traditionally children were often not named for several weeks,
and even then were often given temporary names of endearment,
such as Mimi or Chuchu for a girl, and Mammoush or Babboush
for a boy, until the child's character became apparent. However,
the PA ruled that every child should be named at once so that the
family could receive a milk ration. This meant that parents and

team leaders were quick to report births, which were duly recorded by the PA secretary.

According to Ethiopian Christian tradition, boys are christened on the fortieth day after birth and girls on the eightieth. The baptismal or 'christening' name depends on the day of the month the child was born or christened and often refers to the saint to whom the day is dedicated. The child is not usually called by its christening name, which remains a secret, or is limited to family use. However, the choice of godparent is often a way of marking friendships.

Christening was an event to which relatives and friends were invited and an occasion when food and beer were served. The social importance of a christening may be gauged by the fact that Mammo, who used to live in Village Three but moved to the Integrated Site of Iggu Kofalé, invited his friends from the village to come to his son's christening. About a dozen settlers, including three Muslims, made the journey and spent the night there. In Village Three the lack of a church presented an impediment to christenings. The most devout insisted on taking their child to the church of St Mary, built by the settlers from the Integrated Site at Chanqa Bururi, half an hour's walk away. One of the village priests also conducted baptisms under a tree. However, during the era of collectivisation priests suggested that people were no longer bothering to have their children christened, on the grounds that it was difficult to obtain permission to leave work to go to the church, and gave the excuse that it was too far.

Circumcision of both boys and girls was not performed by a specialist, nor was it carried out at any particular time or with any noteworthy ceremony, although it tended to take place within the first few weeks after the child's birth. Among the Oromo from Wellegga girls were not circumcised until shortly before marriage, a custom which the Wello settlers considered barbaric. They nevertheless believed that circumcision of girls was essential. Circumcision of boys was also general but a few parents did not have their sons circumcised if they had lost several children before, or if the child had some disability, for example a speech problem. Boys were also not circumcised if their mother had had a difficult delivery or had been ill, for the shedding of blood was considered a time when evil spirits were prone to attack the child.

When the wife of the PA chairman had a difficult first delivery, his

mother approached me to try to persuade her son not to have the
child circumcised, on the grounds that the wife's mother was subject
to spirit possession, and that the spirit might attack the child via
the mother when the child was made to bleed.

Wedding rituals[10]

Weddings presented a challenge for settlers to re-establish their
traditions and rituals. Although the administration tried to regulate
marriage and divorce through a committee, weddings were organised by settlers spontaneously. In the case of first marriages they
re-enacted traditional wedding rituals as faithfully as possible,
given the limited means at their disposal. Ceremonies became more
elaborate as settlers could afford to spend more on preparations.
At one wedding a man remarked:

> Weddings are signs of our growth: on the journey we married with
> roasted grain for a feast; when we arrived here we used aid grain;
> two years ago we ate our own maize and beans. Last year some
> served chickens; now we are eating goat. Who knows: maybe one
> day we will eat beef!

The salient features of traditional marriages, from the engagement and negotiations to the actual feast, were reinstated. For a
first marriage, the groom's mother sought two elderly widows to
go with her to speak to the bride's mother. If the outcome was
favourable, elders were sent with the groom's father and an engagement was negotiated, including specification of how many elders
and 'best men' would go to collect the bride.

The actual engagement ceremony was the third stage, which
usually took place a year before the wedding and was called 'the
anointing of butter'. At this ceremony the groom's mother anno-
ints him and his best men on the forehead and knees. The party
then visit the bride's family, whose mother also anoints them. This
ritual was reinstated in the village even though settlers, not having
cows, had to buy the butter. Traditionally the groom's mother
accompanied the party, carrying a bunch of olive leaves, symbolic
of growth. Since olive trees could not be found, a similar-looking
leaf was substituted.

In the village traditional Muslim wedding rituals are faithfully
observed. The toes of the bride and groom are ceremonially cut
by a woman who has not divorced. The groom and his best men

Wedding procession, headed by the groom's mother

are decorated with black markings around their eyes and a cross
on their foreheads. The party set off with the groom carrying a
whip brought from Wello, the symbol which sets him apart from
his best men. The men chant, raising their sticks and the militia
their guns. Elders lead the marriage party, carrying fly whisks,
wearing their best clothes and draped in cloths.

The rivalry, competition and ritualised aggression which traditionally marked weddings is vigorously re-enacted in the settlement. The bride and the groom's factions vie to put on a more
impressive feast and compete for the allegiance of common friends
and important people. Outsiders and prominent PA members are
invited; the chairman usually brought his radio and gun, his deputy
his fiddle, and the secretary his keys. Guests offered a gift of one,

Government workers at the wedding of the Peasants' Association chairman

and lately two, *birr*, and each contribution is recorded in a book. Each party constructs two rectangular shelters, one for women, the other for men. Maize stalks are used for the walls; the ground is freshened with rushes, and palm leaves serve as table mats.

As the groom's party approach the bride's shelter they are kept waiting. Eventually elders are sent on ahead and the members of the groom's party are counted to see that they do not exceed the agreed number. They have to surrender their staffs as they enter the shelter and stand until the bride's representative asks the groom's, 'What are you standing for? What have you come for?' The groom's representative answers, 'If you will be a father to us, we will be a son.'

At this point the bride's representative would customarily have asked what the groom's livelihood would be; the groom's representative would usually answer, 'A third,' as the groom received a third of his father's produce until he set up his own household. In the village this stage was usually omitted, since, until 1989, sons received produce by virtue of work points they earned. However,

at a wedding I witnessed in 1991 the question led to much discussion. It was finally agreed that the son was entitled to half the
produce, and his wife a quarter in the event of divorce.

The type of marriage would also be specified. If a marriage sum
was mentioned this would be returnable upon divorce. If, as was
the norm in the village, the marriage was 'in equality' the bride
had the right to claim half the common property upon divorce.
Finally, the bride's representative enquires about the bride-gift
which the groom's party sometimes pretends to have forgotten.
They 'throw down' the gift, these days brought in a plastic bag,
saying, 'We have clothed.'

The groom's party are shown to their seats along the lower row
of the shelter, facing the bride's guests. Before the meal is served
the groom's party are sectioned off from the other guests with a
screen made from blankets and served with food and beer by male
waiters. The elders eat sitting round one basket, and the best men
round another. The bride is brought in wearing her nuptial dress,
a shawl covering her head and face. She and her bridesmaid sit
next to the groom. The guests offer each other mouthfuls of food
and the groom gives his bride a mouthful. After the meal the
servers refuse to clear until a present, called the 'lifting of the meal',
is handed over. During the two years that I was an observer this
sum increased from three to five *birr*. After the meal the blankets
are lowered and coffee and more beer are served. Select guests are
offered potent spirits.

The ceremony of 'tying' the couple is performed by a religious
leader, who blesses them. He receives two *birr* for his services,
which are concluded with a coffee ceremony. In a private corner
the *qallichcha* asks the groom and the bride in turn if they give
him the authority to represent them, to which both must assent.
The marriage formula used to contain the oath 'May the King die',
which was replaced with the phrase 'May the Government die'. In
recent times the practice of the couple signing has become current,
especially in Christian areas. In Village Three newly wedded
couples were supposed to sign in a register, but this new practice
was not often adhered to and seems to have been abandoned since
1990.

The ceremony is followed by boasting, chanting and dancing.
The two sides compete at traditional chanting, in which themes of
bravery in battle are mingled with recollections of peasant life.
Elders march up and down between the groom's and bride's

parties, declaiming chants to which the audience responds with a chorus. Youths rise and utter traditional outbursts of defiance. References to their places of origin and the oxen which dominated their way of life bring a mood of reminiscence. Defiant boasting is accompanied by sly aspersions on the other side's valour. The assembly later gives way to dancing, in which men and women at first dance separately but then mingle in couples, surrounded by a clapping circle of onlookers.

Suddenly, the groom's party, having made sure that their cups are full, get up to leave. Traditionally, the bride would have ridden with her husband on a mule. In the village a 'carrier' gives her a 'piggy-back' ride to the groom's parents' house. As the party leave they shoot a short volley into the air.[11] When they reach the groom's house the bridal pair are conducted into the *chagula*, a hutlet prepared for the newly wedded. During the honeymoon the couple are served by the best men. Traditionally, this period would last a fortnight, but in the village the PA allowed only one week, during which the groom and his best men did not lose work points. The day after the wedding night the groom and his best men visit relatives for the 'gift to the best men'. The groom kneels and throws down his whip at the feet of each guest in turn while the best men sing and dance until each guest has given them a small gift: a few coins or a *birr*. After three days or a week the *mels*, or 'return' festivities, occur at the bride's house and, after a washing ceremony, the couple take on their new roles as husband and wife.

Although a person arranging a marriage receives some help from relatives, marriages require the help of team mates. On one occasion a serious quarrel broke out between Muslims and Christians in one team:

> All the team members contributed two *birr*. The bride's father, a Muslim, used almost all the money to buy a sheep for fifty *birr*. The Christians unable to eat meat slaughtered by Muslims were displeased, did not help, and arrived late after market. They were served a bean stew, which many of them did not eat, while the Muslims received meat.

After the event elders were called to try to achieve a reconciliation.

> A spokesman for the Christians argued that two lambs might have been bought, or that a greater contribution might have been made, and all the guests could have eaten meat. The bride's father accused

the Christians of boycotting the wedding and wasting the food. As
he put it: 'They buried my feast; they went to market, putting
money before neighbourliness.'

The elders decided that both parties were at fault but that the
bride's father was most to blame. They considered ordering the
latter to prepare five buckets of beer as a punishment, and the
Christians three buckets. Once the litigants had accepted their fault
and called witnesses to guarantee that they would abide by the
judgement, the elders let the protagonists off and expressed more
concern with establishing a 'way of doing things' for the future:

> 'It is a question of whether we can travel along the same road. The
> past must be forgotten; we need a new way. Should the team
> separate in two? Should we not eat meat? Should we buy two
> sheep?' After much debate the last of these views was favoured.
> Some elders mentioned precedents in Wello, and the need to pre-
> serve a sense of community. 'We used to invite each other and
> prepare special dishes, but that was usually for a few people; now
> we are all mixed up.'

Religious belief and practice

We have seen that cadres were keen to discourage what they termed
'beliefs without scientific foundation'. Obvious targets were 'harmful customs', such as spirit possession, female circumcision, early
marriage of girls, healing practices and religious sessions. The main
overt grounds for opposing religion were the waste of labour time
involved: ceremonies hindered production and all-night gatherings,
often with drum-beating, disturbed the peace. The underlying
objections were ideological, stemming from the belief that religion
was 'the opium of the people'.

The PA leadership maintained a more ambiguous position, since
they were themselves settlers and had devout relatives. Some con-
cessions to religious sentiment were made: for instance, the former
chairman, a Muslim and at first the only settler with a radio, had the
bell rung to announce the beginning of Ramadan. The leadership
attended some religious occasions, participated in religious associations and showed deference to the religious leaders.

Five members of the PA leadership had been trained as 'Peasant
Cadres' and, at least outwardly, did not abide by religious norms.

The former chairman objected to religious books being placed in the village library.[12] He and his deputy, both Muslim, ate meat slaughtered by Christians; the secretary, a Christian, ate meat slaughtered by Muslims. Other members of the PA leadership were firm in outward signs of religious observance. For a farewell party when I left, the Government workers bought a sheep; the PA chairman claimed that invited Muslim PA leaders would eat 'Christian' meat. In the event most Muslims refused food and the party did not gain momentum until the drinking, singing and dancing began.

The right to assemble on a few religious holidays was not denied but the erection of a mosque or a church was not allowed, or rather, when settlers made requests to establish them, they were told that self-sufficiency must take precedence and that building places of worship was not a priority. Members of both religious communities resented this policy, which was perceived as an attack on faith, particularly since the policy was still in effect more than four years after the settlers had arrived. One woman spoke of entering 'a place and time without religion'. I shall later describe a new era of religious tolerance which I witnessed during my last visits in 1991.

Islam

Reactions to restrictions on religious freedom varied from accepting the new life to returning home. Several *qallichcha* departed during the first few years and at least two more in 1990. Others decided to work within the system with various degrees of defiance. Some prayed regularly, fasted during Ramadan, held occasional religious sessions and organised feasts at which a goat or sheep would be slaughtered and the devout gathered to celebrate.

By virtue of links with the PA leadership, a few *qallichcha* were able to lead a life of relative ease. The father of the deputy chairman was the head of the Muslim community and was not required to work 'for points'. He remained in effect his son's dependant though he was given his own plot. When the RRC gave the vulnerable small rations, he received his share. He officiated at religious events and read holy texts. Another elderly *qallichcha* was assigned the job of looking after a spring, while a young one was chosen to operate the mill; another was delegated to work on the construction of the clinic in Chanqa, where, as he put it, 'There was time to say prayers at the appropriate time of day.'

A devout elder recalled how he started planning to build a mosque.

> In a forest there was a beautiful tall tree which would make a perfect central pole; I made a mental note of its location, and spoke to a few friends about my plan; we started gathering some wood in our spare time. Then I consulted one of the agricultural extension workers, who was himself a Muslim. After a few days, he told me that in a dream he had seen the mosque fall down, and advised us that the time was premature.

A petition to the PA from Muslim community leaders asking for a mosque remained unanswered. Although no mosque as such was built until 1991, a small hutlet was used for religious gatherings. Groups also built temporary shelters for specific religious events. Moreover, in most teams the house of one or two people who gained reputations as sponsors of religious events became gathering points where religious ceremonies called *wedaja* or *mewlid* were held. Some involved healing sessions, and others were related to particular annual events, notably the Prophet's birthday.

A Muslim *wedaja* ceremony in the village

Such gatherings were expressions of devotion among small groups. Usually, besides religious leaders, only settlers from one or two teams were involved. Groups of five to fifteen Muslim men gathered usually on a Wednesday or Friday to chew *chat*, pray and chant under the *qallichcha*'s leadership. Mehammed Seyd's was one such house.

> On the designated day, part of the house was sectioned off from the rest with a permanent cane partition; blankets were added for privacy. The floor was decorated with a layer of fresh reeds forming a soft, clean and fresh-smelling surface. Men with sandals took them off. The party awaited the arrival of the most senior religious elder. Coffee was then served while incense burned, and the chief elder blessed the coffee server. Finally, *chat* was given by the host to the most senior *qallichcha*, who blessed the provider, and periodically distributed a limited amount to other participants. Once the right atmosphere had been created and the stimulant properties of *chat* had begun to take effect, the leaders started chanting. Participants then joined in with the appropriate chorus. The leader changed the rhythm and tempo, and others followed suit to the best of their ability, while the rest would intone the chorus.[13]

Certain Muslim festivals, such as the Prophet's birthday and the beginning and end of Ramadan, involved larger-scale groupings. Over the past few years Ramadan has coincided with the hottest months of the year, turning the fast into a difficult ordeal when settlers had to work long hours in the fields. During the first year, when many were weak, cadres urged them to eat, and only the most devout fasted. In successive years more people joined the fast. Some elders, many of whom according to custom had 'seen grandchildren', even added an extra six days to the fast. Some were more rigorous about fasting than others, and this led to occasional veiled criticisms. A few households ate food discreetly in their houses. Teams taking the fasting seriously with hardly a defaulter would form a *tertib*, a gathering for prayer and coffee held on a rotating basis in each other's houses every evening during the Holy Month. At the end of Ramadan several dozen devout men gathered for communal prayer. The *id-al-fatr* feast was held in two or three areas in the late afternoon. It was attended by increasing numbers of people. In 1986 only a few teams took part; by 1987 over 200 people gathered. In 1988 for the first time two oxen were slaughtered. Households contributed single or double shares of five or ten *birr* respectively and each carcass was divided into as many lots as there were shareholders. An attempt was made to ensure that each portion comprised a fair share of all types of meat, especially the much prized tripe, liver and intestines.

Such feasts were the most obvious attempts at community organisation outside the PA sphere. There was a gradual increase in the scale of the enterprise, with more people taking part, and beef replacing mutton or goat. Certain men emerged as organisers of such occasions, which reflected power struggles within the community.

Christianity

Christians also showed a range of strategies in the face of religious intolerance. One priest who left early on wrote from Wello that, if settlers built a church, he would return and serve it. A young deacon left and joined the nearest Integrated Site, where he served in a new church dedicated to St Mary. One of the Christian leaders, however, became integrated within the PA. He had served as a priest in the army, and was chosen as PA treasurer and later as storekeeper. Others adopted an attitude of defiance. A deacon living in a row where only he and his brother were Christians placed a wooden cross on top of his house. One of the priests refused to work on Sundays and wrote a petition to the PA stating that he was prepared to work overtime in lieu of hours others worked on Sundays. The main conflict was thus expressed in terms of labour time. Settlers could not obtain permission to go to church every Sunday and the priests feared people would turn away from religion. Permission was, however, granted on holidays, such as *Timqet*, or Epiphany, Easter and *Mesqel*, the day commemorating the finding of the True Cross, when gatherings were held at the top of the hill.

One might think that the absence of a church would affect Christians more than the lack of a mosque did Muslims, since the latter could pray anywhere, while Christians required a church for baptism, prayer and burial.[14] In fact Christians managed to maintain their religion, partly because church was not their only religious experience, and partly because baptism, burial and prayer could occur without a church.

After a Christian burial, a Muslim elder (who had himself been a

Christian earlier in his life) chided the Christians for not having
built a church. Another elder suggested starting to collect wood.
But the main priest, who was a member of the leadership, advised
caution. He suggested that they should wait and see what happened
in the case of Village Six, which had started to build a church.
Privately, he expressed the opinion that since the Muslims were in
a majority they should take the initiative and build a mosque before
Christians could build a church. The PA secretary, who came from
a Christian background, remained silent. He later confided that he
felt that building a church would lead to religious tension, and that
priests running the church would become a burdensome group of
unproductive people.

When a church was established by the nearby Integrated Settlements of Chanqa Bururi and Iggu Kofalé, many settlers from the
village attended the consecration on 12 February 1987.

The ceremony was led by a representative of the Orthodox Church
from the *Awrajja* capital at Dembi Dollo. A priest from Village
Three officiated with priests from the Integrated Sites in the inner
sanctum of the church; four militiamen from the village were among
the cortège parading in step, with their Kalashnikovs over their
shoulders, in front of the deacons bearing the *tabot* [representation

The consecration of St Mary's Church

of the Ark of the Covenant]. The procession circled the church
three times, preceded by priests chanting, beating drums, carrying
censers, crosses and colourful umbrellas. Women formed circles
dancing together, and groups of youths chanted, jumping rhythmi-
cally with raised sticks. The ceremony was also attended by prominent personalities from Chanqa, including merchants and hoteliers,
several of whom were old-time settlers from the north. They contributed candles and large sums of money.[15]

A number of Christians from Village Three moved either to
nearby Integrated Sites or to other Conventional Sites, partly on
religious grounds and partly to join relatives. Thus half a dozen
Christians went to Village Six, which has a majority of Christians
from Lasta, who decided to build a church. Three times local Party
officials insisted that they must pull down the edifice. The settlers
petitioned the Orthodox Church in Dembi Dollo, and received
support to go ahead.

The lack of a church did not mean that faith was on the wane.
Peasants' Christian allegiance was largely mediated through the
Virgin Mary and saints, mainly Michael, George and Gabriel. Individuals had special affinities to particular saints and joined others
in a *mehaber*, or religious association, dedicated to that saint; these
were one of the main foci of Christian religious experience, which
defined community affiliation in a narrower way than the parish.
In early resettlement days the *mehaber* was the only focus for
Christian worship outside life-cycle events and important annual
religious ceremonies. Members met once a month in each other's
houses on a particular saint's day. The host prepared beer and
bread, blessed by a priest, the association's 'spiritual father'.

Taddese's *mehaber* involved thirteen people from several teams, all
Lastans. The spiritual father was the chief priest. Members met once
a month on the 27th of each month, the day dedicated to the
'Saviour of the World' [i.e. Jesus]. On 5 April 1989 it was
Wedajnew's turn. Members gathered in his compound at dusk. They
approached the priest to receive his blessing by kissing his cross.
He performed blessings, saying, 'May *mehaber* members remain
well, be blessed, and help each other.' He then recited special blessings for the person who had prepared the beer, and gave thanks to
Jesus. Food and beer were served. After the spiritual father's blessing, food was consumed, stories were told and dancing began.

Although in theory only *mehaber* members attended, prominent

PA officials were sometimes invited. This meant that one could often see Muslims sitting in at Christian *mehabers*. However, they usually left fairly promptly after the meal. This showed mutual recognition between a traditional religious-based association and the PA's secular authority: modern power respecting traditional religion, which in turn acknowledged the authority of a new manifestation of law and order.

Several annual Christian festivals were celebrated in larger gatherings, notably *Mesqel* and Easter, the latter the most important annual event in the Ethiopian Christian calendar. The Lenten fast of fifty-six days involved abstaining from livestock products and, for the devout, not eating until 3.00 p.m. Priests, deacons and devout elders maintain a total fast from Good Friday till Easter Sunday. Christians and Muslims sometimes discussed the severity of their respective fasts.

> A Muslim argued that Christians were let off easily, since they ate in the afternoon, while Muslims had to wait till after sunset. A Christian replied that Muslims ate eggs and meat at night, while they had to abstain for up to eight weeks. Another Muslim retorted that no one could afford meat anyway. The Christians grudgingly conceded that the Muslim fast was more arduous.

On Easter Sunday a game, peculiar to the Lalibela area, was played:

> Two teams were formed, the horses and the horsemen. The former carry the latter, who throw a spear at a tree trunk. If they hit their mark they pull the spear out, while another person acts the part of a dog trying to prevent them from retrieving the spear. So long as the horsemen succeeds in hitting the target they continue throwing, and the other team members carry them. When they fail they change places.

Genna, Christmas, was much less important than *Timqet*, the Epiphany festival a fortnight later. Settlers gathered in the open by a small tree. Young men played *gugs*, a traditional type of hockey seen at this time of the year throughout Christian Ethiopia.

A festival of particular significance to the Lastans is the Virgin Mary's day in the month of May. In 1985 the festival was not celebrated, as settlers had only just arrived; in 1986 a few groups had a meal of boiled grain. In 1987 several groups slaughtered chickens, and in 1988, one group a goat, another a sheep, and several others chickens. A play, traditionally performed on this occasion, was enacted by one group.

> Two children were yoked as the oxen and a woman walked behind them simulating the ploughman. She pretended to hold the plough and whip the oxen. Then she took boiled maize and broadcast it, simulating sowing, while throwing some in her mouth. The spectators watched with a mixture of amusement and nostalgia. This performance in a setting where settlers did not have oxen was a powerful re-enactment of their past way of life.

Another feature was the making of vows in front of the group.

> People would offer what they had promised the previous year if their wish had come true, and fresh vows were made. Two men promised goat kids, one if he heard news that his parents were well, the other if his wife gave birth to a son. Several people made promises without specifying wishes: a man pledged a lamb, another three *birr* of liquor, and a third four *birr* of sugar; three women offered a pot of beer and bread each, and a young woman vowed to provide a bundle of wood.

Social gatherings: coffee and qub

Coffee

In the village there was little outside the team and PA structures by way of spontaneous organisation or secular mutual assistance between households. Sometimes a few people joined forces to buy a goat or sheep, divided it, and took its meat to their respective houses. Neighbours gathered regularly to drink together. Coffee accompanied every lunch and supper, some drinking it even in the morning before work. Coffee has both social and religious significance. Each coffee session consists of three named boilings, each weaker than the previous. It is considered rude to leave before the second boiling, and hosts will apologise if a guest arrives only for the third.

Coffee was a scarce commodity in Wello; excessive consumption was seen as a sign of decadence, and children were not allowed to drink it, on the ground that it was habit-forming. Among Muslims, coffee was always accompanied by a blessing, in which the woman who has prepared it places the pot next to her, stands up and bends over towards the leading elder or household head, hands outstretched, palms upwards, in supplication. He then commences the blessing, which consists of a series of felicitous wishes and benevolent invocations uttered with increasing speed, raising and lowering his right hand in a gesture representing a showering of blessings. The woman draws the blessings towards her with rapid finger movements and the utterance 'Amin' after each blessing. The blessing increases in speed till the climax, when the man sends a spray of spittle towards the woman, pulls her hand towards him, and kisses the back of her hand; she in turn pulls his hand towards her and kisses it. Only during special ceremonies will a male server perform the role of the woman in the ceremony.

During the month of Ramadan, neighbours sometimes formed a *tertib*, an association in which the members contributed money for the purchase of coffee, and then took turns every evening preparing food and coffee, which was the climax. After three drinkings the *Fatiha*, or opening verse of the Qur'an, was recited.

Prior to the nineteenth century Christians in northern Ethiopia did not drink coffee. The bean was considered a distinguishing marker between Muslims and Christians,[16] much as *chat* is today. However, coffee drinking later became widespread. In the village Christians sometimes performed blessings with coffee, though this was not obligatory except on special occasions such as saints' days.

In fact there was hardly a social occasion in which coffee did not play a leading role. At funerals and credit association gatherings ten cents was often expected as a coffee contribution. At weddings the *nika*, or Muslim marriage vow, was sealed with coffee. Coffee was boiled among neighbours outside their houses on the first of the month. One elderly woman explained: 'An old woman's door-step becomes respected when coffee is roasted.'

The coffee ritual among both Muslims and Christians is ideally accompanied by incense burning.[17] One elderly woman told me that this was particularly important in the new environment 'to acclimatise the benevolent spirits to the new surroundings'. Despite its cost, settlers would buy incense on special occasions. In the early years small pieces of wood were burnt instead, though religious elders criticised this as miserly. In recent years incense has become a prerequisite of coffee sessions.

Qub: *rotating credit associations*

As already noted, settlers formed multi-purpose rotating credit associations, throughout much of Ethiopia called *iqub* and short-ened to *qub* in Wello. Their first and initially most salient role is to bring together a group of people to pool a specific amount of grain or sum of money, allocated in turn to the members by lot. The institution thus performs the role of a banking system, enabling people to save and obtain a larger amount of grain or money than is likely through individual saving. Secondly, the association may act as a form of social security. Thus if an association member requires a large sum of money, for instance for a celebration, s/he may be allowed to receive that month's sum without the draw being held. Thirdly, the institution provides an occasion for social gatherings, which bring people together on the basis of locality, employment, ethnicity or gender; alternatively it can bring people together who otherwise would not meet because of differences in sex, age, religion, ethnicity or occupation. *Qub* were formed almost as soon as the settlers arrived. The first-year cadres recorded disapproval of this 'noxious habit' but could do little to prevent it. *Qub* tended to be team-based, requiring contri-butions in kind.

In Team Nine twenty-five settlers joined to form a grain *qub*. Members met once a fortnight on the day rations were distributed, when each member contributed a tin of grain. Indris was chosen as secretary, since he was literate. He kept a list of members' names in an exercise book; he checked that each member had brought a tin of grain and ticked their names off; then he rolled little slips of paper for each member. The person who won the draw was there-after barred from receiving another lot until all members had their turn. After a complete round the *qub* was dissolved and a new one started.

A few *qub* had a distinctly social character and transcended geographical team boundaries; one such was that of Abba Weda-jew, the driving force behind its establishment.

Abba Wedajew was the principal weaver and several others joined his *qub*. Payment was set at one *birr* and ten cents per week, the latter for the host to prepare beer and bread. Although the sum was difficult to raise, several members were in a position which allowed them to tap extra sources of income, such as weavers, the PA secretary, and a Government worker. Members included a majority of men, but several women attended in their own right. Muslims and Christians participated in almost equal proportions. The *qub* comprised both Amhara and Oromo speakers, and settlers from different parts of Lasta, Desé and Lalo Qilé. Five out of twenty-five were weavers, and one was the PA secretary; the rest were ordinary settlers. Most members were from Teams Eight and Nine, but there were also some from three other teams. The *qub* even included two people who were not from the village: an Oromo from Village Four and an Ethiopian Nutrition Institute worker.

Relations beyond the village

Social life in Village Three was largely self-contained. The organis-ation of the village into a PC, and the consequent control over labour, compelled settlers to become inward-looking. There were, however, a series of ties with the world beyond.

Firstly, the village was administratively linked with two neigh-bouring resettlement sites, Eighteen and Four. Village Three was twinned with the former by the first-year cadres. Villagers also had strong personal links with Village Eighteen for reasons of kinship, religion and marriage. Village Eighteen was further from the markets, and settlers from there came past Village Three. A *qallichcha* from Village Eighteen proclaimed the dawn prayer, aud-ible in Village Three. Several *qallichcha* from Village Eighteen were often invited to take part in ceremonies.

Links between Village Three and Village Four, half an hour's walk to the south, were also important. Initially settlers in Village Three had to use the mill in Village Four, though the position was reversed when a mill installed by Concern began to function in 1989. The establishment of the SC linking the two villages further strengthened the twinning. Settlers from Village Four came regu-larly to obtain rations of salt and other items from the Cooperative Shop, while Village Three sometimes bought vegetables from Vil-lage Four, which had irrigated fields. Links based on common areas of origin resulted in some population exchange through inter-marriage and the reunion of relatives.

Settlers in Village Three also had links with relatives in almost all the other twenty Conventional Sites in the Qéto complex. Frequent family separations had occurred in the resettlement pro-cess and many found close relatives in other villages. During the

era of the collectives, restrictions on labour time reduced opportunities to visit relatives, who tended to meet instead on market
days. In cases of funerals and marriages, however, relatives almost
invariably came to visit, without official permission, and despite
distances of up to 25 km.

The local population

Village Three is surrounded by other resettlement villages and
forested areas. Relations with the local population were therefore
largely limited to the market place. However, the village obtained
dung to make threshing floors from the Oromo PA of Iggu Kofalé
and sought to borrow its oxen for threshing. Moreover, the PA
hired a locksmith in Iggu Kofalé to secure boxes for valuables.
Individual settlers went to Iggu Kofalé to ask for dung to build
hives. Special relationships also developed, since settlers from Village Three were good customers for *chat*, which local peasants in
Iggu Kofalé sell. However, coffee and honey became sources of
tension when settlers stole from local people, who appealed to the
administration. An agreement was eventually reached between
local and settler PAs whereby the Oromo left their hives on land
allocated to the settlement until the harvest season, when they
came to collect their honey and remove their hives. Settlers who
picked coffee on land outside the settlement's confines were liable
to prosecution; offenders caught in the act were beaten.

Settlers, through their labour, also had an impact on the economy further afield. On some Conventional Sites, such as Jarso,
settlers worked part-time for local farmers at peak agricultural
periods; during the first year at a rate of one *birr* per day. In
subsequent years greater activity resulted in tighter labour controls.
Among settlers on Integrated Sites, working for locals continued
because of greater freedom. It was not uncommon for settlers who
left Conventional Sites to seek wage-labour rather than return to
Wello.[18]

Three forms of employment were available. Firstly, young boys
often worked as house servants in towns. Shimellis, who was ten
in 1987, left his mother to become a servant in a rich man's house
in Qaqé. She missed him but was also proud when he came to visit
wearing new clothes and even shoes.

Secondly, young women could find work in town bars as wait-
resses and prostitutes. This option was pursued by young women

with aspirations to independence who had quarrelled with husbands, or did not want to be married against their will. Some found work as servants in rich people's houses; others became additional wives; a few returned disabused, having missed their relatives. Tiringo spent over a year working in a rich man's house. She learnt enough Oromo to get by. After six months the mistress of the house suspected her husband was having an affair with her; she was expelled and decided to return.

Thirdly, men could obtain wage labour in rural areas. Work was easy to come by at coffee-picking time. Local farmers, some of them former landlords employing tenants, were willing to enter agreements with settlers and paid them either in money on a daily basis, or in kind with a share of the harvest. Settlers worked during weeding and harvesting time, earning one *birr* plus food or two *birr* without food. In areas where there was plenty of land and an acute labour shortage, notably in Gidami and Muggi, local farmers employed settlers as sharecroppers. The terms were favourable, as Yimam explained:

> Since they could not find workers, they offered a fair deal; they ploughed land for you and sowed crops. All you had to do was weed the maize regularly and harvest it. You then received half. I stayed nine months and earned 500 *birr*; half went on food and the rest on clothes.

While the cooperative system was in force, settlers who had left and decided to return were either given hard labour for three days to two weeks or fined between twenty and sixty *birr*, depending on how long they had been away.

Other resettlement areas

Because of the massive exodus entailed by resettlement and the extent of family separation, most settlers in Village Three had relatives in other resettlement areas. Close links were established with two Integrated Sites, located on the way to market. Chanqa Bururi also has its own roadside market. Special relationships developed between the two villages. Two settlers from Village Three moved to Iggu Kofalé. In one case this resulted in an exchange:

> Mammo was leader of Team Eight. His sister, Sinedu, married a

man in Iggu Kofalé, but quarrelled with him, and came to live next to her brother in Village Three, where she became a household head. Meanwhile Mammo had a disagreement with the leadership and decided he would rather try his luck in Iggu Kofalé. For the christening of his son he invited his old friends from Village Three.

Relations between the two sites were not always amicable; they share a boundary which was subject to dispute. On one occasion a villager taking wheat to Chanqa for grinding was met by men from the Integrated Site who tried to force him to exchange the wheat for maize. In the ensuing fight they stole his money.

While links with Iggu Kofalé were based mainly on personal relationships and trade, links with Chanqa Bururi were based largely on religion, for its settlers built a church which Village Three Christians attended.

As for other Conventional complexes, settlers had relatives in Gambélla, Asosa, Pawé and Anger Guttin. Some family reunions were organised by the RRC, resulting in a woman joining her brothers in Village Three. Many had no idea where their relatives were. The most common way of finding out was by sending letters back to Wello. Most did not wait for the Family Reunion Programme, and effected their own spontaneous reunion. They sometimes had some difficulty in obtaining permission for reunions, since the authorities and PAs were wary of people leaving settlements. The following accounts give an idea of how such family reunions occurred. The first is by Welela, one of the oldest women, who recalled how she was separated from her children and then moved from Lolchisa village in Jarso to Village Three in order to be reunited with her daughter.

> The bus took my daughter first; she went following her husband. My eldest son went to collect his two children, who were in the countryside. He said, 'I will go with my entire family. I won't leave them behind.' Meanwhile I registered and left with my second son. My daughter was lost to me. I knew not where she was, I assumed she must be dead.

Welela went on to describe how a lad from Village Three found his parents in Lolchisa, where she was.

> Deggu, a young lad, left his parents and resettled with his godfather, Channé, who, on his way to market, saw people reading. He stop-

ped and listened. They were reading out letters from people from
Lasta resettled in Lolchisa, sent in the hope that someone might
know of their lost relatives. Channé was amazed to hear the names
of Deggu's parents. He did not even know they had resettled.
Channé wrote to Deggu's parents and when they received a reply
Deggu asked the PA for a *meshegna* [document releasing him on
legitimate grounds].

Through Deggu, Welela learnt that her daughter was in Village
Three and decided to brave the journey, despite her age.

Deggu brought a number of letters from Lasta people. I asked him
about my daughter but he was a young lad and could not remember
her. We sent a letter, without much hope, and were overjoyed to
receive a reply. We heard that the journey on foot was only three
days, so my son came to visit my daughter and brought back news
of her well-being. But once I knew that Dirrib was alive I could
not keep still. I said: 'I would rather it be said [of me], "She died
on the road" rather than not seeing her eye [to eye].' The journey
took me five days. At the end they had to abandon me and call for
help, for I was too weak to continue. When I found my child and
grandchildren I decided to stay here. No sooner had I arrived than
her children's father died. Now I am worried for my son, who has
remained in Lolchisa. My children are scattered all over the land,
in Lasta, Lolchisa and here.

During the first four years the right to visit relatives in other
areas was denied to most settlers because of the fear that they
would not return. Only a few in leadership positions obtained
permission to visit relatives. A former chairman and his deputy
visited relatives in Asosa. A brigade leader who visited his brother
in Gambélla compared it unfavourably with Qéto and revealed his
prejudice regarding the local Anywa people:

You have to cross a wide sea [the Baro river] to get there. It is a
real desert, the heat is unbearable; apart from cotton, crops do not
grow well. Qéto is an oasis in comparison, it is highland; this is
Wello. People who complain about the climate here have seen
nothing. The local people there are amazing; they don't have houses
to live in and sleep in the bush; the women give birth in the forest.

Until the fifth year ordinary settlers could not obtain identity
papers, without which they were liable to be stopped on the way.

Restrictions on visiting relatives were resented by settlers, who wrote letters and composed poems on the subject. Zennebe received a letter from a relative living in another resettlement who wrote chiding him in verse:

> When we were about to leave in '77 [i.e. 1984]
> Being torn from relatives was very saddening,
> But now when there is plenty of food in the stores
> No person can be found [to say] How are you?
> And to spend time conversing together.

Restrictions did not deter many from visiting relatives without permission, especially in cases of deaths and marriages. Several settlers visited relatives in other Conventional Settlements, notably Jarso, Anger Guttin and Asosa. Settlers in Integrated Sites did not lose points if they were absent, and a number came to visit relatives in the village. In a few cases settlers wanted to take relatives away or have them join the village. The administration was reluctant to facilitate spontaneous family reunions unless a good case could be made:

> Abba Isheté was separated from his wife and three children. By asking travelling settlers he eventually located his children in the village. He returned to obtain permission to take them back to the Integrated Site in Horro Gudru. He was in no doubt that his village was preferable by far to Qéto: 'We plough with oxen on a private basis and grow a wide variety of crops, including *téf* and barley.'

Settlers from Integrated Sites nearer market towns and on main roads seemed more positive about the benefits from trade and consumer goods available in the towns and preferred their life to what they saw of Conventional Sites. Settlers from more remote areas, such as Gidami, were more mixed in their assessments. They recognised that they could grow a greater variety of crops and had more freedom and larger plots, but noted with envy Village Three's health services and assistance received in the form of clothing, the mill and the shop. One of their number concluded:

> You are in the centre of the country, we are on the edge. You are nearer home, we are far from anywhere. Goods such as clothing and salt have to come from so far that they are impossibly expensive. It is further to visit, and finding transport is difficult.

Wello and other areas

Settlers were not issued with identity cards until the fifth year and therefore could not travel legally unless, as leadership members, they obtained temporary documents from the WPE. This treatment of settlers as second-class citizens was counterproductive. Without deterring departures, it discredited resettlement. Abba Hasen, a former deputy PA chairman and staunch believer in resettlement, was disillusioned:

> We now have a new Constitution. It guarantees rights to all Ethiopians. Others enjoy the freedom to travel.[19] Have we lost our nationality simply because we are settlers? Peasants will never fully accept resettlement unless they can visit their homeland and others will not be attracted.

Shortly afterwards Abba Hasen and his wife left for Wello.

Restrictions resulted in a trade in illegal documents. Visitors brought blank pieces of paper with a PA seal and settlers had letters written authorising travel to see relatives. Some seals were fabricated in Wellegga and sold for five to ten *birr*. Unscrupulous persons thus made money selling falsely stamped pieces of paper. Forgeries were often discovered and settlers intercepted on buses. However, the checking was random and settlers often managed to get through using old identity cards, false documents or by giving bribes. Some settlers on buses got through while others on the same vehicle were stopped:

> Abba Husén lived in Village Three with two brothers. One of them left for Wello when he heard that his son had been imprisoned on suspicion of murder. Abba Husén was pining for his adult daughter who had remained with her husband. He married a woman in Village Three, but his heart was set on returning. Eventually he left with his wife and her daughter. At a checkpoint he was taken off the bus. He had forty-one *birr*, which were confiscated, and the PA imposed a fine of ten *birr*. His wife and her daughter continued their journey and arrived safely in Wello. He too has since left.

Large numbers of settlers were intercepted. Their documents and money were confiscated, the latter being handed over to the RRC office in Chanqa. Sometimes they were questioned as to their motives for leaving. Usually they were promptly sent back to their

villages, where they faced either a week to a fortnight's labour, or
a fine of ten to fifty *birr*. The experience was degrading and upset
all settlers. Many who were at first stopped simply tried again.
Defiance at the restrictions was expressed in the following couplet:

> I will go to Wello, I shall not be prevented.
> The road is open: it does not hinder [you].

Several reasons were given for wanting to return to Wello. The
commonest was illness related to the climate. Many complained of
the 'air' or 'wind' in Qéto. Others could not accustom themselves
to the diet or were suffering from complaints which they believed
could be cured by Wello traditional healers. Others simply wished
to visit relatives. Tilayé received a letter in which his relatives urged
him to visit them, come what may:

> We are all well; we hunger for you more than *injera* and thirst for
> you more than water. To us you are further than the stars. We live
> more than the dead, but less than the living. Without meeting you
> our soul will not flourish; all settlers come to visit, but you have
> not come. When you have a father such as Asres Demisé and a
> mother such as Serebet Asfaw how can you remain three and a half
> years without seeing us? Try to come; if you cannot get permission
> what problem would result from your coming and returning all the
> same? May the Saviour of the World enable us to see each other.

The PA files contained a number of petitions by settlers requesting permission to go to Wello for a close relative's funeral or
wedding. Even requests by members of the leadership were sometimes ignored; for instance, one official asked permission to go to
the wedding of his daughter; another wanted to go and fetch his
cousin, whose parents had died.

In 1990 such restrictions were relaxed. Settlers could obtain
identity cards and were allowed to travel freely. However, they
still had to obtain a letter from their PA and have it stamped by
the settlement office and *Awrajja* administration. During my visit
in January 1991 several settlers were away in Wello.

After the change of government in April all restriction disappeared; at the time of my visit in August a number of my settler
friends had left to visit their relatives.

Departures

Although considerable numbers left to work in the west or to return home, it is difficult to estimate how many people were involved, since accurate records were not kept, especially in the first six months. The population of Qéto decreased by a third over its six-year history. Official RRC figures for Qéto provide a figure of almost 6,000 departures in the first four years, i.e. a rate of 15%, or 4% per year. Although this figure is probably too low for the early stages, the RRC has fairly good estimates of population changes from the time its census was carried out towards the end of 1985. The population of Village Three declined over the first five years by over a quarter, despite the increase in the birth rate. Official PA figures suggest that 557 people left Village Three up to January 1991; this represents 28% of the population. A list of those who left, started two years after the settlers arrived, records 441 settlers leaving in about four years up to January 1991, suggesting an annual departure rate of 6%, roughly ten per month.

Table 16: Village Three population by sex and household head

Year	Household head			Dependents			Total		
	M	F	+	M	F	+	M	F	+
1985	581	43	624	432	920	1,352	1,013	963	1,976
1986	504	53	557	422	931	1,353	926	984	1,910
1987	503	50	553	443	859	1,302	946	909	1,855
1988	447	69	516	419	850	1,269	866	919	1,785
1989	333	56	389	369	664	1,033	702	720	1,422

Source: Village Three PA figures.

By 1989 the departures had not subsided; in a year prior to my visit in April 145 settlers, representing 8% of the villagers, had left. By the end of January 1991 an additional 167 people had left, i.e. 9% in less than two years, which suggests a gradual reduction in the rate of departures. By voting with their feet settlers were making a statement about their view of settlement life. While most of those who went to Wello did not return, it is worth considering why at least two dozen returned. Some, including the PA chairman, secretary and treasurer, had obtained official permission. These people were trusted, and known to have a stake in the resettlement venture. Many others went without permission in the hope they would not be caught. Some returned within six weeks, others spent as much as a year away. A number returned to the village to collect family members whom they had left behind. The PA was therefore suspicious of those who returned; some came back with the intention of remaining, but others, planning to leave with their family, were biding their time. Others had no ties left with their homeland. One young militiaman, who went to visit his family, commented: 'Wello has become a country of old men, women and children. The rest have gone to resettlement, military service or to seek labour in towns. I could not find my age-mates, I had no desire to remain.' Some found themselves in a dilemma, with a family in both places. One young man, who had married a woman in the village and had a son by her, also had a wife and daughter in Wello. He wryly commented: 'Now I have a door in both places!'

The main reasons for returning related to difficulties faced in Wello. The greatest problem for those who returned was that they were usually denied access to land. Although in some cases a close relative was able to retain some of it, 'settlers' land' was subject to reallocation. If returnees stayed in rural areas they thus became dependent on relatives, otherwise they had to seek wage-labour in other areas or in towns.

For many the decision to leave was by no means easy. They had established a new life but retained ties with their homeland. This ambivalence is expressed in the following couplet:

> My heart has become twins like the ears [the handles] of a water
>   carrier,
> One of them [wishing] to leave, the other [wanting] life [in the
>   village].

Seventy-five per cent of those who left were adults; settlers who had small children felt that they could not leave because of them, as expressed in the following couplet:

> Oh, children: what a tie. Oh, children are a rope.
> What is there about a hut to keep you back? You can simply close it
> and leave.

When I asked one young woman why she had not accepted any offers of marriage she replied: 'So long as I dream of my mother, whom I abandoned in Wello, I shall not marry and establish a life here.'

At the same time many felt that their homeland was being forgotten, particularly by small children, who could not remember life before resettlement, and by those who were born in Wellegga, who did not even know what *téf injera* tasted like. As Fato mused, 'Our country has turned into a dream. When food and water are available people eat, drink and forget.'

One of the most important factors affecting decision-making was reports about conditions in Wello. Such news spread rapidly. Hardly a week went by without a visitor coming, for peasants from Wello were not restricted in the same way as settlers, and Wello people had no fear of travelling long distances. One elderly woman exclaimed: 'Where relatives have trodden relatives will also tread.'

Some of those who came assisted people wanting to leave, or were looking for lost relatives, but most simply came to visit relatives. Visitors would pull out a stack of letters, often written on the off-chance that a lost relative might be found. In addition communication through the official post increased dramatically, in an area where there had previously not even been a Post Office. Settlers regularly received mail, not only from Wello, but from other regions: from militiamen, relatives who had settled spontaneously and settlers in other sites. The volume of correspondence exchanged through informal networks was far greater. One settler told me that when he decided to visit relatives in Wello, though he told only a few people of his intention a week before, he was entrusted with more than 150 letters.

Settlers also hesitated to return to Wello because of fears that environmental conditions would deteriorate. The news of drought in 1987 was quick to reach the village and long-term prospects did not seem secure in a land 'which had betrayed us'. This explains why many made up their mind to establish themselves in the new land, and would not consider returning even if a bus came to take them. Some even expressed indignation at others leaving. As Abba Seyd put it: '[Since the famine] we have been like baby children born again and growing up. The Government brought us up. As for those who are leaving, it is like hitting the eating basket with a stick [i.e. showing ingratitude].' Another settler compared the reasons why many young people initially left Wello with their wish to return there, revealing a circular view of events: 'Some of these youngsters left, not because of the famine, but because they were impetuous. Then we went through hard times. Now when there is enough food they have become restless again and want to leave. The young never learn.'

Fighting between Government and opposition forces in Wello and the knowledge that the peasant population were caught in between was another deterrent to returning. Most of those who left in 1988 were from Desé; settlers from Lasta, where fighting was intense, were less prone to go home.[20] Some were explicit in stating that the combination of famine and war was the principal factor deterring them from even thinking of return.

Relations with relatives in other areas

Nothing could be further from the truth than the image of the isolated universe of the peasant with no experience of, or links with, the outside world. Settlers in Village Three had contacts with relatives in all regions of Ethiopia. Nor was this initially due to resettlement, although the vast diaspora undoubtedly contributed to a broadening of settler perceptions and resulted in much ethnic mixing.

Settlers had relatives in many towns. Some were soldiers, others traders; a few were earlier settlers who, before the Revolution, had left in search of better opportunities. The greatest concentration of contacts outside Wello was in Addis Ababa. Several settlers had lived there for short periods in the past and had stayed with relatives or people from the same area. One settler had been in the Imperial Bodyguard; another spent six months with a woman with whom he grew up, who was married to a Japanese. Although many had relatives in the capital few knew their whereabouts. Settlers from Desé tended to have relatives living in the market district, where there was a concentration of Muslims, while the Christians lived in areas where there were Lastan migrants.[21] If one considers only parents, spouses, children and siblings, nineteen settlers had relatives in the capital and all but three were in contact with them. Four of these relatives had visited the village. The largest category of relatives in Addis Ababa was children.

Yeshi had been living in Addis Ababa for twelve years. As a teenager filled with a sense of adventure she left home with a cousin and had stayed with a distant relative in the capital. As she put it: 'We were young and did not know what kinship meant.' At first she found work as a servant, but gradually set herself up as an independent woman making baskets, living on her own in a rented room. She married twice and each husband left her with a child. She took her second husband to court, and was awarded alimony. Through visitors from Wello she learnt that her family had resettled. For a long time she had thought they were all dead. She wrote to them and contact was re-established after more than a decade.

Yeshi's father had died, and she decided to visit her mother, brother and sister in 1988:

She brought them salt and chilli powder, a roasting pan, a dress for her sister, a scarf for her mother, and a jumper for her brother. She thought of bringing her sister back to Addis Ababa, but they quarrelled. Her sister had been told by her mother that they should share a bed, but Yeshi's sister felt uncomfortable with the idea. Yeshi was also upset at the way her presents were treated. A pillow case she had brought things in was sold, and her mother cut the scarf in two to keep part of it clean for later use. Yeshi was indignant and felt that this was a sign of rural miserliness. She knew the sacrifices she had made to bring them presents, and felt that their life was not bad, especially since they owned sheep. Not that she would have dreamt of giving up town life to live with them, though she threatened her son, who was playing truant from school, that she would send him to herd his uncle's sheep. In June 1989 she decided to visit her family again, this time taking both children with her. During her visit her mother died; Yeshi was glad to have seen her 'resting place'.

Of the six settlers who had siblings in Addis Ababa, four had brothers there and two, sisters. One of the latter worked in a bar and the other in a hotel. All four brothers had long been established in the capital, and had done reasonably well, supporting large families: one was a trader, another a priest, a third a petrol pump attendant, and the fourth a guard. Four settlers had parents in Addis Ababa, three of whom were mothers. In all cases the settlers were adults and the parents had settled in the capital before the Revolution. The parents had left their children in Wello and had not maintained strong links with them. Two women had husbands who left them for work in Addis Ababa.

Settlers' relatives living in the capital showed a range of attitudes towards them: some refused to have anything to do with them, either because of resentment that they did not ask for help, or because, as urban dwellers, they had cut their links with the countryside. On the other hand some were concerned enough to send the occasional letter and sometimes a photograph. In a few cases relatives living in Addis Ababa tried to help their relatives financially, sending occasional sums of money or goods, such as salt, incense and clothing. Two daughters and one brother had been to visit their relatives.

Conclusion

This chapter has focused on 'traditional' forms of social organis-ation and their development within a restrictive environment imposed by State structures. Three types of interaction resulted. First, some idioms, such as child naming, reflected the new settle-ment environment. Secondly, compromises were reached between former practices and the new administration: for instance, the PA allocated points to women for looking after newly delivered mothers, team members in mourning and best men serving the newly wed. Recognition was mutual, as the PA leadership was invited to religious events. Thirdly, tradition asserted itself, as in the resurgence of wedding rituals, traditional healing practices, religious gatherings and rotating credit associations. Religion was maintained, despite the lack of places of worship, and festivities were celebrated in gatherings of increasing size and expense.

Settlers developed contacts with others living in nearby villages and visited relatives in settlements and in their homeland. Despite, and perhaps also because of travel restrictions, many decided to leave. Some went to work for local people, while others returned to Wello. A few of the latter decided to return once more to the settlement, since their homeland was no longer the place they remembered: without relatives, land and oxen, they could but become dependent. Moreover, famine and warfare were not con-ducive to a future in a land which had already 'betrayed' them once. Many therefore set their minds to creating a life for themselves in the new environment, with all its limitations. However, even the most enthusiastic resented the restrictions on travel which had turned settlers into second-class citizens. The mass exodus of people to different regions resulted in a surge of correspondence with relatives throughout the country, many of whom came to visit, sometimes re-establishing lapsed relationships and helping their settler kin.

Notes

1 Some 509 deaths were recorded, i.e. a quarter of the initial population, or an annual rate of fifty-six per thousand. Since deaths were dated from January 1986, only 163 were recorded until January 1991, an average of thirty-three per annum, i.e. an annual rate of seventeen per thousand.

2 The Deputy Chairman of the Peasant's Association saw me at a Muslim burial and said: 'You see what our graves are like, far too much trouble.'

3 In using the term Amhara to denote Christian, the priest, who is Oromo, was adopting the parlance of the Desé Muslims, who referred to Christians as 'Amara', even though the Dése Muslims speak Amharic while the Christian Oromo do not.

4 It is possible that the significance of the qiré is greater among Muslims in Wello than among Christians, for whom the church forms a focus of community.

5 For a discussion of how news of a death is gently broken see Molvaer (1980, pp. 96–7).

6 No data on perinatal deaths were kept in Village Three. A midwife from Village Eighteen kept a book which revealed that, out of 137 children she had delivered in fourteen months, three were born prematurely and died, two were born dead, and one was classified as a miscarriage.

7 Within six months sixty-eight children were born; in a period of almost five years from March 1986 to January 1991 there were 384 children born in the village, an average of eighty a year. RRC figures for Qéto record 3,669 births in the four-year period from 1985 till 1989, which gives a mid-period birth rate of twenty-four per thousand.

8 Some writers report that a birth is greeted by women ululating; the number of ululations discloses the child's gender, between four and seven for a boy and two and three for a girl (e.g. Walker, 1933, p. 1).

9 Negussie (1988, p. 177).

10 The description concentrates on Muslim wedding ceremonies, since Christian weddings have been described among the Amhara (Messing, 1957, pp. 223–7; Abebe Ambatchew, 1956) and the Oromo of Wellegga (Holcomb, 1973, pp. 107–42).

11 Despite attempts to ban this practice after a serious accident it is still practised and no wedding would be considered proper without it.

12 Several Muslim leaders asked for specific religious texts. On one occasion a young qallichcha asked me to buy him a Qur'an translated into Amharic, since, unlike the elders, his knowledge of Arabic was poor. After a few days he returned the volume because of the chairman's objection.

13 Much of the reading was from Arabic, with which the qallichcha were conversant, and which gave them authority through knowledge reserved to the initiated. However, a form of chanting favoured by settlers involved poetry in Amharic chanted in rhyming verse written in Arabic script (see A. Pankhurst, 1991b).

14 McCann wrote, 'The parish provided the rural population with its basic orientation in space and time' (1987, p. 91).

15 One trader donated 200 out of the total of over 500 birr.

16 Isenberg and Krapf (1843, p. 190).

17 In the Christian tradition the use of incense was supposed to be restricted to the church but a different type of incense became commonly used in the house.

18 A. Pankhurst 1991a.

19 The Constitution stated: 'Ethiopians are guaranteed freedom of movement. Every Ethiopian has the freedom to change his place of residence within the territories of the PDRE' (Article 49.1–2).
20 In two years up to March 1989 only 22% of those who left were from Lasta and in the last year that proportion dropped to 12%.
21 Such as the churches near the French embassy.

VIII

Marriage, divorce and the State

> We met in this place because the Government brought us here. We are a burden, but the Government still helps us. Why? Because of the agreement it entered [by bringing us here]. You too must clothe your wife [with a] dress, according to your agreement.
>
> The Marriage and Divorce Committee chairman, advising a husband

In this chapter I consider the interactions between State and settlers at the household level by focusing on questions of marriage and divorce. I discuss marriages across religious and linguistic boundaries and increase in women household heads. The revival of the custom of offering a bridal dress, and demands during litigation by women who had not received one, revealed the importance of the gift as a way of legitimising marriages. The dress was the standard form of compensation, a way for women to obtain a share of common property, or argue for divorce, and a symbol of commitment to the marital relationship and ultimately a life in the village.

In the second part I describe the Marriage and Divorce Committee, set up to stem the tide of divorce, the rise and fall of the committee and its power struggle with the neighbourhood elders. I examine the reasons given for divorce and discuss the committee's ambiguous position on issues concerning gender relations, notably adultery, wife-beating and sexual access. Finally I examine questions raised by the constitution of the People's Democratic Republic of Ethiopia (PDRE), notably monogamy, women's rights to consent and children born out of wedlock.

Marriage and resettlement

Marriage was arguably the most important social relationship in the village, for it was the basis for the formation of most households. In Chapter IV we heard reasons why many young people were prepared to resettle on their own. When asked whether they had been married before, some would laugh and give answers like: 'We were not thinking of marriage at that time'. Such answers show that they did not have clear ideas about what was awaiting them and did not envisage resettlement as a long-term option. Many who were married had left their spouses behind. Some had tried to persuade one to come with them but found that s/he preferred to remain behind with wealthy, aged or infirm parents. A number had been separated from spouses during the famine, while a few had quarrelled during the hard times.

In the reception centres single people wanting to resettle were asked where their family members were. Some, fearing they might not be accepted, claimed they did not have a family. Several women were left stranded in shelters by husbands who changed their minds about resettling. Many who joined single sought a partner. For single men the need was immediately felt, as they needed a woman to cook. For women it was a question of finding a man to 'dig for them' in the new land. The Government also promoted the formation of couples. Settlers reported pressure on single women, and to some extent single men, to marry. In 1988 as many as 14% of households had been formed through marriages *en route*. Since many such unions were short-lived the number of people forming couples on the way must have been higher.

Settlers who found partners on the journey referred to their unions by the standard word for marriage, and the term 'road marriage' also gained currency. This is not surprising, since the concept of marriage was flexible in Amhara society, and 'marriages for the journey' were a feature of trading and military expeditions in imperial days (Walker, 1933, p. 41). The main criterion people used to seek a partner in the shelters seems to have been common origin. Speaking of their 'road marriages', young settlers would explain their reasoning: 's/he was a child from my country'. 'Road marriages' were pragmatic affairs involving little ceremony and consisting of a pooling of resources, i.e. combining aid rations. One young woman recalled, 'We simply put our rations together and were married.' Asked if any gift was involved, a young man answered laughingly: 'The Government married us; it gave us a common blanket as a marriage gift.' However, several such marriages received religious blessing. One *qallichcha* recalled marrying six couples *en route*.

In Village Three the first-round cadres noted with concern the presence of single people and that men were leaving their wives and going back to Wello. The cadres decided to arrange marriages for single people. Yesuf recalls how one of them persuaded him to marry Toyba:

> I was not thinking of marrying, but Alemneh took me aside and told me about Toyba. Her parents had died in Village Eighteen and her brother had deserted, taking their blankets. She was left alone. Alemneh said, 'I will speak to her and arrange your marriage.'

Another man proudly recalled that he was the winner in a sort of 'husband parade'. His wife's husband had left and she came to see the cadres, who suggested that she should choose another.

> There were a group of us standing near the offices. One of the cadres said: 'Those of you who are single go and sit there.' Five of us sat down. He turned to her and said: 'Choose the one you want.' She looked at us all, and said: 'I will have him.'

In January 1986, ten months after the settlers arrived, a marriage registry book was opened. Twenty-six marriages were registered in the following six months. Each entry had the name, age, ethnic identity and signature of both spouses and sometimes their house number, as well as the name and signature of an elder or prominent PA member, who was termed the 'judge for the two of them', and the name of a 'marrying comrade', or cadre who witnessed the marriage. This reflected the second-round cadres' close involvement in village affairs. After their departure, the practice of the 'marrying comrade' signing was not continued.

Marriage was undoubtedly a crucial factor in settlers establishing themselves. As Table 17 shows, in the first four years half the adult settlers married in Village Three. Almost a quarter married for the first time and over a third remarried. Marriage and subsequent divorce were not infrequent in the settlers' homeland. Several studies show that the divorce and remarriage rate is high in Amhara society.[1] Reminick (1973) mentions people marrying up to fifteen

Table 17: Number of marriages in Village Three, 1985–8

| | Spouse(s) | | | | | | | |
	0	1	2	3	4	5	>5	Total
Men	243	166	62	15	7	0	2	495
Women	238	191	49	14	4	2	0	498
Both	481	357	111	29	11	2	2	993

Source: Author's survey (1988).

times. Almost half Weissleder's (1965, 1973) sample married more than once and almost a third more than twice. H. Pankhurst (1990) reports an average of 3.3 marriages per household head; almost three-quarters of her sample had married more than once, and half more than twice. This study also notes high serial marriage. Table 18 shows all marriages the settlers were involved in, including those prior to resettlement.

Table 18: Total number of marriages of Village Three settlers

| | Spouse(s) | | | | | | | |
	0	1	2	3	4	5	>5	Total
Men	53	143	156	78	35	14	16	495
Women	14	179	160	69	38	24	14	498
Both	67	322	316	147	73	38	30	993

Source: Author's survey (1988).

Two-thirds of the adults, 604 (65%), had married more than once; almost a third, 288 (31%), more than twice; and 141 (15%), thrice or more. If we consider those who married in Wello, but not since resettlement, the rate of remarriage is significantly lower than the overall rate.[2] Comparison of Tables 17 and 18 suggests that the rate of remarriage increased substantially through resettlement. During the village's short existence no fewer than 155 settlers (17%) married more than once in four years, forty-four (5%) more than twice and fifteen (1%) thrice or more.[3] It may be suggested that marital instability was a form of coping mechanism, through which settlers were adapting to their new social environment (A. Pankhurst, 1988d).

Divorce and promiscuity caused cadres much concern. Haile Mikaél recalled: 'You could observe much freedom in the settlers' sexual relations. They would go down to the river; women and men bathed together immodestly. We taught the women to refrain from this and take water back to wash at home.'[4]

Religious conversions and linguistic barriers

Religious conversions were not unusual in Wello but were increased by resettlement.[5] Most of the marriages across religion involved Christian men and Muslim women (forty-one cases, 93%). Traditionally in such marriages one of the spouses would have had to convert. However, conversion was not the prerequisite it used to be. Almost half the couples (eighteen cases, 40%) lived together, to the displeasure of the elders, without converting. Some of those involved said, 'We thought we would wait and see who preferred to convert.' Some spouses pretended to have converted, while others underwent a proper ceremony. Several Christian men had Muslim wives baptised. A few Muslim women likewise had religious leaders slaughter meat for Christian husbands to eat during conversion ceremonies.

Most of the cases where one spouse converted involved Christian men or Muslim women converting, not vice versa.[6] Settlers were aware of this tendency. Muslims claimed that the conversion of Christian men was a sign of Islam's superiority, while Christians argued that the fact that Christian women did not convert was proof of their virtue. The underlying reason for the trend was demographic. Muslims from Desé and Qallu tended to travel in families, and women left their husbands to come with their parents. The Lastans on the other hand, especially the men, tended to be single when they set out.[7] A survey in October 1985 showed that there were almost twice as many divorced women as men, but twice as many single men as women.[8] While women could remain single as households heads, men had to seek wives.

So long as couples could live together without anything testing their affiliation, religion did not play an important part. However, two factors brought it to the fore: the birth of children and the consumption of meat. When a child was born baptism became the acid test. In one marriage dispute where neither party would convert, the committee noted that the wife was pregnant, and one member said: 'The child will be the judge; he will decide for them.

The baptism is decisive, it will make them choose one way or the other.'

The second factor causing problems was the consumption of meat, which traditionally had to be slaughtered by a male member of the faith. In the first few years opportunities for the consumption of meat were rare, for settlers had hardly any livestock and market prices were prohibitive. As livestock breeding increased, the meat issue became significant. Some chose to ignore the question by eating privately without others knowing. Public occasions, however, forced individuals to commit themselves. At least two former Christian men claimed to have fallen ill when eating meat slaughtered for Muslims. One was a militiaman:

> We quarrelled over meat. When I went on service I tried Muslim meat; it would not go down my throat but came up covered in blood. Recently I bought some Christian meat in town and brought it back to my wife. We ate it together and she was not ill, so she should convert.

The other man declared: 'my inwards began to burn like a volcano'. When he went to the priests asking for rebaptism they refused, claiming that he had sinned knowingly, but later agreed upon payment of three *birr*. A young Muslim woman who converted upon marrying a Christian was afflicted by 'spirit possession' and returned to her parents.

As the issue of conversion became salient, spouses in divorce cases used religion to claim compensation for converting. This was not without a precedent in Wello; elders spoke of a sum paid 'for breaking the neck cord'[9] to converting Christians. In a settler case the husband claimed that his wife had agreed to convert in exchange for a dress; she denied the claim. The committee suggested that the husband should find a solution: 'You can send elders to plead with her, she can be tricked, there are plenty of ways of cajoling her into converting; otherwise you should convert yourself, or divorce her!'

The husband claimed that he should be compensated for changing religion but the elders, who were mostly Muslim, replied that he should adhere to his voluntary conversion and 'take his wife back in'. In the end a divorce was granted. Often it was evident that religion was used as a bargaining counter when issues in reality had more to do with access to female labour or the husband's misuse of common property.

Marriage across both religious and linguistic barriers was rare. There were nine cases of marriages across linguistic lines, four of which also cut across the religious divide. Eight cases involved Oromo women. Four involved marriages of Muslim Oromo women from Qallu with Muslim Amhara men from Desé, only one of which proved lasting. Three involved marriages between Christian Lastan men with Muslim women from Qallu. One of these marriages lasted barely a month, a second ended when the man left and the third was the subject of litigation at the Marriage and Divorce Committee. Lastly, there were two cases of marriages between Wello Amharic-speakers and Oromo-speakers from Lalo Qilé: a divorced woman from Desé married a man from Lalo Qilé, and had a child by him but he did not leave his former wife and plot; similarly a Lalo Qilé woman whose husband died leaving her with two small children married a Lasta man whose wife had refused to leave her parents to accompany him. They have lived together harmoniously for six years: she and her children have learnt Amharic.

Single women and the household plot

The northern Ethiopian marriage system is predominantly virilo-cal. Unless he was very poor or his wife's family very rich, a man preferred to bring his wife to his house. Resettlement brought about a significant change: most marriages occurred within the village. One reason for this was its size. The presence of a thousand adults provided many potential marriage partners. Another reason was that, given the strict work rules during the first four years, opportunities for contact with settlers from other villages were limited. Nonetheless, a few intermarriages did take place. The main basis for such marriages was propinquity. Several men sought wives across the river in Village Eighteen, and a few in Village Four. Another criterion was common origin. At least three Christian Lastan women left to marry other Lastans living in distant Village Six. A Muslim Desé woman married a man in Village Twelve, five hours away, where her brother lived. Three Lalo Qilé men, two of whose wives had died, went to their homeland, a day's walk away, to bring back another wife.

Social occasions were a third focus for intermarriage. Two men met their wives when they went to market. A woman who came from Village Nine to attend a funeral in Village Three ended up marrying a man living there. A man from Village Seven who came for a wedding married a woman in Village Three. Most of the marriages with people from other villages were short-lived and spouses tended to return to their families.

We have seen that the allocation of plots to household heads meant that settlers were divided into two basic categories: household heads and their dependants. Most women fell in the latter category. The proportion of households headed by women doubled from 7% to 14% between 1985 and 1989. Although single women were entitled to a plot many did not claim one but joined relatives; just as traditionally women with rights to land did not usually press for them. The PA was more likely to permit occupation of vacated plots than occupation of new plots on the edge of the village. Plots were allocated when a young man or newly wedded couple set up house or when members of a household broke up upon divorce. A young man could apply to the PA for a plot and would often obtain one, especially if he played an influential role in the Youth Association. It would have been unthinkable for a young woman to apply for a plot on her own. However, the number of single women with plots grew, for three reasons: deaths, departures and divorces.

Many settlers lost spouses, particularly early on, when mortality was high. Men almost always remarried unless they had daughters old enough to run their household. One elderly man, whose wife died, went to live with his married daughter but retained his plot. Several widowers remarried more than once because they had been left by their spouses, often because of disagreements with children. Many widows, on the other hand, chose not to remarry. Those who did often retained their plot and insisted that the new husband join them.

Many women were left behind when their husbands decided to leave the settlement. Some husbands, especially those married in the village, promised to return but few did. Many left their wives encumbered with young babies. Tsegga married three men successively, all of whom left. Her child by her second husband died and she vowed not to marry again. However, she came under pressure from her neighbours, and gave in.

Although women also left the village 60% of all 'deserters' were male, and the proportion was much higher among adults. Many

women left behind often did not remarry, hoping that their husbands would return, fearing that a new husband would leave them
or because they preferred the status of a single woman.

Divorces were an important cause of the growth in female-
headed households. A third of the settlers (350 settlers) remarried
in the village. Generally, the spouse seeking divorce, usually the
woman, left the plot. In cases of adultery or bigamy the plaintiff
often retained the plot. Since such charges were usually brought
by women, the man often left the plot to join the woman he had
been frequenting.

Given the existence of female-headed households with access to
household plots, a man seeking the woman's hand had to agree to
her terms. In the following case a man who married a woman with
a plot could not persuade her to leave it and 'go out' with him to
a new one.

> Beshir, an elderly widower who had been living with his married
> son, left his house to join an elderly woman named Desé who had
> been separated from her husband during the famine and was living
> with her three children. She refused to move, asking to see the new
> house, knowing full well that it could only be an abandoned hut
> requiring renovation. He pleaded in vain that he had gathered logs
> and hay. The elders were amused at this hen-pecked husband and
> suggested that he should build a sturdy house to persuade her to
> move. In the end the couple divorced. Beshir returned to live with
> his son. Desé married again, moving to her new husband's plot,
> having ensured that her son was registered as household head and
> would retain her plot.

The independence of women with plots was noted with bitterness by men unable to find a wife and living alone. Kasaw, whose
wife died and was abandoned by two subsequent spouses,
exclaimed: 'The women have become satiated since they have been
given plots. They say they won't leave their place. They say to us,
"You didn't have the house built yourself, the Government gave
it to you." '

Meanings of the dress

Traditionally the *sine qua non* of marriage gifts was an outfit for
the bride. As one elder put it: 'Even if it means selling his ox he
must clothe her.' Famine-engendered poverty created an anomal-

ous situation which, paradoxically, revealed the importance of 'clothing a wife' as a way of legitimising the marriage bond. During the famine and the initial stages of resettlement not even a minimum gift could be presented. There was no question of a man buying his wife a dress, let alone the customary complete costume. However, as a measure of self-reliance was generated through increased crop production and transformed into investment in smallstock, the custom of offering a dress was gradually reinstated, and new marriages were concluded with clothes of increasing value. By the end of the second year a dress was expected for first marriages. Later a waistband, shawl and scarf were usually added. At a wedding I witnessed in April 1989, shoes were also provided. By January 1991 the Qallu custom of providing a Maria Theresa dollar to be worn round the neck as proof of engagement had even been adopted by other settlers.

The new wealth led to disputes among spouses who had married in the early stages with no gift. Women who had been married 'for nothing' began to press for the bride-dress that had not been given. A woman's representative would argue that it was only because of the hard times that no dress had been demanded. One woman's father declared: 'Other men have bought their wives dresses while my daughter is wearing the clothes I gave her, and which she wore when she went in [i.e. when she married].'

Disputes arose when husbands promised a dress at the marriage but after the event did not provide one. Other grievances were turned into a means of demanding a 'retrospective present'. In one case in which a husband had not given a bride-dress, and later fathered a child outside wedlock, the wife began pressing for the traditional 'full dress': 'If he says "my wife" [i.e. shows he is serious about his marriage], let him compensate me from head to toe: shoes for my feet, a scarf for my head, the dress and tunic that are my due; otherwise he shall divorce me.'

Offering a dress was thus a way of giving a seal of legitimacy to earlier hurried unions arranged during hard times. The reassertion of bride-gifts can be interpreted as an indication of a return to normality, marking an end to the crisis period. There was often much negotiation about bridal dresses. Disagreements sometimes occurred when young women wanted fashionable synthetic dresses, with floral or striped patterns, while their parents favoured thicker traditional cotton. In the following case a dispute arose about the quality of the clothing:

The bride's father had insisted that the shawl should not be made in the village out of coarse cotton but of finer cotton made in town. The groom's father stressed the need to keep demands within their means, but agreed to the request. 'I will buy the material according to our level, which is not what it used to be; but what matters is not the money, but that we become relatives.' Although the bride chose her dress on an expedition with the groom, her father later argued that she had been shown only two kinds of cloth, and had been duped into accepting a cheap shimmery material.

Elders listened to the case and a reconciliation was reached whereby the groom and his father bought a watch for the bride, a custom they had seen among their Oromo neighbours in the village. One of the elders concluded by emphasising the need for mutual support and the role of marriage as a way of forgetting the past and building a future.

> The girl is our daughter too, and the boy our son. Haven't we been consoling each other and marrying each other on the road ever since fate abandoned us? The children who marry comfort their fathers, saying, 'Don't cry.' Reconciliation is necessary, not just for the families, but for our neighbourhood and community. This is the way we can continue to live together and create kinship.

Men whose wives left them complained that they could not persuade even an elderly woman to join them without buying her a dress. The cheapest cost twenty *birr*, and demand for better dresses increased steadily until a husband had to spend around 100 *birr* – a substantial outlay for settlers whose only source of cash derived from selling grain or livestock. One man unable to find a wife exclaimed: 'When you look for a woman they want wealth.' Women sometimes spoke of having been duped with the bait of a dress, only to find themselves abandoned when pregnant. On the other hand, men who had bought a dress and had subsequently been abandoned tried to recoup the investment through court proceedings. In one dispute a husband exclaimed: 'She has been gathering cloth while I provide for her; if she leaves she must also leave the cloth.' An elder answered reprovingly: 'How can you say, "Give me my cloth and go"? Divorce her!'

'Clothing a wife' stood for marriage, not only at the outset of the union, but also when it came under stress. Even in marital disputes between couples who had married in their homeland, claims for compensation were usually phrased in the idiom of clothing. The standard form of compensation was the purchase of a dress, *kuta* or tunic, waistband or a combination thereof. Moreover, demanding a dress became a way for women to secure a share of common property and thereby prevent it from being entirely appropriated by husbands. In marital disputes the dress became a test of the husband's sincerity. The dress was thus the most obvious way of transforming property into an investment in a social relationship.

The purchase of a dress was a clear sign of involvement in a marriage. Elders addressed husbands with shorthand phrases for the notion of commitment such as 'If you say "my wife", clothe her and take her.' A dress was a wife's guarantee: should her husband leave her, she would retain at least part of the common property.

If a husband whose wife left him did not send elders to beg her to return, offer compensation to appease her or present a guarantor to underwrite his pledge not to repeat his offence (if, as local idiom put it, he did not 'say "my wife" '), it would be held against him. Repeated refusal to present a dress could be cited as evidence against him. Whatever the husband's offence, the dress was used as a form of redress, and compensation was synonymous with clothing. A dress was spoken of in a number of ways suggesting that it made the wife forget or overlook the offence. She was referred to as a young girl who could be cajoled into returning. The dress was called 'something to make cool', i.e. to lessen her anger; 'to make cheap', i.e. to minimise the offence; and 'to deceive', i.e. to dupe, or entice, the wife into returning. In one instance in which the husband was accused of adultery the elders called him aside, as was their wont, and said: 'How shall we make her enter [your house]? You say you won't divorce, [but] you have wronged; how shall we reconcile you? How shall we make her stay with you? We need 'something that will make [the grievance] cool [down].'

Husbands who were asked by elders to buy their wives a dress tried to resist on three grounds: (1) They rejected the principle, arguing that clothing was the Government's responsibility. However, elders pointed out that others had clothed their wives. (2) Husbands argued that their wives already had clothes and that buying dresses was not a priority. This argument was rejected on the grounds that clothes a wife brought with her, or were given by her father or the Government, did not exonerate a husband from his duty. (3) Husbands, while accepting the clothing principle, argued that they did not have the means. This was acceptable to the elders, since it established a basis for negotiation. The elders then concentrated on establishing what assets the couple had and what Government items – grain, clothing and livestock – had been sold. The husband would be asked to call a guarantor, and a deadline would be set by which time he would undertake to 'clothe his wife'.

The offering of a bride-dress was an indication that men were investing not only in marriage but also in resettlement life. While many young men bided their time till they could make enough money to leave, others spent their earnings on buying their wives a dress, thereby investing in both a social relationship and a commitment to remain.

The social significance of clothing was clearly understood by the elders but not by the representatives of the external world: the cadres who stood for the State and the aid agency which represented international aid and launched a sewing programme to make and distribute free clothes. The cadres saw expenditure on a dress as a waste of precious resources, and a threat to household food security. In one case a cadre intervened on behalf of a young husband who refused to buy his wife a dress.

> I felt sorry for the lad when he said, 'I have been told to buy a dress, what shall I do?' You elders say, 'Sell maize or chickens and buy a dress,' but think of it yourselves: prices are very low now. If he sold all his points, would that be worth a decent dress? At present market prices two quintals of maize may fetch twenty to thirty *birr*, but that will not buy a dress. Tomorrow morning what will they eat? Instead of saying, 'Sell your points and buy a dress,' suggest that they establish a 'warm house'. Once their reserves have been sold, will the dress be food or a blanket? Think about the problem it would create in the future. Don't you know that the Government is about to stop giving food rations?

The cadre offered to help by giving the wife precedence when the sewing programme, initiated by Concern, began making dresses. He suggested that the elders back down from their position, and offered to give the couple priority for the expected clothing. The committee, though by no means unaware of the difficulties, did not agree. After the cadre had left, the secretary addressed the husband and declared that the leadership's concern was no reason for him to deny his responsibilities, or to treat his wife badly, especially since she was pregnant. He proposed a compromise whereby the husband would buy a dress when his wife gave birth:

> It is true that we are all 'pensioners of the Government' [i.e. receiving aid]. We do not have our own private wealth. We were destitute and struggled and finally came here. We are still in the hands of the Government; we are not self-reliant and we must be aware of our own begging. The law and the member of the leadership have taken pity on you; they say they will give you precedence. That is no reason for you to oppress her. She is your wife; tomorrow morning she will give birth. She will face problems; a dress would lighten her burden. It is something you must think about yourself and act upon yourself.

When the husband agreed to clothe his wife the secretary commended him, promising him support:

> You speak well in saying, 'I will clothe her,' and we will do what we can so that she says 'my husband' and stays; by fulfilling your agreement, and saying, 'My wife is my wife, my life is my life,' you are behaving well towards your wife and the mother of your child. What I say is that, even if they give you these clothes, your gift will be her 'delivery clothes'. The dress will make her happy.

The husband, however, continued prevaricating. His wife returned to her father's house. A few months later the husband left the village.

The distribution of free clothes contrasts with the notion of responsibility for which the elders were arguing. The RRC distributed locally made clothes as well as donations from aid agencies. Since these garments were a random assortment, tensions inevitably arose as people felt left out or suspected favouritism. Much of the best clothing allegedly went to men in positions of power in the PA and even to cadres. Some clothes were not particularly appropriate but were nevertheless much prized.[10] Aid agencies occasionally brought high-quality clothing but there was not enough to go round. Settlers preferred to sell such items in the local market for exceedingly low prices.

Concern set up a sewing programme in Qéto to pass on skills

to a few women from each village who were to train others. The
cloth was considered light, appropriate material, and was provided
free. The design was loose-fitting for the heat and the women's
dresses were adjustable to allow for pregnancy.[11] The fact that the
agency relied on charity to obtain the material was not realised by
the men, who argued, 'When the agency has the money, why are
they stingy? Why this light, poor-quality material? Why don't
they bring us good clothes?'

Although the women who acquired skills benefited, and received
points like male workers, the programme in its original form presented a major weakness which could have defeated its purpose.
The fact that the material and clothes were provided free, and
that the scheme was not self-financing, could have perpetuated
dependence, and led to the scheme's collapse when the aid agency
left. Free distribution did not allow of choice and responsibility.
Clothes distributed free were not imbued with the same social value
as the bride-dress paid for by the groom as a sign of commitment
to marriage. Concern later brought about an improvement by
introducing payment for the clothes. Half the income was to go
to the women working on the programme and half was to be used
for purchase of materials. However, since the liberalisations the
SCs became weaker and the PAs became involved in the clothing
programme. Unless a means of purchasing materials independently
of Concern is organised the scheme is unlikely to continue when
the aid agency leaves.

The State in marriage and divorce

The marriage and divorce committee

The setting up of a Marriage and Divorce Committee represented
a curious attempt by the State to intervene at the household level.
The committee was established by the administration in response
to what was termed the 'divorce problem'. For the leadership
divorce raised administrative, moral and political issues. Households splitting often meant allocating new plots and houses. Single
women as female heads of households were considered a burden,
since collective labour had to be allocated to dig their plots. Moreover, female household heads were perceived as weakening moral

standards. In cases of adultery elders sometimes exclaimed, 'It is the women heads of household that are creating problems.' Break-up of marriages due to adultery was also seen as a political issue, since the letter of the 1986 Draft Constitution prohibited bigamy and the spirit of the final text supported monogamy. The 1987 Constitution explicitly stated that 'marriage shall enjoy the protec-tion of the State'.

By far the most frequent conflicts were domestic disputes, and cadre records abound in cases of spouses 'disturbing the peace'. Marital disputes were initially considered by the PA. A committee comprising the chairman, his deputy, the secretary and the treasu-rer was designated the 'Husband and Wife Executive Committee'. Only one record existed in the WPE files, dating from February 1986:

> Their dispute is disturbing the neighbourhood. They were sum-moned and agreed to divorce, but we have no directive. They were divorced not by us, but by elders. Since it seems to us that they did so in order to expand their land, and since this matter could be an agitation which could expand to all the peasants, we draw your attention to it so that it can be clarified on your part and that you can issue a directive.[12]

When disputes arose the usual procedure was for neighbours to alert elders who lived nearby, or came from the same area, as the protagonists. The elders would then attempt to bring about a reconciliation by reprimanding both sides, though they would make clear who they thought was to blame. They would suggest that the fault should be overlooked if it was a first offence, or suggest payment of compensation if it was serious, or had been repeated.

Quarrels between spouses occupied so much time that a Mar-riage and Divorce Committee was set up in January 1987 to hear cases twice a week. In a little under a year and a half up to May 1988 it had dealt with sixty-four recorded cases. This meant that 12% of couples brought serious cases to the committee. Many disputes were resolved by elders at the neighbourhood level and did not reach the committee. Other disputes heard by the commit-tee were not registered, since litigants were always first referred to neighbourhood elders.

The Marriage and Divorce Committee presented a paradox. On

The Marriage and Divorce Committee at work

the one hand it was a body set up by agents of the State, i.e. cadres in collaboration with the PA; as such it was a new, exogenously established institution. On the other hand it was composed of elders who deliberated on the basis of established cultural values and local customs; as such it was built on traditional ways of thinking and customary forms of reconciliation.

The committee was composed of seven elders and a secretary, who was also the PA deputy chairman. The committee was specifically designed to include elders from different traditions, both religions (five Muslims and two Christians) and both language groups (six Amhara and one Oromo). This composition somewhat overrepresented the Muslims and underrepresented the Oromo.

Participating in the committee provided elders with a sense of recognition and an illusion of power. However, the committee did not mean the same thing to all its members. One of them, Abba Yimer, saw it as recognition of the value of 'eldering', i.e. negotiation and arbitration in which elders were traditionally involved. He once exclaimed: 'The eldering that is from ancient times has not been annulled. It is as before. The Government says today to the elders, "Look at grievances and reconcile." This Revolution has accepted the "ancient way".' Another elder, Abba Addisé, pointed to their reliance on external authority, saying: 'No, there are things that we don't know. Have you not read the directives of the Constitution?'

Abba Addisé was attracted by the bureaucratic side of the committee – its files, written statements and signatures – but recognised that elders no longer held authority. The undermining of elders' 'traditional' influence was accentuated by resettlement. Abba Yimam succinctly stated, 'Refugeehood is conducive to lying.' He meant that since the settlers came from different places people could pretend to be what they were not, and did not know the reputation of each other's elders. Though most did not know it, Abba Yimer had a reputation stretching far and wide: 'People used to send mules from distant places for him to come and litigate.' In the settlement personal reputations had to be rebuilt in a context where 'traditional' attributes of successful elders, namely land, livestock and positions of authority, were no longer available.

The committee provided the only village-level forum where marital disputes could be discussed. This was no doubt the attraction for the committee chairman, a charismatic figure who jested that he knew 'the movements of all 500 peasants and their wives'. He enjoyed asserting his authority by referring to the Constitution but often moved 'from judging to eldering' and suggested compromises. He liked to think that village affairs were of concern to the higher authorities and seemed to feel that the village was the hub of the universe, and the committee its central stage.

The committee and neighbourhood elders

The attempt to institutionalise litigation through the committee may at first sight seem to have lent clout to traditional forms of 'eldering'. Committee members were themselves elders, actively involved in neighbourhood litigation. Discourse in committee sessions, the form of litigation, and the aims and strategies of the committee all resembled traditional neighbourhood 'eldering'. There were, however, three crucial differences which suggest that the committee, while seemingly acknowledging the 'elders' way', was in fact undermining the role and authority of neighbourhood arbitration by formalising litigation through writing, relying on PA authority and referring to the Constitution.

The written word was paramount. The committee would not

conclude a case until the secretary had recorded a case summary.
Litigants were asked to make their statements, which they had to
sign. The members also signed 'for their unanimous verdict'. The
secretary, who was the PA deputy chairman, was the only literate
committee member. The elders signed with a thumbprint, a humili-
ating experience.

The committee's powers were severely curtailed by its reliance
on the PA. Difficult cases were referred to the leadership and
'criminal cases' and property division to the PA Law Court. The
committee liked to see itself as occupying the moral high ground,
i.e. sorting out the legal/spiritual side of disputes while referring
financial or criminal matters to the PA. In theory the committee
had the power to enforce its decisions. In practice the elders'
verdict was ignored. Since their strength lay in working towards a
compromise, they often did not attempt to enforce decisions. They
told litigants that they were offering advice as elders, not as judges,
and warned them that if they went to the Law Court there would
be no compromise.

By referring to the authority of the Constitution, a written
document linking the village to the external Ethiopian world, the
committee replaced the local elders' authority by edicts of an
exogenous text. The Constitution was referred to as the 'directive'
or 'the decree'.

The committee began to undermine the position of the elders
by insisting that cases involving divorce should be referred to it
for ratification. The committee needed elders to look into disputes
and bring them to its attention, but wished to control their verdicts.
The committee's role was thus to appropriate the positive value of
the 'elders' way', using it to legitimise the PA's involvement in
marital affairs in an attempt to control divorce.

The committee was concerned at the numbers of divorces
granted by local elders, often dissolving marriages the former had
not even heard about. It therefore insisted on being present at
marriage contracts. The difficulty of coordinating the presence of
the signing parties – the couple, their representatives, the committee and the Youth Association scribe – for what seemed a formality
meant, however, that many marriages went unregistered or were
not witnessed by committee members. In such cases, where marital
disputes were brought before the committee, its members
expressed indignation, asking for the elders who 'signed' and the
couple to be summoned and rebuked.

For many months the committee felt unable either to control the marriage and divorce process or to limit what it saw as the compromising role of neighbourhood elders. A letter was addressed to the PA on 28 August 1987 making the point clearly:

> It is recalled that we have been delegated to the Marriage and Divorce Committee which has been meeting since 13 February 1987. From that day on we have been working in accordance with custom. If there is a problem we encounter without being able to deal with it, it is that the peasants in each neighbourhood, in each team, have taken the matter as a joke. They divorce there and, without informing us, marry. Since they have caused us difficulties, coming to us quarrelling without our knowing about the marriage, and since it has become difficult for us to give verdicts, and since we have raised the issue in meetings more than once and not received an answer, we are making [this] known to you in a report so that, having given it due consideration, you can correct the matter in accordance with the law.

In trying to extend its control over marriage and divorce the committee undermined the role of neighbourhood elders for the sake of its own position. While seemingly upholding the values of traditional litigation, the hallmark of the elders, it contributed to the demise of their last remaining powers which time and misfortune had not succeeded in divesting them of.

The committee and gender issues

The committee, whose mandate was to protect marriage, had an ambiguous role. It was composed solely of elders supposed to represent 'culture'. However, it was also the guardian of modern values of women's rights embodied in the Constitution. The committee would sometimes tell a husband that it was there to ensure that a woman's rights were respected. Women were encouraged to speak for themselves even though the committee tried at the same time to make use of the traditional authority of the wife's representative. A woman's grievances were often taken as excuses rather than valid reasons for a divorce. When one was granted the committee was usually more concerned to ensure that the husband agreed to pay maintenance for children than alimony for the wife. It argued that a child could not be 'dropped', leaving responsibility for its upkeep to the Government. The committee therefore always tried to postpone a divorce until an infant's birth. The father was then asked to provide grain for it on an alternate monthly basis. However, the amount was never stipulated and men often tried to avoid their obligations.

The committee tried to ensure an equal division of property upon divorce. It pointed out that the Government had provided goods to households, and that they therefore had to be shared equally. Much emphasis was placed on the principle of equality in marriage. In a case in which a young man did not want to share a third blanket with his wife, a member declared: 'You married stating that the union was for better or for worse, on equal terms. Your wife has a right to half of what you possess.'

The principle of equal division was applied to points earned during the year in which a divorce took place. The cadres instructed the committee to warn couples seeking divorce that the husband would have to surrender half his 'points'. Many men were at first incredulous and later angry to hear that they had to part with half their income. When women started earning points, in the case of divorce the total was supposed to be added and divided in two. In practice husbands often tried to renege on their obligations and sometimes succeeded.

Most cases brought before the committee concerned people who had been married in the village (89%). Settlers married in Wello represented only 8% (five cases) while two cases involved 'road marriages'. Divorce proceedings tended to be initiated by women. In a quarter of the cases (sixteen) both parties agreed to divorce before coming to the committee. Of the remaining cases more than four times as many wives (thirty-nine) as husbands (nine) were plaintiffs.

Although the committee's brief was to check divorce, 73% of the cases in fact ended in separation. Divorce was most frequently granted when both litigants had agreed to it. The committee adopted the principle that the spouse who initiated a divorce should leave the plot, but it was the wife who usually left. A third of the women and half the men who divorced remarried within the time of my fieldwork; a few, more than once. Men who did not remarry had sisters or daughters to cook for them. Some women returned to live with their parents; the rest set themselves up as household heads.

A variety of reasons for divorce were brought forward. Out of sixty-four cases the most common reasons were adultery (twenty-two cases), spouses leaving the house (thirteen cases), wife-beating (twelve cases) and illness (eleven cases). Issues mentioned less often were the sale of joint property (five cases), husband's refusal to buy a dress (four cases), sexual access (three cases), religion (three cases) and wife's extreme youth (two cases).

Adultery was not considered sufficient grounds for divorce, though members considered female adultery more serious than male. Most adultery charges involved the husband (eighteen cases). The usual remedy suggested was for the culprit to sign that he or she would not frequent the named accomplice and that guilty husbands should buy their wives dresses in compensation.

Ten out of thirteen who left their spouses were women, usually as a protest of maltreatment. Three men claimed to have been 'expelled'. For a man the departure of his wife was considered a serious problem, for it left him without anyone to cook for him. For a wife, leaving her husband was the traditional way to draw attention to her grievances, and to force her husband to send elders to 'beg' for her return. In such cases the committee invariably tried to persuade her to return by asking the husband for a guarantor to vouch for him. If maltreatment recurred it tried again in the hope that the quarrel would 'cool down'. Attempts were also made to pressurise relatives among whom the wife had sought refuge to send her back.

Wife-beating was not considered a crime worthy of divorce. Unless there was proof of bodily injury, the committee tended to dismiss such cases as insignificant. If the wife was pregnant they were outraged at the thought that the child might be hurt. In one such case the wife's brother, acting as her defendant, stated: 'Beating your wife is not a crime. I do it from time to time, so do you, but laying hands on her when she is nine months pregnant is inexcusable.'

Many women were, however, vocal and declared that their rights had been protected since the Revolution. One exclaimed: 'If he thinks he can beat me like a donkey, he is wrong; since the Revolution our rights are respected. We will not wash our husbands' feet.' When wife-beating was linked with other issues, such as the sale of joint property, the committee took a harder line. If the husband refused to offer compensation clothes, he was open to attack. An elder argued that a husband wanting to discipline his wife must also accept responsibility for clothing her: 'You can't simply take what the Government has given you both and beat her, saying the Government will clothe her. Either clothe your wife or divorce her!'

A spouse's illness was considered grounds for divorce only if the other spouse consented. Several women who could not look after their husbands gave them permission to marry a second wife. The committee sought to stall divorce proceedings if one spouse alone claimed to be ill and the other, usually the husband, did not wish to divorce and claimed he would look after his wife or find a woman to do so. The committee therefore made it difficult for the wife to obtain a divorce unless she had powerful relatives to back her or received support from a health agent.

Some marital disputes revealed tensions in the household cycle which already existed in northern Ethiopia. A number of disputes were not between the spouses but between one of them and the other's parents. While couples were still living with the husband's parents, in accordance with the traditional patri-virilocal pattern, disputes frequently developed between the wife and her mother-in-law. When such cases came before the committee, the young couple were invariably urged to move out and set up their own household. In a case where a husband was living with his wife's mother, he was constantly chided for not setting up his own household. Where the couple had moved into their own house several disputes occurred, when husbands complained that wives were spending too much time with their parents.

Sexual access and contraception

Although the committee was largely concerned with adultery cases, sexual access was not a major issue. In at least ten cases the husband was accused of unfaithfulness while his wife was pregnant. One woman who had had two children within eighteen months and did not want another complained: 'I am suffering, carrying one child on my back and the other in my arms. I have three children. Now my husband is getting into position for a fourth. In addition to the two children he troubles me. How can I sleep?' The committee was against divorce and argued that the husband had to look after his children and work for the family. The wife suggested that her eldest son from a former marriage could become the household head but the committee declared him too young. One member suggested that the couple should sleep apart but the husband replied that they had only one blanket. Another member suggested that they should refrain from intercourse for six months or a year but the husband objected. The members remonstrated with him; one of them even said: 'The Government forbids such behaviour.' When a member suggested that they try contraception, which had just become available in the village clinic, the wife replied: 'He says he won't accept the thing which comes from the doctor.' The case was postponed. At a further session a cadre came to give advice, revealing his perspective:

A child born on top of another causes problems. We do not have the means to look after it. The problem widens, starting from one family, and ends up throwing the country into difficulties. When we say today we must live according to our means, we can only have children we can support. It won't do to say, 'The Government's hand is broad and the aid will come, I will get what I need from the Government's stores; I will do as I please.' The Government does not bring aid from its own store but gets it from agencies by begging. Our problems cannot be overcome by begging alone; we must found a new life according to our means.

The cadre outlined his version of a better world with fewer children (he himself had six):

Now women work as well as men; if this woman carries children on her back and stomach how is she going to earn a living? If we breed children in rapid succession they cannot receive the love and care they need from their mothers. Moreover, having children in close succession endangers a woman's life; the womb must rest. We must not simply look from one point of view and seek to satisfy short-term desires; we must see the consequences of our actions. Man's brain is superior to animals' because we can think. If we follow blind interest we are no different from other animals, we become like baboons and monkeys.

He went on to stress that the State protected women's rights:

Some of you men may have been ordering women about, abusing your brute force; this is oppression, it won't do now, it is unacceptable. Women are now organised, with their own association; your wife can appeal against you. You are subject to the law. If you create problems you will be taken to court and punished.

The cadre concluded on a paternalistic note of caution and advice to try contraceptives:

> Cooperative life is not easy and our efforts have not flourished so far. Our wants are great, but our means are small. We now live in small huts struggling against rats and termites. Until things get better we must plan our lives and pass on what we have to coming generations. Is this not what wise fathers do on their deathbeds? Is my way of speaking clear? Separate your beds, consult the doctor and consider taking the pills.

The Constitution: negotiating tradition and change

The committee became the setting where Government policy regarding the family came into contact with village household life. The following discussion of cases in the light of the State's values and objectives, as stated in the Constitution, conveys some of the complexity of the litigation process. The committee was not a mere puppet of the State and sometimes worked round the letter of the law. Moreover, State policy itself was not always clear and its objectives were sometimes in conflict. The Constitution's concern with woman's consent in marriage ran counter to its goal of protecting marriage. Just as representatives of the State set up a committee to protect marriage, so the committee required the support of patriarchal authority to prevent divorce. The PA legitimised its extended control over marriage and divorce by setting up a 'traditional' committee, which in turn legitimised its position with reference to the new Constitution, as a source of authority.

State policy on marriage became an issue in the village at the time of the drafting of the 1987 Constitution, which was the most important formal step in the establishment of the PDRE. The draft was published on 7 June 1986 and submitted to organised nationwide discussion. The final text was published six months later, on 30 January 1987, and approved by referendum in February that year. The most significant change introduced in the final text, following widespread dissent among Muslims, was the removal of the clause prohibiting bigamy. Article 38 on marriage had read:

> Marriage is based on the consent of a man and a woman who have attained maturity. Bigamy is prohibited. Husband and wife have

equal relations in their family relations. Marriage shall enjoy the protection of the State. Children have the same rights whether born in or out of wedlock.

Three issues featured prominently in the committee's proceedings: (1) maturity and consent; (2) the legality of unions, and polygamy versus bigamy, and (3) the rights of offspring in cases of divorce and births out of wedlock.

Maturity and consent

Reference to maturity was a barely veiled attack on the traditional custom of early marriage. The definition of maturity was not discussed, but the committee used the concept of a woman being 'not yet ready [for marriage]'. The age of spouses in the PA register was approximate, since age was not an indigenous concern but rather reflected what was considered acceptable. Elders sometimes spoke of an ideal minimum of sixteen but several women were registered as fifteen and one as fourteen. Registration was usually a mere formality. One case involving the arranged marriage of a young girl generated controversy.

A man from Lasta married his young daughter to a lad without close relatives. The girl's father admitted that his daughter was very young but argued that it was traditional for a young indigent lad to seek protection with the father of a woman he would later marry. Several Lasta elders supported this view and testified that 'marriage with a time limit' was customary. Although the Desé elders had no experience of such a custom, the committee accepted the proposition but asked the father to guarantee that the children would not engage in sexual intercourse. A date was set for a proper marriage. The chairman decided that the marriage would not be registered 'according to the directives which came now', but a written agreement would be made.

This case shows the committee seeking a compromise between the values of the Constitution and those of tradition. The Constitution was referred to directly by one member who claimed that the 'directive' stated that the girl had to be eighteen and must not be 'pushed by her parents'. Desé elders, who did not give their daughters in marriage as young as Lasta girls, found the custom reprehensible. One of them stated, 'We don't marry off our girls until they can carry a large water pot.'

In another case the committee was intransigent against a young Qallu woman of fifteen who left the husband to whom her mother and stepfather had married her. She argued that she had not chosen to marry him, but had been forced by her mother; that the man was not her age-mate and that his children did not respect her. The committee pointed out that she had already married thrice and rejected her plea that she was too young. It tried in vain to make her return to her husband; she remained with her mother.

The issue of consent raised much debate because it questioned parental marriage arrangements. When a couple came to register, each signed for themselves and a judge signed for both. This was a departure from tradition, where each party had a representative. However, in subsequent litigation a woman was usually represented by a man, who was often asked to sign. The term *wabi*, literally 'giver', 'witness' or 'guarantor', was used for the representative who ideally was the person who gave her in marriage. The woman's 'giver' could thus be interpreted as the witness of the 'gift' and its 'guarantor'.

During committee sessions the elders sometimes addressed the *wabi* and listened to his account but at other times told him to be silent and let the woman speak. The committee thus moved between the 'traditional' and 'contemporary' perspectives. Nor was the discourse one-way: litigants also argued from both viewpoints. In one case, even the cadre shifted between the two positions. How is this double-speak to be explained? Were the committee and litigants using 'contemporary' discourse to undermine 'traditional' values; or were they using 'contemporary' rhetoric while adhering to 'traditional' values?

At first sight it would appear that the committee was attacking the 'traditional' role of the *wabi* by suggesting that the woman should speak for herself. But this was a tactical move to weaken his position. The sophistry with which the issue of women's representation was manipulated is apparent in a case where the mother's involvement was condoned while the brother's was opposed:

> The committee heard the mother's compromising speeches and the wife's and her brother's belligerent stance. It told the brother the matter did not concern him, since it was an affair between the

husband and wife, but at the same time said it *did* concern the
mother. The chairman even referred to the Constitution to justify
the exclusion of the brother, saying: 'It does not concern you, we
administer husbands and wives; the directive is here, we administer
looking at it.' The young wife tried to play the same game by
arguing at times that her brother and not her mother spoke for her,
while arguing that she had a right to speak independently of her
mother.

The committee often acknowledged 'contemporary' values by
asking the woman to speak for herself. Women were usually the
initiators of divorce proceedings and often precipitated their
demands by leaving their husband and returning to their *wabi*.
The committee often relied on invoking the patriarchal authority
of the *wabi* to return his ward in order to achieve the aim of
holding marriages together. The *wabi* often responded by refusing
to hand the woman back. In one such case the committee argued
in the 'traditional' idiom that the woman's brother should reprimand his ward and return her. She was spoken of as a girl to be
'scolded and pinched'. Her brother argued that he did not want
to be her *wabi* any longer but the committee refused to let him
off the hook. When it was suggested that the matter be brought
back to the committee if the quarrel continued, he reluctantly
agreed on condition that her husband 'signed in front of the committee' that he would buy her a dress, refrain from hurting her
and bring a guarantor. The chairman summed up the matter thus:

> Let him clothe her 'on you' [i.e. while you remain her *wabi*], you
> reprimand her and put her in, let them go into their house. We do
> not want to dwell on the past; we are working for the future. What
> we are saying to you is this: you remain the *wabi*, be straight in
> your 'wabiship', fulfil your role as brother, he his as husband, and
> she hers as wife.

The committee was thus caught in a contradiction. The official
doctrine denied the right of the *wabi* to represent his ward while
expecting the committee to preserve the marriage, which could be
achieved only by relying on the *wabi* to coax her into returning to
her husband. Paradoxically, in order to achieve the 'contemporary'
objective of 'protecting' marriage, it had to rely on 'traditional'
patriarchal authority, thereby going against 'contemporary' values
of women's right of consent and self-representation.

This contradiction occasionally erupted in a clash, a breakdown of discourse, a postponement of negotiations, or even the brief imprisonment of a *wabi*. This happened in a case when a father refused to hand back his daughter, saying: 'I won't give [her even] if the sky descends and the earth rises . . . Let me hear the directive which says fathers shall be prevented [from representing their children].' The secretary argued that parents should not meddle in their children's marriages but the father refused to back down, arguing that he had rights over, and responsibilities for, his child. He said he would petition and rather be imprisoned than hand her over. The chairman replied that the father had handed over responsibility by giving his daughter in marriage: 'Did you not give her in marriage to him? Is he not her husband? Is she not his legal wife? She is the one to speak.' In an aside revealing alleged instructions to counter parental control, the chairman added: 'It is our fault; [while] the directive is telling us not to accept this "guardianship" we have done so.'

Although the committee had the father imprisoned for a day, in the last resort it had to plead with him. The intervention by a cadre shows a representative of the new order equally adept at moving between 'contemporary' and 'traditional' idioms. He denied parental involvement while appealing to a sense of paternal responsibility.

> It is her choice. It is a sin for parents to become involved after husband and wife are married; you are going beyond the law. Ultimately you will be shamed if she prefers her husband to you; no one can force her to leave him; as parents you should advise her; even if she comes [to you] having committed a fault say [to her], 'What! Have you come dropping your matrimony? You ill-mannered girl; are you going to have me insulted?' It will be said: 'Who brought her up?' Advise them to remain in wedlock. Meet parent-to-parent and counsel each other, they are children today; why don't you make them agree?

After the cadre's departure the secretary reprimanded the husband in 'traditional' idiom and advised him to beg forgiveness of his father-in-law in order to win his support in protecting the marriage. He further referred to tradition, suggesting that in Wello the husband would have been punished and required to pay exacting compensation, or face excommunication.

Act in such a way that her father takes your side. Being a father means that he is your father too, the father who gave birth to her also gave birth to you. Respect him, you are at fault. Ask for mercy and forgiveness in front of us, in front of the elders; you have done wrong and are fully to blame. In our homeland, you would be punished by having to pay not merely a calf [in compensation] but an ox. Moreover, you would be liable to be expelled from the burial group [i.e. the community]. Even if the father dislikes you, respect him; he will then reprimand the girl himself, saying to her, 'You are at fault, return to him.'

Polygamy and bigamy

The second sentence in the Draft Constitution article on marriage was the much-debated bigamy clause which, owing to Muslim protest, was removed from the final text. The draft was in the hands of the PA in the six months before the final publication and during this period the policy of discouraging polygamy took effect.

Although the majority of the village population were Muslim, polygamy was not widespread. Ten men each had two wives; four came with both wives, and the others remarried in the village. Two points need to be emphasised. Firstly, second marriages were correlated with success. Four of the six men who married a second wife were in positions of authority in the PA and Youth Association while another was rich, having brought money with him. Secondly, most of the men involved in polygamous marriages later divorced one wife. Only two of the ten were still married to both wives by the end of my fieldwork. Four men in leadership positions chose to renounce one wife, partly in response to pressure. One of the two remaining cases was the rich man who married a second wife, a single head of household without support; the other came with both wives, who live with him in one house.

Despite the small scale of polygamy, bigamy was a major issue. Much litigation involved adultery and it was claimed that this was tantamount to bigamy. The issue came to the fore in relation to the Draft Constitution's prohibition and erupted when the chairman of another village came to Village Three to represent a woman whose husband had left her. During a lull in the proceedings, I asked him if there was a Marriage and Divorce Committee in his village. The committee listened with evident curiosity as he explained that there were no 'elders of custom' but that the PA considered marital disputes and, if divorce could not be avoided, sent them to a committee to execute the decision. He then recalled his own case:

> I had two wives, one whom I brought from Wello and the other who was divorced by her husband. For two years they lived together without quarrelling or jealousy. Then the cadres asked me to choose between the two, saying, 'The law permits one wife, choose one and the other will be given a separate house.' I could not decide . . . a fine house was built for me. They then had my first wife called and advised her, saying, 'Your husband has left you for another, what will you do? He is about to go into the new house; won't it be better for you to be divorced?' They convinced her, saying, 'Keep this house; if you find a husband we will join you to his household.'

The chairman went on to describe his distress at being divorced from his preferred wife:

> I was called to our 'house of customs'; they said to me, 'Won't you accept our directives?' I could not think what it was about and said, 'Why not? What have I done wrong?' They said, 'Will you agree to what we say?' I replied, 'Of course; if I refuse where will I go?' They said, 'In that case, sign that you agree to divorce from today. Without correcting your stance, we will not go on to others.' I was devastated. I loved the woman and admired her ability to run the household; she was the one who lifted my sorrows. I felt dizzy and scribbled, I know not whether it was my name or not . . . I was distraught. They had married me to the one my heart did not wish for; the wife who was good to me had slipped away from me.

He concluded with the measures subsequently taken:

> There were ninety-five women; some entertained two men, some even three or four. As with me, we divorced all of them and registered the second wives too; a list was drawn up. If those who were divorced are seen around the yards of the women they divorced, they are to be denounced . . . this is how it happened in our village; in the end law rules, it is the directive that vanquishes.

The above account visibly shocked the committee. After the outsider had left, worries were expressed about rumours that the man would denounce Village Three for allowing bigamy. The following day the PA chairman, who had two wives, appeared

before the committee. It was a strange situation in which the
man with power was called to account by a legally subordinate
committee. One of the members explained what had happened the
preceding day and concluded, 'The man said he will take the
matter to the *Wereda*, saying, "Village Three has become a place of
merriment, ignoring the Constitution." '

The PA Chairman responded by approving the elders' concern
but pleading that his case was special.

> You are right; while we at the top are spoiling things it is difficult
> for you to give judgement to the people below, and it should not
> be like that. But I have a problem, she is a mother; truly I prefer
> her to the mother who gave birth to me . . . my turning [to another
> woman] doesn't mean I will abandon her. I would suffer rather
> than that she should have troubles and misery; but as for a wife, I
> have chosen the new one . . . I am not one to spend three days with
> one and three with another but I will not be distanced from her. I
> agree that for your work it is bad if people say, 'Doesn't the
> chairman do things like this?' But the woman is indigent, she is
> elderly, it cannot be said that she will set up another marriage. I
> will help her, with my wealth and my labour, for she came under
> my name. She has no other relatives. If I drop her who is going to
> lift her up?

The secretary explained that they were not asking the chairman
not to support her but simply to legalise the divorce, to which he
agreed. Explaining the top-down logic of summoning the chairman
first, he used a metaphor derived from house building, revealing
the traditional hierarchical mentality. He compared the PA chairman to the *walta*, the piece of wood at the top of the roof, to
which the roof poles are attached: 'It is to be able to say we came
from the top and went down. If it is put right at the *walta* the rest
can be put right slowly.'

The secretary, who also had two wives, felt awkward being a
'judge' while still married to two wives. He volunteered to legalise
a divorce with the woman he was no longer living with and
declared: 'Let us straighten our stand so that we can lead those
below; otherwise it is playing with people.'

This sudden concern with bigamy did not lead to major changes.
Polygamy was not important in the village; most of those who
had married two wives, including the chairman and his deputy,
were no longer in fact living with both. One exception was Seyd,

who came from Wello with a wife, married a second in the village and later another from Village Eighteen.

> Seyd's first wife left and returned to Wello. His second wife, Ansha, wanted a divorce on the grounds that he was unfaithful and refused to dig her plot. While she was pregnant Seyd married a third wife. However, when the latter discovered that he was married, she initiated divorce proceedings. The committee used delaying tactics but she took the matter to the Qéto WPE Committee, which sent a letter to the Village Three cadres asking for the matter to be given priority by the Marriage and Divorce Committee.

Seyd responded to the bigamy charge with the claim that he had divorced his second wife, a claim which she at first denied. However, since she had always wanted a divorce, a religious leader carried out the formalities on the spot, witnessed by elders. The committee saw Seyd's sudden divorce as a ploy and insisted that he remain with Ansha, since the marriage with his third wife was bigamous. Ansha wanted to abide by the divorce and refused to surrender the divorce document. The committee summoned the signatory elders to rebuke them and try to retrieve the document. The chairman hoped to set an example which would serve as a caution to other neighbourhood elders.

> One day people say, 'We are married,' the next they say, 'We are divorced.' Elders are divorcing people in the fields . . . We have not called you to demonstrate our authority but so that it will be said, 'Those people have been given advice'; people will listen if the prominent religious leaders and elders that you are say, 'They have given us advice, we will not divorce' . . . how can elders divorce all those who came married from Wello? They are divorcing the wives of 500 peasants. Even now this so-called Village Three is infamous because of Seyd Yimer. You heard the letter from the *wereda* which instructs the cadres to refer the matter to us; even they could not solve the matter. In future keep your reputations clean, retrieve the document lest the whole province say, on reading your names, 'Who are these people who divorce people on the ground [i.e. illegally]?'

The concern with polygamy and bigamy has since abated. In 1991 I learnt that the new PA secretary, in accordance with the former pattern, had married a second wife.

Children born out of wedlock

The last sentence in the Constitution's article on marriage guarantees equal rights to children born in and out of wedlock. In Christian tradition a man could recognise the rights of an adulterine child if he wished, but did not have to. Among the Muslims the genitor had no obligations towards an adulterine child unless he legalised the union with the mother. A contradiction developed between the traditional concern with legalising a marriage leading to progeny in order to protect the child's rights and the Constitutional concern with legalising the child's rights while preventing a bigamous union from being recognised. Muslim tradition would not accept the illegitimate child but recognised the man's right to more than one marriage. The legislation recognised the rights of the adulterine child but would not legalise a second union. In the following case a wife argued for divorce on the grounds that her husband had fathered a child by another woman. She attempted to present payment of maintenance to the child's mother as proof of bigamy.

> The elders argued that adultery was 'merely thieving', something everyone did. It was nothing new, 'something which existed from the morning'. The secretary articulated both traditional and constitutional points of view within a single speech. He chastised the man for not legalising the marriage according to traditional Islamic law and suggested that the fact that the child fathered out of wedlock was born so soon after a child was born in wedlock was a sign that the father was cursed. At the same time he stressed that the Government was rightly concerned with protecting the rights of 'illegitimate' children.

In accordance with its brief to uphold marriage and counter divorce, the committee argued that fathering a child out of wedlock was not sufficient grounds for divorce, and the chairman invoked the Constitution to justify this position.

> Stay calm and listen. The directive will speak to you to prevent you going wrong; we are arguing holding it next to us. It is the decree which gives us advice; we will look at it; it does not accept casuistry. What the house says, what is said here clearly, is that if the man gives birth by mistake, that person who is born has equal rights. It does not say he was mistaken and should divorce her.

However, the attempt to manipulate the law was not merely

one-way; the wife tried to argue that the husband's involvement with the other woman was tantamount to bigamy in 'contemporary' terms and hence legitimate grounds for divorce. She asked rhetorically, 'Does the Government say sleep with two [women]?' When the committee pointed out that the husband did not legalise the marriage, the wife's mother argued in 'traditional' terms that awarding maintenance was unfair, since her husband would in effect be supporting two women. 'When her food is divided and goes to the other woman is it not dividing it for two? When her grain and points are divided is that right? It means that he is going to give his points to her and eat my daughter's.' The committee argued that the support was strictly for the child, whom 'the Government won't allow him to drop'. The wife countered defiantly: 'Will I give my points for his bastard? Don't I have a child? I won't return to him. If I am to share grain I have worked for with his bastard, he and I have no matrimony.'

The committee offered to make the husband sign an undertaking that he would not frequent the other woman. The chairman stressed the need to find a compromise. 'Leaving the judging aside and entering the eldering', he concluding by suggesting that the husband should compensate his wife by buying a dress and that she should accept the payment of maintenance for the other woman's child.

The Marriage and Divorce Committee was disbanded four months after the end of my fieldwork, apparently because of a complaint lodged by a woman to the *wereda* WPE Committee headquarters, situated in Village Five. She had obtained a divorce but was not satisfied with the terms. Her husband had agreed to leave the plot and house to her, to provide maintenance for their child and pay her twenty *birr* compensations – but she wanted more. The cadres ordered the committee to disband. During a visit I paid to Village Three in April 1989 some of the elders on the committee expressed regret that a fulfilling part of their lives had ceased and spoke wistfully of the time they were in a position of authority. Others, including the chairman, felt relieved at having been released from the burden of the responsibility. With the disappearance of the cadres and disbanding of the committee, this experiment of State intervention in domestic affairs came to an end. Since then neighbourhood elders have regained some of their former prestige and the PA no longer seeks to regulate marriage and divorce.

Conclusion

In the period under discussion, domestic relations in the village were shaped by the involvement of the State, which sought to promote marriage and discourage divorce. Resettlement resulted in dislocation and family separation. The instability of settler life led to an increase in divorce and remarriage. In this context, the restitution of the bridal dress came to symbolise re-establishment and an assertion of independence through the transformation of material wealth into a commitment to the fragile marital bond.

The creation of the Marriage and Divorce Committee represented an attempt to use tradition to curb divorce, as well as to uphold the Constitution by proclaiming the values of monogamy and the rights of women and children. The committee found itself in an ambivalent position as representative of both tradition and the new order. The committee was gradually able to extend its influence over neighbourhood litigation by referring to the authority of the Constitution. Although the bigamy clause was repealed in the final text, in the interim the ideology of monogamy prevailed. The committee relied on the patriarchal authority of the wife-giver, using traditional values in ways which undermined the woman's right to self-representation. Although using the authority of the State seemingly to legitimise traditional values in litigation, the committee's deliberations weakened the elders' role in marital affairs. However, the committee's stance was considered too compromising; the experiment was cut short and neighbourhood elders have regained the upper hand.

Notes

1 Messing (1957, p. 184); Levine (1965, p. 103); Weissleder (1965, pp. 199–204 1973); Hoben (1973, p. 149); Reminick (1973, p. 322); Poluha (1989, pp. 63–6); H. Pankhurst (1990, p. 164).
2 Some 350 (45%) adults married more than once, 122 (16%) married more than twice and sixty (8%) more than thrice.
3 It is interesting to note that the remarriage rate among those who married in the village for the first time was extremely high. Fifty out of 162 (30%) married more than once, fourteen (8%) more than twice, and four (2%) more than thrice.
4 Letter, 22 August 1989.
5 At least forty-four marriages occurred between Muslims and Christians during the first four years, involving thirty-nine men and thirty-seven women. This

accounts for 8% of couples and a fifth (19%) of those who married in the village.

6 Ten Christian men but only one Christian woman converted; nine Muslim women but only two Muslim men converted.

7 The demographic imbalance was clearly marked: 53% of the adults from Desé were women, a figure which rose to 58% for the fifteen-to-twenty-five age group. On the other hand, women represented only 45% of the 426 adult Lastans.

8 The figures were 120 divorced women, as opposed to sixty-seven divorced men, and 134 single men as opposed to sixty-five single women.

9 Christian Ethiopians traditionally wear a neck cord called *mateb*, given to them at the time of baptism.

10 Western gender notions notwithstanding, the Peasants' Association storekeeper prided himself on a 'granny's' dressing gown and a young man was never seen without a frilly women's swimming head-cap.

11 An initial hiccup was overcome when it was realised that the design did not allow for easy baring of breasts for feeding.

12 Memorandum from the PA leadership to the WPE Committee, 4 February 1986.

IX

Conclusion

State intervention in the lives and movements of individuals and groups of people has become an issue of growing importance. Although resettlement represents an extreme and therefore a more clear-cut case, it is becoming increasingly difficult to study 'communities' as if they were discrete isolates. Boundaries between the indigenous and exogenous become blurred when the very existence of people as a group is an artificial creation of Government design. Settler adaptation, livelihoods, relationships and self-perceptions were influenced less by ecological factors than by the pervasive influence of State policies. This book is therefore part of an increasing anthropological interest in the relationship between localities and nations.

In the encounter between the settlers and the State, the effects of the aid environment placed pressure on people to resettle and resulted in specific adaptations in the village. A combination of political, economic and social forces explains why and how resettlement took place. The failure of peasant survival strategies led many to surrender their autonomy and become dependent on the State. The rationale of the Government's programme was rooted in the impact of famine, Ethiopia's independent past, and its leaders' aspirations for a brighter future. The haste with which the programme was implemented left little time for planning, and resulted in much hardship, coercion and family separation. Settlers were, however, attracted to resettlement for a variety of reasons; their decisions were affected by combinations of factors including wealth, age and gender; individual motivations nevertheless took effect within the context of social pressures of family, kinship, peer and community.

The horror of the shelters remains a vivid recollection in settler consciousness. Once in the village, the settlers began to adapt to their new physical and social environment. Their lives were shaped by their relationship to the State, whose agents imposed a cooperative mode of production, and instituted a hierarchy based on literacy and military skills. Families responded to an aid environment by splitting households, and team units became the basis of social organisation. Settlers sold some food rations, and later the produce distributed to them, to pursue a strategy of transforming grain into investments in livestock. Social life was constrained by official opposition to traditional beliefs, and restrictions on free time and movement. In the domestic sphere the State sought to promote marriage and discourage divorce through the Marriage and Divorce Committee; its members were caught between representing tradition and the new order, symbolised by the 1987 Constitution, which embodied values of monogamy and the protection of women's and children's rights.

Over the five years 1985–89 the settlers experienced radical changes. While the provision of aid was initially inadequate, State support in terms of material and personnel soon became disproportionate in national terms, and could not be sustained. However, the structure of production perpetuated dependence. As the State began to withdraw both its hands, its care and its control, the 'children of the Government', as the settlers sometimes called themselves, became its orphans. Given a collectivised system which was abhorred and uneconomic, the future of large-scale settlements such as Qéto when the study was carried out seemed precarious.

X

Epilogue

The study which formed the core of this book reflects village life in a settlement during 1987–8. Subsequent visits in 1989 and 1991 have helped to place that chronicle in a context of contemporary historical change. Two points need stressing: first, the village was not divorced from changes in other parts of Ethiopia, most notably liberalisation of the economy in the final year of the Mengistu regime and after the subsequent change of government. Indeed, the village is part of the world at large; indirectly it was affected by the mood of *perestroika*. The second point is that the settlers have, in a sense, come full circle, through the imposition of collectivisation and an attempt to introduce socialism, back to the ideals of smallholder peasants, the ethos of household independence and social life based on neighbourhood values and religious affiliations. Beneath the appearance of radical change is the subtext of continuity which has prevailed over exogenous attempts to impose alien reforms.

During my first return visit in April 1989 I was struck by a sense of community which revealed itself in the face of adversity. Plans partially to privatise land holdings suggested that the village land holdings were too small, and the administration proposed that 'excess' households should be moved. The settlers voiced strong opposition to what they called 'resettlement on top of resettlement'. They likened it to going back to '77, i.e. 1984–5, the year they left their homeland. They spoke in terms reflecting a sense of village belonging, relatedness and common destiny. Some mentioned the four years they had lived together, 'Muslims and Christians as brothers and sisters'. Others spoke of their toil to make the land bear fruit and become 'our dung', rendered fertile through human effort. One woman stated: 'We are the milk of one cow, the crop of one field.' Settlers also expressed a sense of 'rootedness' and belonging to Village Three in comments such as 'Now this country is [like] Wello for us.' In the event the move was cancelled, and this parochial drama was not turned into another resettlement tragedy.

My second visit, in January 1991, revealed a new sense of optimism and hopes for a brighter future. The main change had been brought about by decollectivisation. From a situation where communal agriculture was the norm and private farming the exception the reverse had come about. This apparently resulted in increases in yields as farmers put more time, energy and care into their own private plots. More important, however, it released people from rigid work rules, and allowed them to make their own decisions regarding production and the use of time. The freedom to choose when to visit relatives, take part in social and religious events, go to market or leave the village brought about a marked improvement in the quality of settler life.

A second, no less important, change was in the status of settlers, who had been a privileged group receiving disproportionate Government assistance, and paying no taxes, while simultaneously remaining second-class citizens denied freedom of movement. By the end of 1989 those with identity cards could obtain a letter from their PA and have it stamped by the administration enabling them to travel. At the time of my visit many settlers were visiting relatives in other settlements and in their former homeland. On the other hand they have taken on their responsibilities, paying taxes and health care charges.

Changes in social and religious life were remarkable. A marriage I attended was celebrated in style for several days. The bride-dress was more elaborate, and professional singers from another village rendered the occasion even more impressive. Muslims had constructed a mosque and spent much time in traditional neighbourhood ceremonies. Christians went to nearby St Mary's Church on holy days, for christenings and to bury their dead. I accompanied friends to the large church of St George in Village Six for the annual feast day, which drew hundreds of settlers bringing contributions of food and donating money generously. Settlers were resplendent in their Sunday best; a priest of the Ethiopian Orthodox Church from the regional capital, Neqemté, commented: 'Who would believe that these were destitute settlers a few years back?'

Settlers were better dressed. You no longer saw children without clothes or people in tattered garments; many wore several layers of clothing. Settlers who were selling jewellery when they arrived began buying some. There were other signs of prosperity. During the first few years those with sheep or goats were the exception; by early 1991 even the poorest owned smallstock. Settler houses were better furnished. Whereas before they sold aid items, by then they were buying household utensils. Outside each house was at least one large grain store, and there were several smaller ones indoors.

However, this did not mean that all settlers were entirely content with their lives. Many pointed to the privileges still enjoyed by the leadership and militia, for whom most still had to work two days a week. Other settlers complained of the burden of taxation. For health care they had to go to another village and pay for medicine. A few settlers even left, in part owing to the effects of liberalisation. They included several in leadership positions, such as the chairman, and a few elderly persons without family help who had been supported by the collective. Finally, although the diet had improved, and people occasionally ate eggs and meat, the maize-based diet was qualitatively inferior to the *téf*-based one to which they were accustomed.

Radical transformations swept across Ethiopia in the spring of 1991 as this book was going to press; fortunately, I was able to revisit the Village for a third time in August, and can therefore conclude with a few observations as to how the change of government may affect the settlers' lives.

During the period of turmoil no fighting took place in the Qéto area and the takeover by the Oromo Liberation Front occurred without bloodshed. The settler militiamen were disarmed, funds from SCs and PAs were confiscated, and meetings were called at which new PA leaders were elected. The last vestiges of collectivisation were removed; settlers were no longer required to work for the leadership and militiamen, and freedom of movement was reasserted.

In the new political climate ethnic consciousness came to the fore. Settlers anticipated discrimination from liberation fronts which had previously condemned resettlement. However, a change of heart seems to have taken place, and settlers were told that they had nothing to fear. They were free to remain or leave as they wished. The rationale offered was that, since the settlers were from Wello, which had once been settled by Oromo, even those who had lost their language and adopted Amharic were considered Oromo and were therefore welcome in Wellegga.

The reader may wonder whether the people whose lives have been portrayed in this book will settle for a new world or return to their former homeland. Although by the time of my penultimate visit, over a quarter of the settlers had left, remarkably few followed them during the time of unrest and in the five months after the change of government. However, at the time of my last visit the harvest had not yet been gathered and people planning to leave may have been waiting to sell their crops.

The situation remains fluid, but assuming that the present climate of goodwill prevails, several factors suggest that most settlers will remain in the village. Firstly, the changes in the last eighteen months have removed repressive policies, most notably collectivisation and restrictions on travel. Secondly, conditions remain precarious in the settlers' homeland, with its soil degradation and high population pressure. Although peace at last prevails, the spectre of famine has not been laid to rest. Thirdly, the settlers' former land was generally redistributed and their property was appropriated by those who remained behind. Finally, a web of social relationships has developed within the village; the universe of the settler is rooted in marriages, friendships and neighbourhood gatherings. More and more children born in Qéto know not the taste of *téf*; Wello is to them merely a fairyland evoked in the adults' reminiscences.

Ultimately, settlers' decisions will probably be influenced by the policies of the Transitional Government and the liberation fronts. Some settlers hope that the Government will assist them in returning to Wello and that it will promulgate new land reform legislation for their benefit. Given the massive economic problems facing the country and land shortages in the North, it seems more probable that the Government will adopt a *laissez-faire* course; in Ethiopia, as in most parts of the world, State interventionism seems to be on the wane.

If the settlers are left to their own devices and their right to remain in Wellegga is upheld, the majority may well decide to stay. Already during my penultimate visit, settlers confided that, when they visited relatives in Wello, they had been distressed at being stigmatised as settlers. Likewise in Wellegga they objected to being labelled 'settlers', a term which they considered derogatory. In their own eyes they had ceased to be immigrants and thought of themselves as peasants living in Wellegga. When I expressed surprise at this new-found identity, one man wryly noted that the word for settler, *sefari*, rhymes with *asaffari*, meaning shameful.

Settlers have made the transition from famine victims to success-ful peasants. Although prospects are brighter than ever before, in the long term two issues may jeopardise the future of Village Three and similar settlements.

Firstly, the sustainability of agricultural production, even sup-ported by State inputs, remains precarious. Mechanisation no longer seems a viable option. Prior to the recent troubles the number of operational tractors was dwindling and high costs of fuel and maintenance coupled with low prices for maize meant that the programme had to be heavily subsidised. After the damage incurred during the period of unrest it seems improbable that the MOA will consider reinvesting in settlements which may be unable or unwilling to pay for tractor services. Ox-plough cultivation, the only alternative and the one which the settlers prefer, is by no means assured. Despite the oxen programme introduced by Con-cern, the ratio of oxen to households remains low. The high inci-dence of trypanosomiasis has resulted in alarming losses, notably during the period of instability when veterinary drugs could not be supplied. Oxen fatalities highlight the need for the Qéto area to be firmly linked into regional and national veterinary programmes.

Secondly, and most importantly, the integration of settlers within the local economy has become the most salient issue. In Wellegga at the time of writing ethnic tensions, which arose during the period of unrest, seem to have been defused. However, the promotion of harmonious relations between settlers and local people within a framework of regional development remains the single most important challenge for the future.

Bibliography

Ethiopian authors are listed as is customary by first name.

Ethiopian government

Central Statistical Office (1984) *Ethiopia 1984: Population and Housing Census Preliminary Report*, Office of the Population and Housing Census Commission, Addis Ababa.

— (1985a), 'Report on the results of the 1981 demographic survey', *CSO Bulletin* 46.

— (1985b), *Population of Weredas and Towns by Sex and Average House-hold Size Based on the Preliminary Census Results and Population Projections by Age, Sex and Rural and Urban for Total Country and Regions 1984–1995*, National Committee for Central Planning, Addis Ababa.

— (1986), 'Area by Region, Awraja, Wereda in sq. km., Gasha, Hectare', *CSO Bulletin* 49.

Constitutional Drafting Commission (1986), 'Draft Constitution of the People's Democratic Republic of Ethiopia', *Ethiopian Herald*, 7 June.

— (1987), 'Revised Draft Constitution of the People's Democratic Republic of Ethiopia', *Ethiopian Herald*, 30 January.

Council of Ministers (1988a), *Activities of the Resettlement Source Areas: Study Report* [Amharic, Meggabit 1980], Addis Ababa.

— (1988b), *Resettlement in Post-Revolutionary Ethiopia: Results, Problems and Future Direction* [Amharic, Miyazya 1980], National Committee for Natural Disaster Rehabilitation Host Regions Study Committee, Addis Ababa.

Ethiopian Highlands Reclamation Study (1983–5), see MOA/FAO.

Imperial Ethiopian Government (1968), *Third Five Year Development Plan 1968–1973*, Ministry of Planning and Development, Addis Ababa.

Ministry of Agriculture (1989a), *Production Assessment Report from 77–8 to 80–1 EC* [Amharic, Yekkatit 1981], Resettlement Coordination Office, Addis Ababa.

— (1989b), *Assessment Report of Agricultural Development Work in Resettlement Areas during 1977–81 EC*, Meggabit 1981, Addis Ababa.

— (1989c), *Study Report Concerning Land Fragmentation and Reallo-*

cation, [Amharic, Sené 1981], Land Use Planning and Regulatory Department, Addis Ababa.

Ministry of Agriculture and Settlement (1978), *The Settlement Authority at a Glance*, August, Addis Ababa.

Ministry of Agriculture/FAO (1985), 'Ethiopian Highlands Reclamation Study, resettlement strategy proposals', *EHRS Working Paper 28*, Colaris, J., with the assistance of Yibrah Hagos, Addis Ababa.

Ministry of Land Reform and Administration (1969), *A Policy Oriented Study of Land Settlement*, Burke, V., and Thornley, F., Addis Ababa.

— (1972a), *Settlement as Government Land Use*, Addis Ababa.

— (1972b), *Draft Policy of the Imperial Ethiopian Government on Agricultural Land Tenure*, August, Addis Ababa.

— (1974), *Low Cost Settlement Projects*, June, Addis Ababa.

National Committee for Rehabilitation from Environmental Problems (1984), *Structure and Work Guidelines of the National Committee for Rehabilitation from Environmental Problems* [Amharic, Tiqimt 1977], Addis Ababa.

National Revolutionary Production Campaign – Central Planning Supreme Council (1982, 1983), *Agricultural Development in the 10 Year Guiding Plan*, V, *Development of Settlement Programme*, Parts I and II [Amharic], July, January, Addis Ababa.

Office of the National Committee for Central Planning (1984a), *Assessment of the Six Year Plan Implementation (1971–6 EC)* [Amharic], Addis Ababa.

— (1984b), *Action Programme Prepared to Solve Problems Arising from the Drought* [Amharic, Hidar 1977]. Addis Ababa.

— (1984c), *Ten Years Perspective Plan 1984–5 – 1993–4*, August, Addis Ababa.

— (1987), *1988 Plan for Existing Settlements* [Amharic, Nehasé 1979], Department of Natural Resources and Human Settlement, Addis Ababa.

— (1988a), *Human Settlement, A Draft Plan for Five Years (1990–94)* [Amharic, Hidar 1981], Department of Natural Resource Development and Conservation, Addis Ababa.

— (1988b), *1989 Plan for Existing Settlements* [Amharic, Sené 1981], Department of Natural Resource Development and Conservation, Addis Ababa.

Planning Commission Office (1973), *Strategy Outline for the Fourth Five Year Plan*, Addis Ababa.

Regional Planning Office for Western Ethiopia (1985), *General Report on Resettlement Activity in Western Ethiopia in 1985* [Amharic, Tir 1980], Addis Ababa.

Relief and Rehabilitation Commission (1985), *The Challenges of Drought:*

Ethiopia's Decade of Struggle in Relief and Rehabilitation, H & L Communications, London.

— (1987), *Eshet*, I, Quarterly publication of the Relief and Rehabilitation Commission, Addis Ababa.

— (1988), *Settlement Activities and Agricultural Development in Settlement Areas* [Amharic, Tir 1980], Addis Ababa.

Wellegga Environmental Problems Rehabilitation Committee (1985), *Report of the Wellegga Environmental Problems Rehabilitation Committee until Nehase 30/77* [Amharic, Nehasé 1980], Neqemté.

International organisations

Concern (1986a), *Concern's Programme in Jarso and Ketto Settlements: Evaluation Team Report, Nov.-Dec. 1986*, Sandford, R., *et al.*, Concern, Addis Ababa.

— (1986b), *Ketto Community Survey*, December, Concern, Ketto.

— (1987), *Integrated Villages in the Vicinity of Ketto Conventional Resettlement*, McGuire, J., and Fesseha Asfaw, Concern, Ketto.

— (1988a), *Developing Artisanal Production in Resettlement Schemes*, Report for Concern of a Survey at Ketto and Jarso, Scott, A., Hardingham, M., and Elkington, P., ITDG, Addis Ababa.

— (1988b), *Tsetse and Trypanosomiasis Situation at Ketto Resettlement, Wellega Region, June 1988*, Getachew Tikubet and Mulugeta H. Sellassie, Concern, Addis Ababa.

Food and Agriculture Organisation/United Nations Development Programme (1983), *Assistance to Land Use Planning and Implementation of Large Scale Settlement for Rural Development*, DP/ETH/80/015, FAO, Rome.

— (1986), *Land Settlement Projects in Ethiopia*, Gentings, H., FAO, Addis Ababa.

Intermediate Technology Development Group, see Concern (1988a)

International Bank for Reconstruction and Development (1974), *Appraisal of Drought and Rehabilitation Project Ethiopia*, General Agriculture Division, East Africa, IBRD, Washington.

International Labour Organisation (1970), *Report to the Government of Ethiopia on Integrated Rural Development*, ILO, Geneva.

United Nations Development Programme/Relief and Rehabilitation Commission (1983), *A Study of Nomadic Areas for Settlement* (4 vols), UNDP/RRC, Addis Ababa.

United Nations International Children's Emergency Fund (1988), *Integrated Rehabilitation Project Baseline Survey*, December, Addis Ababa.

United Nations Office for Emergency Operations in Ethiopia (1986), *Report on the New Resettlements in Ethiopia 1984–6*, Addis Ababa.

World Bank (1985), *The Experience of the World Bank with Government-sponsored Land Settlement*, Report 5625, World Bank, Washington.

Other sources

Abebe Ambatchew (1956), 'Betrothal among the Sawan Amhara', in *University College of Addis Ababa Ethnological Society Bulletin*, V, pp. 244–5.
Adane Mekonnen (1988), 'Health Status in Resettled and Indigenous Populations in Kelem Awraja, Wellega Region, Southwestern Ethiopia', M.Sc. thesis, Department of Community Health, Faculty of Medicine, Addis Ababa University.
Alasebu Gebre Sellassie (1984), 'Women in settlement sites', *National Workshop on Women in Agricultural Development*, Awasa.
Alemneh Dejene (1990a), 'Peasants, environment, resettlement', in Pausewang, S., Fanta Cheru, Brüne, S., and Eshetu Chole (eds), *Ethiopia: Options for Rural Development*, Zed Books, Boulder and London, pp. 174–86.
— (1990b), *Environment, Famine and Politics in Ethiopia: A View from the Village*, Lynne Rienner, Boulder and London.
Apthorpe, R. (1966), 'A survey of land settlement schemes and rural development in East Africa', in *East African Institute of Social Research Conference Papers*, no. 352, Kampala.
— (ed. 1968), *Land Settlement and Rural Development in Eastern Africa*, Transition Books, Kampala.
Baeteman, J. (1929), *Dictionnaire amarigna-français*, Imprimerie Saint Lazare, Diré Daoua.
Bartels, L. (1983), *Oromo Religion, Myths and Rites of the Western Oromo of Ethopia: An Attempt to Understand*, Collectanea Instituti Anthropos VIII, Dietrich Reiner, Berlin.
Bender, M. L. (1975), *The Ethiopian Nilo-Saharans*, Artistic Printing Press, Addis Ababa.
Berterame, S., and Magni, L. (1988a), 'Potters between adaptation and survival in Beles resettlement area, Ethiopia', *Xth International Conference of Ethiopian Studies*, August, Paris.
— (1988b), 'Local markets and exchanges in Beles resettlement area', *IDR Workshop on Famine Experience and Resettlement*, December, Addis Ababa.
Bishop, R. (1984), 'An evaluation of the Ethiopian resettlement programme', *EHRS Working Paper*, 5, MOA/FAO, Addis Ababa.
Brokensha, D. (1963), 'Volta resettlement and anthropological research', *Human Organisation*, XXII, pp. 286–90.

Budge, E. A. Wallis (1928), *A History of Ethiopia, Nubia and Abyssinia*, I, Methuen, London.

Burke, B. E., and Thornley, F. T. (1969), *A Policy-oriented Study of Land Settlement* (2 vols) MLRA, Addis Ababa.

Cernea, M. (ed. 1985), *Putting People First: Sociological Variables in Rural Development*, Oxford University Press, Oxford.

Cerulli, E. (1956), *Peoples of South-west Ethiopia and its Borderland*, International African Institute, London.

Chambers, R. (1969), *Settlement Schemes in Tropical Africa: A Study of Organisations and Development*, Praeger, New York.

Clapham, C. (1988), *Transformation and Continuity in Revolutionary Ethiopia*, Cambridge University Press, Cambridge.

Clark, G. C. (1971), *English History: A Survey*, Clarendon Press, Oxford.

Clarke, J. (1986), *Resettlement and Rehabilitation: Ethiopia's Campaign against Famine*, Harney and Jones, London.

Clay, J. W., and Holcomb, K. (1986), *Politics and the Ethiopian Famine 1984–1985*, Cultural Survival, Cambridge, Mass.

Clay, J. W., Steingraber, S., and Niggli, P. (1988), *The Spoils of Famine: Ethiopian Famine Policy and Peasant Agriculture*, Cultural Survival Report 25, Cambridge, Mass.

Cohen, J. M., and Isaksson, N. I. (1987), *Villagisation in the Arsi Region of Ethiopia*, Swedish University of Agricultural Sciences, Uppsala.

Colaris, S. J., with Yibrah Hagos (1985), *Ethiopian Highlands Reclamation Study: Resettlement Strategy Proposals*, MOA/FAO, Addis Ababa.

Colchester, M., and Luling, V. (1986), *Ethiopia's Bitter Medicine: Settling for Disaster*, Survival International, London.

Colson, E. (1971), *The Social Consequences of Resettlement: The Impact of the Kariba Dam Resettlement on the Gwembe Tonga*, Manchester University Press, Manchester.

Constable, M., and Belshaw, D. (1985), *A Summary of Major Findings and Recommendations from the Ethiopian Highlands Reclamation Study*, MOA/FAO, Addis Ababa.

Curtis, D., *et al.* (1988), *Preventing Famine: Policies and Prospects for Africa*, Routledge, New York.

Cutler, P., and Stephenson, R. (1984), *The State of Food Emergency Preparedness in Ethiopia*, International Disaster Institute, London.

Dawit Wolde Giorgis (1989), *Red Tears: War, Famine and Revolution in Ethiopia*, Red Sea Press, Trenton.

Dessalegn Rahmato (1987), *Famine and Survival Strategies: A Case Study from North-east Ethiopia*, Institute of Development Research, Food and Famine Monograph No. 1., Addis Ababa University, Addis Ababa.

— (1988a), 'Some notes on settlement and resettlement in Mettekel Awraja

(Gojjam Province)', *Proceedings of the Ninth International Congress of Ethiopian Studies*, I, Nauka Publishers, Moscow, pp. 116–34.

— (1988b), 'Settlement and resettlement in Mettekel, western Ethiopia', *Africa* (Rome), LXIII, pp. 14–43.

— (1989), 'Rural resettlement in post-Revolution Ethiopia: problems and prospects', *Conference on Population Issues in Ethiopia's National Development*, ONCCP Population and Development Planning Division, July, Addis Ababa.

de Waal, A. (1989), *Famine that Kills: Darfur, Sudan, 1984–5*, Clarendon Press, Oxford.

Dirks, R. (1980), 'Social responses during severe food shortages and famine', *Current Anthropology*, 21, pp. 21–44.

Donham, D., and James, W. (1986), *The Southern Marches of Imperial Ethiopia: Essays in History and Social Anthropology*, Cambridge University Press, Cambridge.

Eshetu Chole and Teshome Mulat (1988), 'Land settlement in Ethiopia: a review of developments', in Oberei A. (ed.), *Land Settlement Policies and Population Distribution in Developing Countries*, Praeger, New York.

Fernea, R. A., and Kennedy, J. G. (1966), 'Initial adaptation to resettlement: a new life for Egyptian Nubians', *Current Anthropology*, VII, pp. 349–54.

Fikre Zergaw (1970), *Settlement Schemes: Theory and Practice (Ethiopia)*, MLRA, June, Addis Ababa.

Flood, G. (1976), 'Nomadism and its future: the Afar', in Abdul Mejid Hussein (ed.), *Rehab: Drought and Famine in Ethiopia*, International African Institute, London.

Gill, P. (1986), *A Year in the Death of Africa*, Paladin, London.

Goering, T. J. (1971), *Some Thoughts on Land Settlement in Ethiopia*, Planning Commission Office, Addis Ababa.

Goyder, H. and C. (1988), 'Case studies of famine: Ethiopia', in Curtis, D., *et al.*, *Preventing Famine: Policies and Prospects of Africa*, Routledge, New York, pp. 73–110.

Gragg, G. (1982), *Oromo Dictionary*, Michigan State and Chicago Universities, East Lansing.

Greer, G. (1986), 'Resettlement, Ethiopia, 1985', in *The Madwoman's Underclothes: Essays and Occasional Writings 1968–85*, Pan Books, London, pp. 273–99.

Grottanelli, V. (1940), *I Mao. Missione Etnographica nel Uollega Occidentale*, I, Accademia d'Italia, Rome.

Guidi, I. (1901), *Vocabolario amarico-italiano*, Istituto per l'Oriente, Rome.

Habte Mariam Marcos (1973), 'Regional variations in Amharic', *Journal of Ethiopian Studies*, XI, 2, pp. 113–29.

Hancock, G. (1985), *Ethiopia: The Challenge of Hunger*, Victor Gollancz, London.

Hansen, A., and Oliver-Smith, A. (eds 1982), *Involuntary Migration: The Problems and Responses of Dislocated People*, Westview Press, Boulder.

Hareide, D. (1986), *Report on the New Resettlements in Ethiopia 1984–6*, United Nations Office for Emergency Operations in Ethiopia, Addis Ababa.

History of Villages Three and Four, Qéllem Awrajja Qéto Settlement Scheme (1987), [Amharic, Miyazya 1979], Sisay Derrese *et al.* (third-round WPE cadres).

Hoben, A. (1973), *Land Tenure among the Amhara of Ethiopia: The Dynamics of Cognatic Descent*, Chicago University Press, Chicago.

— (1986), 'Assessing the social feasibility of a settlement in north Cameroon', in Horowitz, M., and Painter, T. (eds), *Anthropology and Rural Development in West Africa*, Westview Press, Boulder.

Holcomb, B. (1973), 'Oromo marriage in Wallaga Province, Ethiopia', *Journal of Ethiopian Studies*, II, 1, pp. 107–42.

— (1985), *Ethiopian Resettlement: The Evidence*, Survival International, London.

Huntingford, G. W. B. (1955), *The Galla of Ethiopia: The Kingdoms of Kafa and Janjero*, International African Institute, London.

— (1989), *The Historical Geography of Ethiopia from the First Century AD to 1704*, Oxford University Press, New York.

Isenberg, C., and Krapf, J. (1968), *The Journals of C. W. Isenberg and J. L. Krapf, detailing their Proceedings in the Kingdom of Shoa and Journeys into other Parts of Abyssinia*, Frank Cass, London.

James, W. (1980), 'From aboriginal to frontier society in western Ethiopia', in Donham, D., and James, W. (eds), *Working Papers on Society and History in Imperial Ethiopia: The Southern Periphery from the 1880s to 1974*, African Studies Centre, Cambridge, pp. 37–67.

Jansson, K., Harris, M., and Penrose, A. (1987), *The Ethiopian Famine*, Zed Books, London.

Kloos, H. (1990), 'Health aspects of resettlement in Ethiopia', *Social Science and Medicine*, XXX, pp. 643–56.

Kloos, H., and Aynalem Adugna (1989), 'Settler migration during the 1984–85 resettlement programme in Ethiopia', *Geojournal*, XIX, pp. 113–27.

Last, G. C. (1975), *Settlement Programmes and the Education Sector*, MOE Planning Unit, November, Addis Ababa.

Legesse Begashaw (1988), 'Resettlement, a tool of regional development with special reference to western Ethiopia', in Treuner P., *et al.* (eds), *Regional Planning and Development in Ethiopia*, 2, IDR, Addis Ababa.

Levine, D. N. (1965), *Wax and Gold: Tradition and Innovation in Ethiopian Culture*, University of Chicago Press, Chicago.

Lockhart, D. (1984) *The itinerário of Jerōnimo Lobo*, Hakluyt, London.

Lulseged Asfaw (1975), *The Role of State Domain Lands in Ethiopia's Agricultural Development*, Report 106, University of Wisconsin, Land Tenure Centre.

MacArthur, J. D. (1971), *Some Aspects of Land Policies in Ethiopia*, Report to MLRA, University College of North Wales, Bangor.

— (1972), *The Development of Policy and Planning of Land Settlement in Ethiopia*, Report to MLRA, University of Bradford, Bradford.

McCann, J. C. (1987), *From Poverty to Famine in Northeast Ethiopia: A Rural History 1900–35*, University of Pennsylvania Press, Philadelphia.

McMillan, D. (1987), 'The social impacts of planned resettlement in Burkina Faso', in Glantz, M. (ed.), *Drought and Hunger in Africa*, Cambridge University Press, Cambridge.

Médecins sans Frontières (1985) *Mass Deportations in Ethiopia*, MSF, Paris.

Mekuria Bulcha (1988), *Flight and Integration: Causes of Mass Exodus from Ethiopia and Problems of Integration in Sudan*, Nordiska Afrikainstitutet, Uppsala.

Mérab, P. (1921–30), *L'Abyssinie sous Ménélik, II, Impréssions d'Ethiopie*, Leroux, Paris.

Mesfin Wolde-Mariam (1984), *Rural Vulnerability to Famine in Ethiopia 1958–1977*, Vikas, New Delhi.

Messele Negash (1973), 'Agricultural land settlement', *Proceedings of the Fourth Annual Research Seminar*, IDR, Addis Ababa.

Messing, S. D. (1957), 'The Highland-Plateau Amhara of Ethiopia', Ph.D. thesis, University of Pennsylvania.

Metu N. Belatchew, assisted by O'Bray, E. (1988), *Support to Women's Associations on Settlement Schemes: An Evaluation*, FAO/RRC Project, July, Addis Ababa.

Molvaer, R. K. (1980), *Tradition and Change in Ethiopia: Society and Cultural Life as Reflected in Amharic Fictional Literature*, Brill, Leiden.

Montandon, G. (1913), *Au pays ghimirra: récit de mon voyage à travers le massif éthiopien (1909–11)*, A. Challmel, Paris.

Negaso Gidada (1984), 'History of the Sayyoo Oromoo of Southwestern Wallaga, Ethiopia, from about 1730–1886', Ph.D. thesis, University of Frankfurt.

Negussie, B. (1988), *Traditional Wisdom and Modern Development: A Case Study of Traditional Peri-natal Knowledge among Elderly Women in Southern Shewa, Ethiopia*, Studies in Comparative and International Education, No. 13, Institute of International Education, University of Stockholm.

Niggli, P. (1986), *Ethiopia: Deportations and Forced Labour Camps*, Berliner Missionswerk, Berlin.

Oberei, A. S. (ed. 1988), *Land Settlement Policies and Population Distribution in Developing Countries*, Praeger, New York.

Oxford English Dictionary (1989), Oxford University Press, Oxford.

Pankhurst, A. (1985), 'Social Consequences of Drought and Famine: An Anthropological Approach to Selected African Case Studies', M. A. dissertation, University of Manchester.

— (1987), 'Seasonality of Infant Natality and Mortality in Ketto Settlements: Some Implications for Assistance', unpublished report, Addis Ababa.

— (1988a), 'Social dimensions of famine in Ethiopia: exchange, migration and integration', *Proceedings of the Ninth International Congress of Ethiopian Studies*, II, Nauka Publishers, Moscow, pp. 65–80.

— (1988b), 'Resettlement in Ethiopia: A Background Paper', unpublished report, Addis Ababa.

— (1988c), 'Social Dynamics of Resettlement: A Village Perspective', unpublished report, Addis Ababa.

— (1988d), 'Responses to resettlement: household, marriage and divorce', *Tenth International Conference of Ethiopian Studies*, Paris.

— (1989a), 'Resettlement in Ethiopia: orphan child or herald of change?', *Conference on Options for Rural Development in Ethiopia*, July, Bergen.

— (1989b), 'The administration of resettlement in Ethiopia', in Abebe Zegeye and Isheno, S. (eds), *Forced Labour and Migration: Patterns of Movement within Africa*, Hans Zell, Bowker-Fauer, London, pp. 319–69.

— (1990a), 'Policy and practice of resettlement in Ethiopia', in Pausewang, S., Fanta Cheru, Brüne, S., and Eshetu Chole (eds), *Ethiopia: Options for Rural Development*, Zed Books, Boulder and London, pp. 121–34.

— (1990b), 'Amakkäläč, the amazing jigger flea: Amharic couplets interpreting a settler environment', *First National Conference of Ethiopian Studies*, April, Addis Ababa.

— (1991a), 'People on the move: the case of settlers leaving Ethiopian resettlement villages', *Disasters*, XV, pp. 61–7.

— (1991b), 'Indigenising Islam in Wello: Ajem, Amharic verse written in Arabic script', *Eleventh International Conference of Ethiopian Studies*, April, Addis Ababa.

Pankhurst, A., and Hezekiel Gebissa (1986), 'Report on a Study Tour of Settlement Schemes in Wollega, 12 October – 9 November 1986', unpublished report, Addis Ababa.

— (1987–8), 'Lej Eyasu's visit and the removal of the Gondäré from Läqämté', *Quaderni di Studi Etiopici*, VIII–IX, pp. 82–93.

Pankhurst, H. (1989), 'The value of dung', *Proceedings of the Conference on Peasant Production Systems in Ethiopia*, August, Trondheim.

— (1990), 'Women, the Peasantry and the State: A Study from Menz, Ethiopia', Ph.D. thesis, University of Edinburgh.

Pankhurst, R. (1986), *The History of Famine and Epidemics in Ethiopia prior to the Twentieth Century*, RRC, Addis Ababa.

Poluha, E. (1989), *Central Planning and Local Reality: The Case of a Producers' Cooperative in Ethiopia*, Stockholm Studies in Social Anthropology, 23, Department of Social Anthropology, University of Stockholm.

Prunier, G. (1988), 'Population resettlement in Ethiopia: the financial aspect', *Tenth International Conference of Ethiopian Studies*, Paris.

Reining, C. C. (1966), *The Zande Scheme: An Anthropological Case Study of Economic Development in Africa*, Northwestern University Press, Evanston.

Reminick, R. A. (1973), 'The Manze Amhara of Ethiopia: A Study of Authority, Masculinity and Sociality', Ph.D. thesis, University of Chicago.

Robertson, A. F. (1984), *People and the State: An Anthropology of Planned Development*, Cambridge University Press, Cambridge.

Sahle Mariam Moges (1982), 'Land Settlement as Rural Development Policy: The Ethiopian Experience', M.Sc. thesis, University of Wisconsin.

Sandford, R., *et al.* (1986), *Concern's Programme in Jarso and Ketto Settlements: Evaluation Team Report, Nov.-Dec. 1986*, Concern, Addis Ababa.

Scudder, T. (1968), 'Social anthropology, man-made lakes and population relocation in Africa', *Anthropological Quarterly*, XLI, pp. 168–76.

— (1969), 'Relocation, agricultural intensification and anthropological research', in Brokensha, D. and Pearsall, M. (eds) *The Anthropology of Development in Sub-Saharan Africa*, Monograph 10, Society for Applied Anthropology, Lexington.

— (1973), 'The human ecology of big projects, river basin development and resettlement', *Annual Review of Anthropology*, II, pp. 45. 55.

— (1955), 'A sociological framework for the analysis of new land settlements', in Cernea M. (ed.).

Scudder, T., and Colson, E. (1972), 'The Kariba Dam project: resettlement and local initiative', in Bernard, R., and Pelto, P. (eds), *Technical Innovation and Cultural Change*, Macmillan, New York, pp. 40–6.

— (1979), 'Long-term research in Gwembe Valley, Zambia', in Foster, G., *et al.* (eds), *Long Term Field Research in Social Anthropology*, Academic Press, New York, pp. 227–54.

— (1982), 'From welfare to development: a conceptual framework for the analysis of dislocated people', in Hansen, A., and Oliver-Smith, A. (eds), pp. 267–88.

Shiferaw Bekele (1988), 'An empirical account of resettlement in Ethiopia

(1975–1985)', *Proceedings of the Ninth International Congress of Ethiopian Studies*, II, Nauka Publishers, Moscow, pp. 127–42.

Simpson, G. (1975), 'A preliminary survey of settlement projects in Ethiopia', *IDR Research Report* 21, Addis Ababa.

— (1976), 'Socio-political aspects of settlement schemes in Ethiopia and their contribution to development', *Land Reform, Land Settlement and Cooperatives*, II, pp. 22–40.

Sivini, G. (1986), 'Famine and the resettlement program in Ethiopia', *Africa* (Rome), XLI.

Sorokin, P. (1975), *Man and Society in Calamity*, Greenwood Press, Westport.

Stauder, J. (1971), *The Majangir: Ecology and Society of a Southwest Ethiopian People*, Cambridge University Press, Cambridge.

Steingraber, S. (1987), 'Resettlement and villagisation in Wollega: report based on refugee testimony collected in Sudan, May–June 1987', *Conference on Oromo Revolution*, August, Washington.

Taddese Wolde (1985), *Report to the WPE*, [Amharic, Hamlé 1977], Qéto.

Tedla Haile Modja Guermami (1930), 'Pourquoi et comment pratiquer une politique d'assimiliation en Ethiopie', thesis, Université Coloniale d'Anvers.

Tegegne Teka (1988), 'The State and rural cooperatives in Ethiopia', in Hedlund, H. (ed.), *Cooperatives Revisited*, Scandinavian Institute of African Studies, Uppsala.

Teshome Mulat and Tennassie Nichola (1988), *Integrated Rehabilitation Project Baseline Survey*, UNICEF, November, Addis Ababa.

Torry, W. I. (1984), 'Social science research on famine: a critical evaluation', *Human Ecology*, XII, pp. 227–52.

Trimingham, J. S. (1952), *Islam in Ethiopia*, Oxford University Press, Oxford.

Turnbull, C. (1972), *The Mountain People*, Simon and Schuster, New York.

Turton, D. and Turton, P. (1984), 'Spontaneous resettlement after drought: an Ethiopian example', *Disasters*, VIII, pp. 178–89.

Ullendorff, E. (1960), *The Ethiopians: An Introduction to Country and People*, Oxford University Press, London.

Van Santen, C. E. (1978), *Six Case Studies of Rural Settlement Schemes in Ethiopia*, MOAS, Addis Ababa.

— (1980), *Ethiopia: Rural Settlement Schemes*, Technical Report, UNDP/FAO, Rome.

Walker, C. H. (1933), *The Abyssinian at Home*, Sheldon Press, London.

Webb, P., and von Braun, J. (1989), *Drought and Food Shortages in Ethiopia: A Preliminary Review of Effects and Policy Implications*, International Food Policy Research Institute/ONCCP, Addis Ababa.

Weissleder, W. (1965), 'The Political Ecology of Amhara Domination',
Ph.D. thesis, University of Chicago.
— (1974), 'Amhara marriage: the stability of divorce', *Canadian Review
of Sociology and Anthropology*, XI, pp. 67–85.
Wetterhall, H. (1972), *Government Land in Ethiopia*, MLRA, Addis
Ababa.
Wood, A. P. (1975), 'Migration and settlement in the forest fringe, Illuba-
bor Province, Ethiopia', Paper 20, *University of Liverpool, African
Population Mobility Project*.
— (1976), 'The resettlement of Wollo famine victims in Illubabor, south-
west Ethiopia', Paper 29, *University of Liverpool, Africa Population
Mobility Project*.
— (1977), 'Resettlement in Illubabor Province, Ethiopia', Ph.D. thesis,
University of Liverpool.
— (1982), 'Spontaneous agricultural resettlement in Ethiopia', in Clarke,
J., and Kosinski, L. (eds), *Redistribution of Population in Africa*, Heine-
mann, London.
— (1985), 'Population redistribution and agricultural settlement schemes
in Ethiopia, 1958–80', in Clarke, J., Khogali, M., and Kosinski L. (eds),
Population and Development Projects in Africa, Cambridge University
Press, Cambridge.

Index